CHAPTER 1: INTRODUCTION TO FASTAPI

FastAPI has emerged as a revolutionary tool in the realm of web frameworks for developing APIs with Python, distinguished by its emphasis on speed, ease of use, and modern features grounded in standard Python type hints. This chapter delves into the core principles and advantages of FastAPI, elucidating why it stands out as a preferred choice for developers seeking to create high-performance APIs.

At its heart, FastAPI is engineered for speed. The framework's architecture is optimized to handle asynchronous operations efficiently, leveraging Python's `asyncio` library. This design enables FastAPI to process multiple requests concurrently, significantly reducing latency and enhancing throughput compared to traditional synchronous frameworks. The underlying mechanism involves non-blocking I/O operations, which allows the server to handle other tasks while waiting for I/O operations to complete. This asynchronous capability is particularly beneficial for applications that require high levels of concurrency, such as real-time data processing or microservices architectures.

Another compelling feature of FastAPI is its integration with standard Python type hints. Python's type hinting system, introduced in PEP 484, provides a way to indicate the expected data types of variables, function parameters, and return values. FastAPI utilizes these type hints to automatically validate request payloads, generate detailed API documentation, and offer autocompletion in IDEs. This integration simplifies the development process by catching potential errors early and improving code clarity. For instance, when defining an API endpoint in FastAPI, developers can use type hints to specify the expected structure of request bodies. FastAPI will then automatically validate incoming data against these specifications, ensuring that only correctly formatted data is processed.

The automatic generation of interactive API documentation is another standout feature of FastAPI. The framework includes built-in support for generating documentation using Swagger UI and ReDoc, two widely adopted tools for presenting API endpoints in a user-friendly format. Swagger UI offers an interactive interface that allows users to explore API endpoints, view request and response examples, and even test the endpoints directly from the browser. ReDoc, on the other hand, provides a more comprehensive and structured documentation layout. Both tools are generated automatically based on the type hints and API endpoint definitions, ensuring that the documentation remains up-to-date with minimal manual effort.

FastAPI's design also prioritizes ease of use. The framework's syntax and structure are intuitively aligned with modern Python practices, making it accessible to both novice and experienced developers. For example, creating an API endpoint in FastAPI involves defining a function with a specific decorator, such as `@app.get()` or `@app.post()`, and specifying the route and method. This straightforward approach minimizes boilerplate code and allows developers to focus on implementing business logic rather than dealing with complex configuration setups.

Moreover, FastAPI supports dependency injection, a design pattern that promotes modular and maintainable code. By using FastAPI's dependency injection system, developers can manage reusable components, such as database connections or authentication mechanisms, in a modular fashion. Dependencies are defined as functions or classes and then injected into endpoints as needed. This approach not only fosters code reuse but also enhances testability by allowing individual components to be tested in isolation.

In addition to its performance and usability benefits, FastAPI adheres to industry standards for security. The framework includes built-in mechanisms for handling common security concerns, such as authentication and authorization. For example, FastAPI provides support for OAuth2, JWT tokens, and other authentication schemes, allowing developers to implement secure access control in their APIs. The framework also encourages the use of secure coding practices, such as input validation and proper error handling, to mitigate potential vulnerabilities.

FastAPI's ecosystem is enriched by its compatibility with a range of third-party libraries and tools. For instance, the framework integrates seamlessly with SQLAlchemy and Tortoise-ORM for database interactions, enabling developers to build robust data-driven applications. Additionally, FastAPI's support for asynchronous frameworks, such as Starlette and Pydantic, extends its functionality and enhances its versatility. These integrations contribute to a rich development environment that caters to various use cases and application needs.

In summary, FastAPI represents a significant advancement in the landscape of web frameworks, offering a blend of speed, ease of use, and modern features that streamline API development. Its emphasis on asynchronous processing, type hinting, automatic documentation generation, and dependency injection sets it apart from traditional frameworks. As we progress through this chapter, we will explore practical examples and delve deeper into FastAPI's capabilities, equipping you with the knowledge needed to harness its full potential in your API development endeavors.

The syntax and structure of FastAPI are crafted to be intuitive and straightforward, aligning closely with Python's own idiomatic practices. The framework draws upon Python's native capabilities, minimizing the learning curve for those familiar with Python's conventions. This simplicity is evident in how FastAPI facilitates the creation of API endpoints. By using decorators, developers can define routes with a clear and concise syntax. For instance, defining an endpoint for a GET request involves annotating a function with the `@app.get("/path")` decorator, where `app` is an instance of the FastAPI class. This approach leverages Python's decorator syntax to map functions to specific HTTP methods and routes, creating a seamless integration between function definitions and route management.

One of the central elements of FastAPI's design is its use of dependency injection. This feature enables developers to modularize and reuse components such as database connections, authentication mechanisms, or business logic. Dependencies are defined as callable objects or functions that FastAPI automatically resolves and injects into the API endpoints as needed. This pattern promotes cleaner, more maintainable code by separating concerns and encapsulating functionality. For example, if multiple endpoints require access to a database connection, a dependency can be defined to establish and manage this connection, ensuring that all endpoints use a consistent and efficient approach.

FastAPI's performance is not solely attributable to its asynchronous capabilities but also to its use of Pydantic for data validation and serialization. Pydantic, a data validation and settings management library based on Python type annotations, is integral to FastAPI's approach. It enforces type checks and data validation at runtime, ensuring that incoming request data conforms to the expected format. This is achieved through the use of Pydantic models, which define the structure and constraints of the data. When a request is received, FastAPI automatically parses the data, validates it against the model, and raises errors if the data is invalid. This process not only enhances security by preventing malformed data from reaching the application logic but also provides clear error messages to the client, facilitating debugging and user feedback.

Another critical aspect of FastAPI is its support for path parameters, query parameters, and request bodies, all of which can be seamlessly integrated into endpoint definitions. Path parameters, embedded directly within the URL path, enable dynamic routing based on variable input values. Query parameters, appended to the URL in the form of key-value pairs, allow for optional input that can influence the behavior of the endpoint. Request bodies, which can be more complex structures, are handled through Pydantic models. FastAPI's ability to parse and validate these various input types ensures that developers can build flexible and robust APIs that accommodate a wide range of use cases.

Error handling in FastAPI is designed to be both flexible and user-friendly. The framework provides mechanisms for defining custom exception handlers, allowing developers to respond to different types of errors with tailored messages or actions. This capability is particularly useful for managing application-specific errors or integrating with external services. By defining custom exception handlers, developers can ensure that the API returns consistent and informative responses when errors occur, enhancing the overall user experience and aiding in troubleshooting.

The integration of FastAPI with modern development practices is further exemplified by its support for automated testing. The framework includes built-in support for testing via the `TestClient` class, which simulates requests to the API endpoints and verifies the responses. This feature enables developers to write unit tests and integration tests with minimal setup, facilitating continuous testing and deployment workflows. FastAPI's compatibility with testing tools such as pytest further streamlines the testing process, allowing for comprehensive test coverage and ensuring that the API behaves as expected under various conditions.

In terms of deployment, FastAPI's compatibility with a wide range of deployment environments is noteworthy. The framework supports various ASGI (Asynchronous Server Gateway Interface) servers, including Uvicorn and Hypercorn, which are optimized for asynchronous applications. This flexibility allows developers to choose the most suitable server for their needs, whether they are deploying locally, in a containerized environment, or on a cloud platform. FastAPI's adherence to ASGI standards ensures that it integrates seamlessly with modern deployment pipelines and orchestration tools, making it a versatile choice for both development and production environments.

The growing adoption of FastAPI in the industry is a testament to its effectiveness and efficiency. Organizations ranging from startups to large enterprises are leveraging FastAPI to build scalable and performant APIs. The framework's ability to handle high levels of concurrency, combined with its ease of use and robust feature set, makes it a compelling choice for modern web development. As the demand for high-performance APIs continues to rise, FastAPI’s position as a leading framework for Python web development is likely to be further solidified.

In conclusion, FastAPI represents a significant advancement in the landscape of Python web frameworks. Its design prioritizes speed, simplicity, and modern features, making it an attractive option for developers seeking to build high-performance APIs. By leveraging Python type hints, asynchronous capabilities, and integrated tools for validation and documentation, FastAPI streamlines the development process and enhances the overall quality of API implementations. As we continue to explore its features and capabilities, it becomes clear that FastAPI is well-positioned to address the evolving needs of web development in the contemporary tech landscape.

within the URL as query parameters, offer flexibility in filtering or modifying the results of API requests. FastAPI manages these parameters through function signatures, where you can specify expected query parameters with default values or type hints. For example, an endpoint that retrieves user information might use query parameters to filter results by age or location, providing an easy and efficient way to customize queries.

Request bodies, typically represented as JSON payloads, are another integral part of FastAPI's functionality. The framework's integration with Pydantic models allows developers to define the expected structure of incoming data, ensuring that the payload adheres to the specified format. FastAPI handles the deserialization of JSON data into Python objects, applying validation rules as defined by the Pydantic models. This process simplifies the handling of complex request data and helps maintain data integrity across different parts of the application.

FastAPI's built-in support for OAuth2 and JWT (JSON Web Tokens) authentication is another feature that enhances its appeal. Security is a critical concern in API development, and FastAPI addresses this with a range of authentication options. OAuth2, a widely adopted authorization framework, is implemented using a simple and extensible system in FastAPI. Developers can configure OAuth2 flows to manage user authentication and authorization with ease. JWT, a compact and self-contained token format, is also supported, allowing for secure and stateless authentication mechanisms. These features enable developers to implement robust security measures with minimal configuration, streamlining the development process and improving application security.

Error handling and exception management are essential aspects of any web framework, and FastAPI provides a flexible system for addressing these issues. The framework's approach to error handling involves defining custom exception classes and using exception handlers to manage and respond to errors. FastAPI allows developers to specify custom error responses for different types of exceptions, enhancing the clarity and usability of API interactions. This capability is crucial for providing informative and user-friendly error messages, which can greatly improve the client experience and facilitate debugging.

The performance optimizations in FastAPI are complemented by its efficient use of resources. The framework is designed to minimize overhead and maximize throughput, which is particularly evident in high-load scenarios. FastAPI achieves this efficiency through several mechanisms, including its use of asynchronous I/O, optimized request processing, and minimalistic design principles. The result is a framework that not only performs well under typical conditions but also scales effectively to handle large volumes of requests.

Another notable aspect of FastAPI is its comprehensive support for testing and debugging. The framework integrates seamlessly with testing tools and libraries, allowing developers to write and execute tests with ease. FastAPI's design facilitates the creation of unit tests, integration tests, and end-to-end tests, enabling a thorough validation of API functionality. Additionally, the interactive documentation provided by Swagger UI and ReDoc serves as a valuable debugging tool, allowing developers to manually test endpoints and inspect responses during development.

In summary, FastAPI offers a modern and efficient solution for building APIs with Python, distinguished by its speed, ease of use, and robust feature set. Its integration with standard Python type hints, support for asynchronous operations, automatic generation of interactive documentation, and comprehensive authentication and error handling capabilities make it a compelling choice for developers seeking to create high-performance APIs. The framework's emphasis on simplicity and performance ensures that it meets the demands of contemporary web development while maintaining a focus on developer productivity and application security. As you embark on your journey with FastAPI, you will find that its thoughtful design and advanced features provide a solid foundation for creating powerful and scalable APIs.

CHAPTER 2: SETTING UP YOUR DEVELOPMENT ENVIRONMENT

Establishing a robust development environment is crucial for effectively working with FastAPI. This process involves several key steps, beginning with the installation of Python, setting up virtual environments, and installing the FastAPI framework along with Uvicorn, the ASGI server used to run FastAPI applications. Each of these steps is integral to creating a functional and efficient environment tailored for FastAPI development.

To commence, the first step is installing Python. FastAPI is built upon modern Python features and type hints, which necessitate having Python 3.6 or higher. The latest stable version of Python can be obtained from the official Python website. On the website, you will find installers for various operating systems, including Windows, macOS, and Linux. After downloading the appropriate installer for your system, follow the installation instructions to set up Python. It is advisable to enable the option to add Python to your system's PATH during installation, as this facilitates easier access to Python from the command line.

Once Python is installed, the next step involves setting up

a virtual environment. Virtual environments are essential for managing project-specific dependencies and ensuring that your development environment remains isolated from system-wide packages. This isolation prevents potential conflicts between project dependencies and system libraries. To create a virtual environment, you can use the `venv` module, which is included with Python's standard library. Open a terminal or command prompt and navigate to the directory where you wish to create your project. Use the command `python -m venv env`, where `env` is the name of the virtual environment directory. This command creates a new directory containing a self-contained Python environment.

After creating the virtual environment, you need to activate it. The activation process varies depending on your operating system. On Windows, use the command `.\env\Scripts \activate`, while on macOS and Linux, the command is `source env/bin/activate`. Once activated, your terminal or command prompt should display the virtual environment's name, indicating that any Python packages installed or run will be confined to this environment.

With the virtual environment set up and activated, the next step is to install FastAPI and Uvicorn. FastAPI is the core framework for building APIs, while Uvicorn serves as the ASGI server that runs FastAPI applications. Both can be installed via Python's package manager, pip. Execute the command `pip install fastapi uvicorn` to install the latest versions of both packages. FastAPI provides the functionality for creating API endpoints, while Uvicorn handles the server-side operations, including serving requests and managing asynchronous operations.

As you install FastAPI and Uvicorn, it is beneficial to also consider best practices for managing project dependencies. One such practice is to use a `requirements.txt` file to keep track of the packages and their versions required for your project. This file can be generated by executing the command `pip freeze > requirements.txt`, which outputs a list of installed packages and their versions into a file. This file can then be used to recreate the environment on different machines by running `pip install -r requirements.txt`. Maintaining this file ensures consistency across development environments and simplifies the process of sharing your project with others or deploying it to production.

Another best practice involves using a `.gitignore` file if you are using version control with Git. This file specifies which files and directories should be ignored by Git, helping to prevent unnecessary files from being committed to the repository. For example, you would typically include the virtual environment directory (`env`) and any environment-specific configuration files in the `.gitignore` file to avoid including them in version control.

Managing dependencies also involves keeping your packages up-to-date and ensuring compatibility with your project's requirements. Tools such as `pip-tools` can assist with managing and updating dependencies. By using `pip-tools`, you can generate a `requirements.txt` file from a `requirements.in` file, which specifies the primary dependencies. This approach allows for better control over dependency versions and helps to prevent conflicts or issues arising from outdated packages.

Furthermore, integrating a linter and formatter into your development workflow can enhance code quality and maintainability. Tools such as `flake8` for linting and `black` for formatting can be installed and configured to automatically check and format your code according to best practices. These tools help maintain consistency and adherence to coding standards, making collaboration and code reviews more efficient.

In summary, setting up a development environment for FastAPI involves installing Python, creating and managing virtual environments, and installing FastAPI and Uvicorn. Following best practices for dependency management and incorporating tools for code quality ensures a smooth and efficient development experience. By adhering to these guidelines, you establish a solid foundation for building and maintaining high-performance FastAPI applications.

With the virtual environment activated, the installation of FastAPI and Uvicorn is the next crucial step in setting up your development environment. These installations can be handled via `pip`, the Python package installer, which is included with Python. First, ensure that you have `pip` updated to its latest version by running the command `pip install --upgrade pip`. Keeping `pip` updated ensures compatibility with the latest packages and features.

To install FastAPI, execute the command `pip install fastapi`. FastAPI is a lightweight yet powerful framework designed to work seamlessly with modern Python features and asynchronous programming. It is not dependent on any particular ASGI server, but for development purposes, Uvicorn is commonly used due to its performance and compatibility with FastAPI. To install Uvicorn, run the command `pip install uvicorn`. Uvicorn is an ASGI server that serves as the interface between your FastAPI application and the outside world, handling incoming HTTP requests and delivering responses. It is optimized for high-performance and asynchronous operations, making it a suitable choice for serving FastAPI applications.

After the installation of FastAPI and Uvicorn, it's beneficial to configure your development environment for a smooth and productive experience. This involves setting up best practices for dependency management, ensuring that your project remains organized and maintainable. A fundamental practice in managing dependencies is to create a `requirements.txt` file, which lists all the packages required for your project. This file can be generated using the command `pip freeze > requirements.txt`. This command captures the current state of your environment, including all installed packages and their versions, and saves it to a `requirements.txt` file. This file is crucial for replicating the environment in different setups or for other developers working on the same project.

Furthermore, for more comprehensive project management and dependency handling, consider using `pipenv` or `poetry`. These tools offer additional features over standard `pip` and `requirements.txt` management. `Pipenv`, for instance, manages both your dependencies and a virtual environment in one place, using a `Pipfile` to specify dependencies and a `Pipfile.lock` to lock them to specific versions. `Poetry` offers similar functionality but with a focus on project management and dependency resolution, providing a `pyproject.toml` file to manage dependencies and package configurations. Both tools facilitate a more organized approach to managing project dependencies, ensuring that your development environment remains consistent and reproducible.

In addition to managing dependencies, consider implementing version control for your project using Git. Version control is essential for tracking changes, collaborating with others, and maintaining a history of your project's evolution. Initialize a Git repository in your project directory by running `git init`, and create a `.gitignore` file to exclude files and directories that should not be versioned, such as the virtual environment directory (`env`). To create a `.gitignore` file, you can use a simple text editor to list patterns of files and directories to ignore. For example, the `.gitignore` file might include entries such as `env/`, `__pycache__/`, and `.pyc` to ensure that these files do not clutter your repository.

As you develop your FastAPI application, it's also important to establish a consistent coding style and adhere to best practices. Consider integrating code formatting and linting tools such as `black` and `flake8`. `Black` is an opinionated code formatter that automatically formats your code to adhere to a consistent style, enhancing readability and reducing the likelihood of style-related issues. To install `black`, use the command `pip install black` and format your code with `black .`. Similarly, `flake8` is a linting tool that analyzes your code for potential issues and style inconsistencies, helping maintain high code quality. Install `flake8` with `pip install flake8` and run it using the command `flake8 .` to receive feedback on your code.

Testing is another critical aspect of development that should not be overlooked. Implementing automated tests for your FastAPI application ensures that your code behaves as expected and helps identify bugs early in the development process. FastAPI supports testing with tools like `pytest`, which is a powerful testing framework that integrates well with FastAPI. To get started with `pytest`, install it using `pip install pytest` and create test files that adhere to the `test_.py` naming convention. FastAPI also provides a `TestClient` class, which allows you to simulate HTTP requests and test your API endpoints directly. Using `pytest` in conjunction with `TestClient` enables comprehensive testing of your FastAPI application's functionality and performance.

In summary, setting up a development environment for FastAPI involves several key steps: installing Python, configuring a virtual environment, and installing FastAPI and Uvicorn. It also encompasses best practices for dependency management, version control, coding style, and testing. By following these guidelines, you can create a well-organized, efficient, and maintainable environment for developing FastAPI applications.

Once your dependencies are installed and managed, it is important to ensure that your development environment is configured to facilitate efficient workflow and debugging. This includes setting up a robust development server, configuring logging, and establishing a process for running and testing your FastAPI applications.

To start your FastAPI application during development, you will use Uvicorn as the ASGI server. Uvicorn's command-line interface allows you to specify various options, such as the host, port, and logging level. For a basic development setup, you can run your FastAPI application with the command `uvicorn main:app --reload`, assuming that `main` is the filename of your FastAPI application and `app` is the FastAPI instance. The `--reload` option enables automatic reloading of the server upon code changes, which is particularly useful during development as it eliminates the need to manually restart the server each time you modify your code.

Configuring logging is another essential aspect of managing your development environment. Proper logging can significantly aid in debugging by providing detailed information about application behavior and errors. FastAPI integrates well with Python's standard logging library, allowing you to set up custom logging configurations. By default, Uvicorn outputs logs to the console, but you can customize logging settings to direct logs to files or adjust the verbosity. To configure logging, you can create a `logging_config.py` file where you define handlers, formatters, and loggers. For instance, you might configure a file handler to write logs to a file, a console handler for real-time output, and a formatter to specify the log message format. You then integrate this logging configuration with your FastAPI application by including it in your application's startup events.

Testing is a crucial part of the development workflow and ensures that your FastAPI application behaves as expected. FastAPI's design facilitates testing by leveraging standard Python testing frameworks such as `pytest`. To test your FastAPI application, you can use the `TestClient` class provided by FastAPI, which simulates HTTP requests to your application and allows you to assert responses and behavior. The `TestClient` can be used to write unit tests for individual endpoints, validate response data, and check for correct status codes. A typical test might involve sending a mock request to an endpoint and verifying that the response matches the expected output.

For comprehensive testing, consider using `pytest` plugins such as `pytest-cov` to measure code coverage, ensuring that your tests cover all critical paths in your application. It is also beneficial to incorporate continuous integration (CI) tools into your workflow, which automatically run your tests on each code change or pull request. CI tools can be configured to use your `requirements.txt` or `Pipfile` to install dependencies and execute your test suite, providing automated feedback on the health of your application.

Lastly, it is essential to adhere to best practices in managing and updating your development environment. Regularly review and update your dependencies to incorporate security patches and improvements. Use tools such as `pip-tools` to manage and synchronize dependencies between your project's requirements file and your virtual environment. Additionally, maintain clear documentation of your development setup and configuration to facilitate collaboration and onboarding of new team members.

By following these steps, you will establish a well-organized development environment conducive to building and maintaining high-quality FastAPI applications. Each component, from Python installation to dependency management and testing, plays a critical role in ensuring that your development process is efficient, reliable, and adaptable to evolving project requirements.

CHAPTER 3: CREATING YOUR FIRST FASTAPI APPLICATION

Creating your first FastAPI application is an excellent way to get acquainted with the framework's core concepts and features. This process involves setting up a basic application that includes a simple "Hello World" endpoint. This foundational exercise will help you understand FastAPI's routing system, request handling, and response generation, providing a solid basis for developing more complex applications.

To begin, ensure that your development environment is properly set up and that FastAPI and Uvicorn are installed. With your virtual environment activated and these packages in place, you can start by creating a new Python file that will contain your FastAPI application code. For this example, we will name the file `main.py`.

Inside `main.py`, you will first need to import the FastAPI class from the `fastapi` package. The FastAPI class is the core component of your application and is responsible for managing routes, handling requests, and generating responses. Instantiate an object of the FastAPI class to serve as the application instance. This instance will be used to define your application's endpoints and configuration.

Here is a basic example to illustrate this setup:

```python
from fastapi import FastAPI

app FastAPI()
```

In this snippet, we import FastAPI and create an instance of it, assigning it to the variable `app`. This instance is now the central object that will handle incoming HTTP requests and route them to the appropriate endpoints.

Next, define a route for the "Hello World" endpoint. FastAPI uses decorators to associate HTTP methods and paths with functions that handle requests. To create a simple GET endpoint, use the `@app.get("/")` decorator. This decorator specifies that the decorated function will handle GET requests to the root URL (`/`). Define a function named `read_root` to return the response for this endpoint. The function should return a dictionary with a message that will be converted to JSON automatically by FastAPI.

Here's how you can define the "Hello World" endpoint:

```python
@app.get("/")
def read_root():
  return {"Hello": "World"}
```

In this example, the `read_root` function returns a dictionary with a single key-value pair, `{"Hello": "World"}`. FastAPI automatically serializes this dictionary to JSON and sets the appropriate content type for the HTTP response.

To run your FastAPI application, you will use Uvicorn, the ASGI server. Open your terminal or command prompt, navigate to the directory containing `main.py`, and execute the following command:

```bash
uvicorn main:app --reload
```

This command tells Uvicorn to run the application defined in `main.py`, where `main` is the module name and `app` is the FastAPI instance. The `--reload` option enables auto-reloading, so any changes to your code will be reflected immediately without needing to restart the server manually.

Once Uvicorn starts, you should see output indicating that the server is running and listening on a specific port, usually `http://127.0.0.1:8000`. Open a web browser and navigate to this address. You should see the JSON response `{"Hello": "World"}`, which confirms that your endpoint is functioning correctly.

In addition to serving the API, FastAPI also provides interactive documentation automatically generated based on your endpoints. With the application running, you can access the Swagger UI at `http://127.0.0.1:8000/docs` and the ReDoc documentation at `http://127.0.0.1:8000/redoc`. These interfaces allow you to explore the available endpoints, view request and response formats, and test the endpoints directly from your browser.

To further understand the routing and request handling in FastAPI, consider adding more endpoints or experimenting with different HTTP methods. For instance, you can define additional routes for handling POST requests or include path parameters in your endpoints to handle dynamic content. FastAPI's routing system is designed to be intuitive and flexible, allowing you to build complex applications with ease.

By completing this exercise, you have taken the first

step towards mastering FastAPI. You now have a basic understanding of how to set up a FastAPI application, define endpoints, and run your server. This foundational knowledge will serve as the basis for more advanced topics and applications as you continue exploring FastAPI's capabilities.

To test the "Hello World" endpoint you have just created, you need to run your FastAPI application using Uvicorn. Ensure that Uvicorn is installed in your virtual environment; if not, you can install it using `pip install uvicorn`. Once Uvicorn is installed, you can start your FastAPI application by executing the following command in your terminal:

```
uvicorn main:app --reload
```

In this command, `main` refers to the name of your Python file (without the `.py` extension), and `app` is the instance of the FastAPI class defined within that file. The `--reload` flag enables the auto-reloading feature, which is especially useful during development as it automatically restarts the server when changes are detected in your code.

Upon executing this command, Uvicorn will start the server and provide output indicating that it is running, including the address and port number where your application is being served, typically `http://127.0.0.1:8000`. You can open this URL in a web browser to see your application in action. When you navigate to `http://127.0.0.1:8000/`, you should see the JSON response `{"Hello": "World"}` displayed in the browser.

In addition to serving the application, Uvicorn also provides interactive API documentation via Swagger UI and ReDoc by default. FastAPI automatically generates this documentation based on the defined endpoints and their metadata. You can access the interactive documentation at `http://127.0.0.1:8000/docs` and the ReDoc documentation at `http://127.0.0.1:8000/redoc`. These interfaces allow you to explore the available endpoints, view request and response examples, and interact with your API directly from the browser. This feature is invaluable for testing and understanding how your API works without needing to write separate test cases or documentation manually.

As you develop more complex applications, you'll find that FastAPI's routing system and request handling capabilities extend beyond simple endpoints. You can create multiple routes with different HTTP methods such as POST, PUT, DELETE, and PATCH, and you can define path parameters, query parameters, and request bodies. Path parameters are useful for dynamic routing where parts of the URL are variable, while query parameters allow you to pass optional data in the URL. Request bodies enable you to handle complex data structures sent by the client.

For example, to add a POST endpoint that accepts JSON data, you can define a new route and use Pydantic models to validate and parse the request body. Pydantic models allow you to define the expected structure and constraints of the incoming data. Here's how you can create a POST endpoint that accepts user information:

```python
from pydantic import BaseModel

class User(BaseModel):
    name: str
    age: int

@app.post("/users/")
def create_user(user: User):
    return {"name": user.name, "age": user.age}
```

In this example, the `User` class is a Pydantic model that

specifies the expected structure of the request body: it must include a `name` of type `str` and an `age` of type `int`. The `create_user` function is defined with a `user` parameter that FastAPI automatically parses and validates based on the `User` model. When a POST request is made to `/users/` with a JSON payload containing `name` and `age`, FastAPI will validate the data and pass an instance of the `User` model to the `create_user` function.

It is also important to handle various types of errors and exceptions that may occur during request processing. FastAPI provides mechanisms for defining custom exception handlers to manage and respond to errors in a controlled manner. For instance, you can define a custom error response for a validation error:

```python
from fastapi import HTTPException

@app.get("/items/{item_id}")
def read_item(item_id: int):
  if item_id < 0:
    raise HTTPException(status_code400, detail"Item ID must be a positive integer")
  return {"item_id": item_id}
```

In this example, if the `item_id` is not a positive integer, the function raises an `HTTPException` with a status code of 400 and a descriptive error message. FastAPI automatically returns this error response to the client, making it easier to handle and debug issues.

By following these steps, you have successfully created a basic FastAPI application and explored some of its fundamental features. You now have a foundational understanding of how to define endpoints, handle requests, and manage responses with FastAPI. As you continue to develop more advanced applications, you will build upon this knowledge, incorporating additional features and techniques to create robust and efficient APIs.

To further explore the capabilities of FastAPI, consider adding more complexity to your application by introducing path parameters and query parameters. These features allow your API to handle more dynamic and detailed requests.

Path parameters are integral for creating routes that depend on variable parts of the URL. For instance, suppose you want to create an endpoint that responds with a personalized greeting. You can modify your `main.py` file to include a new route that uses a path parameter to capture a user's name. Here's how you can define such an endpoint:

```python
@app.get("/greet/{name}")
def greet(name: str):
  return {"message": f"Hello, {name}!"}
```

In this example, the route `"/greet/{name}"` contains a path parameter named `name`. The function `greet` takes this parameter as an argument and returns a JSON response that incorporates the name into a personalized message. FastAPI automatically extracts the value of the `name` parameter from the URL and passes it to the `greet` function. For example, if you navigate to `http://127.0.0.1:8000/greet/Alice`, you will see the response `{"message": "Hello, Alice!"}`.

Query parameters offer another way to pass data to your endpoints, but they appear in the URL after the question mark (`?`). Query parameters are typically used for filtering or specifying options for the request. To demonstrate, let's add an endpoint that uses query parameters to optionally include a greeting message. Modify your `main.py` file with the following code:

```python
@app.get("/greet")
def greet(name: str, message: str "Hello"):
  return {"message": f"{message}, {name}!"}
```

In this updated example, the `greet` function accepts two parameters: `name` and `message`. The `message` parameter has a default value of `"Hello"`. When you navigate to `http://127.0.0.1:8000/greet?nameBob&messageHi`, you will receive the response `{"message": "Hi, Bob!"}`. If the `message` parameter is omitted, the function defaults to `"Hello"`, and the response will be `{"message": "Hello, Bob!"}`.

Furthermore, handling request bodies is a crucial aspect of developing APIs, especially for endpoints that require data input beyond simple query parameters. FastAPI uses Pydantic models to define and validate the structure of request bodies. For example, if you want to create an endpoint that accepts JSON data to create a new user, you can define a Pydantic model for the user data and use it in your endpoint. Here's how you can set this up:

First, define a Pydantic model in your `main.py` file:

```python
from pydantic import BaseModel

class User(BaseModel):
  username: str
  email: str
  full_name: str  None
```

The `User` model defines the structure of the request body, including required fields (`username` and `email`) and an optional field (`full_name`). Next, create an endpoint that uses this model to receive and process JSON data:

```python
@app.post("/create_user")
def create_user(user: User):
    return {"username": user.username, "email": user.email, "full_name": user.full_name}
```

In this endpoint, the `user` parameter is of type `User`, which means FastAPI will automatically parse the JSON request body, validate it against the `User` model, and convert it into a `User` instance. If you send a POST request to `http://127.0.0.1:8000/create_user` with a JSON body like `{"username": "johndoe", "email": "johndoe@example.com", "full_name": "John Doe"}`, you will receive a response reflecting the data sent.

By now, you should have a basic understanding of how to set up and extend your FastAPI application. The ability to handle different types of request data, such as path parameters, query parameters, and request bodies, is fundamental for creating robust APIs. With these capabilities, you can build more complex endpoints and start integrating your application with various data sources and external services. This foundation will serve as a springboard for developing more sophisticated FastAPI applications as you delve deeper into its features and capabilities.

CHAPTER 4: UNDERSTANDING FASTAPI'S REQUEST AND RESPONSE MODELS

FastAPI's request and response models are fundamental to building robust and efficient APIs. By leveraging these models, you can ensure that your application handles data consistently and effectively, benefiting from FastAPI's automatic data validation and serialization capabilities. This discussion covers defining request bodies with Pydantic models, handling query parameters, and formatting responses to fully utilize FastAPI's powerful features.

To begin with, defining request bodies is a crucial aspect of creating APIs that accept structured data from clients. FastAPI uses Pydantic models for this purpose, which provide a way to enforce data types and validate input data. Pydantic models are Python classes that define the structure of the data expected in the request body, including fields, data types, and validation constraints.

Start by installing Pydantic if it is not already included in your project. Since FastAPI relies on Pydantic for data validation, it is included by default when you install FastAPI. Here is an example of how to define a Pydantic model and use it to handle request bodies:

```python
from pydantic import BaseModel

class User(BaseModel):
  username: str
  email: str
  full_name: str  None
```

In this example, the `User` class inherits from `BaseModel`, which is provided by Pydantic. It defines three fields: `username`, `email`, and `full_name`. The `username` and `email` fields are required, while `full_name` is optional, indicated by its default value of `None`. FastAPI will use this model to validate incoming request data, ensuring that it adheres to the defined structure.

To utilize this model in your FastAPI application, define an endpoint that accepts a request body of type `User`. Modify your `main.py` file as follows:

```python
from fastapi import FastAPI
from pydantic import BaseModel

app  FastAPI()

class User(BaseModel):
  username: str
  email: str
  full_name: str  None

@app.post("/create_user")
def create_user(user: User):
     return {"username": user.username, "email": user.email,
"full_name": user.full_name}
```

In this updated example, the `create_user` endpoint accepts a `POST` request with a request body that must conform to the `User` model. FastAPI will automatically parse and validate the incoming JSON data, converting it into an instance of the `User` class. If the data does not meet the model's constraints (e.g., missing required fields or incorrect data types), FastAPI will return a detailed error response indicating the validation issues.

Handling query parameters is another important aspect of request management in FastAPI. Query parameters are part of the URL and are used to pass additional data to endpoints. You can define query parameters directly in your endpoint functions by adding them as function arguments. FastAPI automatically extracts these parameters from the URL and validates them.

Consider an example where you want to filter users based on their age and city. You can define query parameters as follows:

```python
from fastapi import FastAPI
from typing import Optional

app FastAPI()

@app.get("/users")
def get_users(age: Optional[int]  None, city: Optional[str]
None):
    Implement logic to filter users based on age and city
   return {"age": age, "city": city}
```

In this example, the `get_users` endpoint accepts two optional query parameters: `age` and `city`. The `Optional` type hint indicates that these parameters are not required. If the client does not provide a value for either parameter, the corresponding variable will be `None`. FastAPI will automatically handle the extraction of these parameters from the URL and make them available in the function.

Formatting responses is the final component in managing API interactions. FastAPI allows you to return various types of responses, including JSON, HTML, and custom response formats. By default, FastAPI will serialize the return value of your endpoint functions to JSON. However, you can customize the response format using the `JSONResponse` class or other response classes provided by FastAPI.

Here is an example of using `JSONResponse` to customize the response:

```python
from fastapi import FastAPI
from fastapi.responses import JSONResponse

app FastAPI()

@app.get("/custom_response")
def custom_response():
  content {"message": "This is a custom response"}
  return JSONResponse(contentcontent, status_code200)
```

In this example, the `custom_response` endpoint returns a `JSONResponse` with a custom content and status code. This allows you to have fine-grained control over the response details, such as setting headers or customizing the response body.

By understanding and utilizing FastAPI's request and response models, you can create APIs that handle data efficiently, enforce validation rules, and deliver responses in a format that meets your application's requirements. These capabilities are central to building reliable and high-performance APIs, providing a strong foundation for developing more complex and feature-rich applications.

Once you have defined your Pydantic models for request bodies, handling query parameters becomes an important aspect of creating dynamic and flexible APIs. Query parameters are typically used to filter or sort data, provide optional configurations, or control the behavior of an endpoint. FastAPI provides robust mechanisms for working with these parameters, allowing you to define them easily and ensure they are validated appropriately.

To work with query parameters, you can define them directly in your endpoint functions using standard Python function arguments. FastAPI automatically treats these arguments as query parameters if they are not part of the request body. You can also specify default values and type annotations for these parameters, which FastAPI uses to perform validation and type conversion.

For example, suppose you want to create an endpoint that retrieves user information based on optional query parameters such as age and city. Here's how you can modify your `main.py` file to include such an endpoint:

```python
from fastapi import FastAPI
from typing import Optional

app FastAPI()

@app.get("/users")
def get_users(age: Optional[int]  None, city: Optional[str]
None):
  results []
  if age:
    results.append(f"Filtering by age: {age}")
  if city:
    results.append(f"Filtering by city: {city}")
```

```
    return {"results": results}
```

In this example, the `get_users` endpoint accepts two query parameters: `age` and `city`. Both parameters are optional, as indicated by their default value of `None`. FastAPI automatically parses these parameters from the URL and passes them to the function. The `Optional` type hint from the `typing` module indicates that the parameters can be of the specified type or `None`. This endpoint will handle requests like `http://127.0.0.1:8000/users?age25&cityNew%20York`, and it will respond with a JSON object that lists the filters applied.

Beyond handling query parameters, formatting responses is another crucial part of creating APIs. FastAPI provides flexible mechanisms for defining the structure and content of responses. You can use Pydantic models to enforce response data formats and types, just as you do with request bodies. This ensures consistency and reliability in your API responses.

Suppose you want to extend your application to return user information in a structured format. First, define a response model using Pydantic, similar to how you defined the request model:

```python
from pydantic import BaseModel

class UserResponse(BaseModel):
    username: str
    email: str
    full_name: Optional[str] None
```

In this `UserResponse` model, the fields are similar to those in the request model, but it may include additional fields or slightly different constraints depending on your requirements. Next, modify your `create_user` endpoint to use this response model:

```python
from fastapi import FastAPI
from pydantic import BaseModel
from typing import Optional

app FastAPI()

class User(BaseModel):
    username: str
    email: str
    full_name: Optional[str] None

class UserResponse(BaseModel):
    username: str
    email: str
    full_name: Optional[str] None

@app.post("/create_user", response_modelUserResponse)
def create_user(user: User):
    return user
```

In this updated endpoint definition, the `response_model` parameter is used to specify that the `UserResponse` model should be used to format the response. FastAPI automatically serializes the response data to match the `UserResponse` model and includes only the fields defined in the model. This ensures that the response is consistent and adheres to the specified format.

Moreover, FastAPI supports more advanced response features such as status codes, headers, and custom responses. For example, you can specify HTTP status codes directly in your endpoint functions using the `status_code` parameter. You can also use the `JSONResponse` class from `fastapi.responses` to create custom responses with specific status codes and headers. Here's how you can create a custom response:

```python
from fastapi import FastAPI
from fastapi.responses import JSONResponse

app FastAPI()

@app.get("/custom_response")
def custom_response():
  content {"message": "This is a custom response"}
  return JSONResponse(contentcontent, status_code202)
```

In this example, the `custom_response` endpoint returns a response with a status code of 202 and a custom JSON body. This flexibility allows you to tailor responses to meet various application requirements and client expectations.

In summary, FastAPI's request and response models enable you to build APIs that are both efficient and robust. By defining request bodies with Pydantic models, handling query parameters effectively, and formatting responses to ensure consistency, you can leverage FastAPI's powerful features to create high-quality APIs. These techniques will serve as a foundation for more advanced API development, allowing you to build scalable and maintainable applications.

To fully grasp FastAPI's capabilities in formatting responses, it is crucial to understand how to utilize Pydantic models for structuring your response data. By using these models, you not only ensure consistent response formats but also leverage FastAPI's built-in validation and serialization mechanisms. This approach enhances the robustness of your API by validating that response data adheres to specified formats before sending it to clients.

Consider a scenario where you need to return detailed user

information from an API endpoint. By defining a Pydantic model for the response, you ensure that the data structure is both predictable and self-documented. Let's define a Pydantic model to represent a user's profile:

```python
from pydantic import BaseModel
from typing import Optional

class UserProfile(BaseModel):
  username: str
  email: str
  full_name: Optional[str]  None
  age: Optional[int]  None
```

In this `UserProfile` model, `username` and `email` are required fields, while `full_name` and `age` are optional. This model provides a clear structure for what a user profile should include and ensures that any data returned from the API adheres to this format.

To use this model in an endpoint, you would modify your FastAPI application to return an instance of `UserProfile`. Here's how you might adjust the `/users/{username}` endpoint to return a user's profile information:

```python
@app.get("/users/{username}", response_modelUserProfile)
def get_user_profile(username: str):
   Dummy data for demonstration
  user_data {
    "username": username,
    "email": f"{username}@example.com",
    "full_name": "John Doe",
    "age": 30
  }
  return user_data
```

```

In this example, the `response_model` parameter in the `@app.get` decorator specifies that the `UserProfile` model should be used to validate and format the response data. FastAPI will automatically serialize the returned dictionary into the `UserProfile` format and validate that it conforms to the model's specifications. If the data does not meet the model's criteria, FastAPI will raise an error, preventing invalid responses from being sent to clients.

Additionally, FastAPI provides advanced features for response customization, such as status codes and response headers. You can define these customizations in your endpoint functions to provide more control over the HTTP responses. For example, if you want to return a specific HTTP status code along with your response, you can use the `JSONResponse` class from FastAPI's `fastapi.responses` module:

```python
from fastapi.responses import JSONResponse

@app.get("/custom_response")
def custom_response():
    content {"message": "This is a custom response with status
code 201"}
    return JSONResponse(contentcontent, status_code201)
```

In this example, the `JSONResponse` class allows you to specify both the content and the status code of the response. This flexibility is particularly useful for APIs that need to return specific status codes based on the outcome of the request.

FastAPI also supports response models for more complex scenarios, such as nested models and lists. For instance, if you want to return a list of user profiles, you can define a response
```

model that represents a list of `UserProfile` instances:

```python
from typing import List

@app.get("/users", response_modelList[UserProfile])
def list_users():
   Dummy data for demonstration
  users [
          {"username": "alice", "email": "alice@example.com",
"full_name": "Alice Smith", "age": 28},
            {"username": "bob", "email": "bob@example.com",
"full_name": "Bob Johnson", "age": 35}
  ]
  return users
```

In this scenario, the `response_model` parameter is set to `List[UserProfile]`, indicating that the endpoint returns a list of `UserProfile` objects. FastAPI handles the serialization and validation of each item in the list according to the `UserProfile` model.

By effectively utilizing Pydantic models for request and response handling, you can create APIs that are both robust and maintainable. FastAPI's automatic validation and serialization features streamline the development process, allowing you to focus on building functionality rather than managing data consistency and error handling. Understanding and leveraging these features will enable you to build high-performance APIs that are reliable and easy to use.

CHAPTER 5: WORKING WITH PATH PARAMETERS AND QUERY PARAMETERS

Path parameters and query parameters are integral to RESTful API design, playing a critical role in specifying and filtering the resources your API interacts with. In FastAPI, these parameters are handled with ease and precision, allowing you to build dynamic and flexible endpoints. This discussion will cover how to define and work with both path and query parameters, including how to validate their values and use them to retrieve and filter data efficiently.

To begin, let's explore path parameters, which are part of the URL and used to specify the resource being requested. Path parameters are typically included in the URL path of an endpoint, enclosed in curly braces `{}`. For instance, if you want to design an endpoint that retrieves details about a specific user, you can use a path parameter to identify the user.

Consider the following FastAPI application snippet that demonstrates how to use path parameters:

```python
from fastapi import FastAPI

app FastAPI()
```

```
@app.get("/users/{user_id}")
def read_user(user_id: int):
    return {"user_id": user_id}
```

In this example, `user_id` is a path parameter. When a request is made to the `/users/123` URL, FastAPI captures `123` as the `user_id` and passes it to the `read_user` function. The parameter is defined as an `int`, which allows FastAPI to automatically handle type conversion and validation. If the `user_id` provided in the URL cannot be converted to an integer, FastAPI will respond with an error indicating invalid input.

Path parameters are essential for creating resource-specific routes. They allow you to dynamically generate responses based on the resource identifier included in the URL. However, to handle more complex data filtering and querying, you will often need to use query parameters.

Query parameters are included in the URL after a question mark `?` and are used to pass additional information or modify the behavior of an endpoint. They can be used to filter results, specify pagination, or control the format of the response. FastAPI makes it straightforward to work with query parameters by including them as function arguments in your endpoint definitions.

Let's enhance the previous example by adding query parameters to filter user data. Suppose you want to allow clients to retrieve user information based on optional parameters such as `name` and `age`. You can modify your endpoint as follows:

```python
from typing import Optional

@app.get("/users/{user_id}")
```

```
def read_user(user_id: int, name: Optional[str] None, age: Optional[int] None):
  filters {}
  if name:
    filters["name"] name
  if age:
    filters["age"] age
  return {"user_id": user_id, "filters": filters}
```

In this updated endpoint, `name` and `age` are query parameters that are optional. They are defined with `Optional` types, meaning they can be provided or omitted in the request. The function collects these parameters into a `filters` dictionary, which is included in the response. For example, a request to `/users/123?nameAlice&age30` will result in the response `{"user_id": 123, "filters": {"name": "Alice", "age": 30}}`.

By leveraging path and query parameters in this way, you can build versatile endpoints that cater to various client requirements. The automatic validation and conversion provided by FastAPI simplify the handling of these parameters, ensuring that your application remains robust and reliable.

Moreover, FastAPI supports more advanced parameter handling, such as combining path and query parameters to create complex filtering scenarios. You can also use FastAPI's dependency injection system to manage parameters across multiple endpoints, facilitating more modular and maintainable code. This advanced usage ensures that your APIs remain flexible and scalable as they grow in complexity.

Handling parameters efficiently is crucial for creating responsive and user-friendly APIs. By understanding and applying the principles of path and query parameters, you can build APIs that are not only functional but also aligned with RESTful design principles. FastAPI's robust parameter handling capabilities streamline the development process, allowing you to focus on building features and delivering value to your users.

To extend our previous example with query parameters, let's consider a scenario where you want to enhance the user data retrieval functionality by allowing clients to filter users based on optional parameters such as `age` and `status`. Query parameters are particularly useful for this type of dynamic filtering, as they can be easily included in the URL and parsed by FastAPI.

Here's an updated version of the user retrieval endpoint that includes query parameters for filtering users:

```python
from typing import Optional

@app.get("/users/{user_id}")
def read_user(user_id: int, age: Optional[int]  None, status:
Optional[str] None):
  filters []
  if age:
    filters.append(f"age{age}")
  if status:
    filters.append(f"status{status}")
  return {
    "user_id": user_id,
    "filters": filters
  }
```

In this example, the `read_user` function now accepts two optional query parameters: `age` and `status`. These parameters are included directly in the function signature with default values of `None`. This approach allows you to include them in the request URL as query parameters, such as `/users/123?age25&statusactive`. FastAPI automatically parses these parameters from the URL and provides them as arguments to the function. If a parameter is not included in the request, its value remains `None`, which you can check within your function.

The `Optional` type hint, imported from the `typing` module, indicates that these parameters are not required. This flexibility allows clients to provide any combination of parameters or none at all. The function then constructs a list of filters based on the parameters provided, which can be useful for debugging or logging purposes.

Another powerful feature of FastAPI's query parameter handling is its support for complex data types and validations. For instance, you can use query parameters to specify a range of values or validate that a parameter meets specific criteria. FastAPI's integration with Pydantic enables you to enforce such constraints easily.

Let's explore how to handle more complex query parameters by defining a model for filtering criteria. Suppose you want to allow clients to filter users based on a set of criteria, including minimum and maximum ages. You can define a Pydantic model for these criteria and use it in your endpoint:

```python
from pydantic import BaseModel
from typing import Optional

class FilterCriteria(BaseModel):
  min_age: Optional[int] None
  max_age: Optional[int] None
  status: Optional[str] None
```

In this model, `min_age`, `max_age`, and `status` are

defined as optional fields. You can now use this model in your endpoint to validate and handle complex query parameters:

```python
@app.get("/users/{user_id}")
def read_user(user_id: int, criteria: FilterCriteria  Depends()):
  filters  []
  if criteria.min_age is not None:
    filters.append(f"min_age{criteria.min_age}")
  if criteria.max_age is not None:
    filters.append(f"max_age{criteria.max_age}")
  if criteria.status is not None:
    filters.append(f"status{criteria.status}")
  return {
    "user_id": user_id,
    "filters": filters
  }
```

In this updated example, the `read_user` function uses the `FilterCriteria` model to handle query parameters. The `Depends` function from FastAPI's dependency injection system is used to extract and validate the query parameters based on the `FilterCriteria` model. FastAPI will automatically validate the data against the model's constraints and provide it to the endpoint function.

Using Pydantic models for query parameters provides several benefits. It ensures that the parameters are validated against specified criteria, it provides clear and consistent API documentation, and it makes handling complex query logic more manageable.

FastAPI also allows you to customize the behavior of query parameter parsing and validation further by using custom types or validators. For example, you can create custom query parameter types to handle specific formats or ranges, or you can implement custom validation logic to enforce more complex rules.

By understanding how to effectively work with path and query parameters in FastAPI, you gain the ability to create flexible and dynamic endpoints that meet the needs of various client applications. Whether you are handling simple identifiers or complex filtering criteria, FastAPI's tools and features make it straightforward to build and manage robust APIs.

To further enhance the flexibility and robustness of your FastAPI application, integrating Pydantic models with query parameters can significantly improve how you handle complex data requirements. Pydantic's capabilities allow you to define structured query parameters that facilitate extensive validation and parsing, which is particularly useful for managing multiple filtering criteria or more intricate validation logic.

Suppose we want to create an endpoint that filters users based on a range of ages. To achieve this, we first define a Pydantic model that represents the filtering criteria:

```python
from pydantic import BaseModel
from typing import Optional

class UserFilter(BaseModel):
  min_age: Optional[int] None
  max_age: Optional[int] None
  status: Optional[str] None
```

In this `UserFilter` model, `min_age` and `max_age` are optional integers that represent the range of ages for filtering users. The `status` field is an optional string used to filter users by their status. By using this model, we can enforce that only valid data types are accepted, and we can perform validation on the values to ensure they meet specified criteria.

With this model in place, you can modify the endpoint to accept a query parameter that adheres to this model. FastAPI allows you to use the `UserFilter` model directly in the query parameters of your endpoint:

```python
from fastapi import FastAPI, Query
from typing import List

app FastAPI()

@app.get("/users")
def get_filtered_users(filter: UserFilter Query(...)):
    Implement filtering logic based on `filter`
   return {
     "min_age": filter.min_age,
     "max_age": filter.max_age,
     "status": filter.status
   }
```

In this example, the `filter` parameter is of type `UserFilter`, and it is marked as required by using `Query(...)`. FastAPI automatically parses the query parameters and maps them to the `UserFilter` model. If the query parameters do not match the model's schema, FastAPI will handle it gracefully, ensuring that only valid data is processed.

The use of `Query(...)` in the endpoint definition allows you to specify additional metadata and constraints on the query parameters, such as default values or descriptions. For example, if you wanted to make the `status` parameter mandatory, you could modify the model and endpoint like so:

```python
from pydantic import Field
```

```
class UserFilter(BaseModel):
  min_age: Optional[int]  None
  max_age: Optional[int]  None
  status: str  Field(..., description"Status of the user to filter by")

@app.get("/users")
def get_filtered_users(filter: UserFilter  Query(...)):
   Implement filtering logic based on `filter`
  return {
    "min_age": filter.min_age,
    "max_age": filter.max_age,
    "status": filter.status
  }
```

In this version, the `status` field is required, and you can also provide additional documentation for the parameter using the `description` argument in `Field(...)`. This enhances the clarity and usability of your API documentation.

Handling path and query parameters efficiently is crucial for developing scalable and user-friendly APIs. By combining FastAPI's intuitive parameter handling with the powerful validation capabilities of Pydantic, you can create APIs that are not only robust and reliable but also easy to use and maintain. As you build more complex applications, these techniques will help you manage data input and output with greater precision and flexibility, ensuring that your API meets the needs of its users while maintaining high standards of data integrity and validation.

CHAPTER 6: IMPLEMENTING DEPENDENCY INJECTION

Dependency injection is a pivotal concept in FastAPI, enhancing modularity and testability by allowing you to manage and reuse components and services efficiently. This mechanism helps you to decouple various aspects of your application, such as authentication, database connections, and caching, thereby improving maintainability and scalability. In this discussion, we will delve into how FastAPI's dependency injection system operates and how you can leverage it for common tasks.

To start, let's understand the fundamental principles of dependency injection in FastAPI. The core idea behind dependency injection is to provide dependencies to your endpoints or other components from a central source, rather than creating them directly within the components themselves. This practice not only promotes cleaner code but also enhances testability by allowing you to easily swap out implementations for testing purposes.

FastAPI's dependency injection system is based on the concept of "Depends," which is a function that defines and provides dependencies. Dependencies can be used to inject services, configuration, or other shared components into your route handlers. Dependencies are defined as functions or classes, and they are invoked by FastAPI whenever the associated endpoints are called.

Consider an example where you need to implement a dependency for managing database connections. First, you would define a function that provides the database connection. This function will be used as a dependency in your route handlers:

```python
from fastapi import FastAPI, Depends
from sqlalchemy.orm import Session
from .database import SessionLocal, engine

app FastAPI()

Dependency function
def get_db() -> Session:
  db SessionLocal()
  try:
    yield db
  finally:
    db.close()
```

In this code snippet, `get_db` is a dependency function that yields a database session. The `SessionLocal` object represents the SQLAlchemy session factory, and `db.close()` ensures that the session is properly closed after use. The `yield` statement is used to provide the database session to the endpoint handlers.

Once you have defined the dependency function, you can use it in your route handlers by including it as a parameter with the `Depends` annotation. This informs FastAPI that the parameter should be resolved using the dependency function:

```python
from fastapi import FastAPI, Depends

app FastAPI()

@app.get("/items/{item_id}")
def read_item(item_id: int, db: Session Depends(get_db)):
   Use the db session to interact with the database
  item db.query(Item).filter(Item.id item_id).first()
  return item
```

In this endpoint, the `db` parameter is injected with the result of the `get_db` dependency function. FastAPI automatically handles the invocation of `get_db`, providing a new database session to the endpoint and ensuring it is closed after the request is processed.

Dependency injection in FastAPI is not limited to database connections. It can also be employed for tasks such as authentication, configuration management, and caching. Let's examine how to use dependencies for authentication.

Suppose you need to implement authentication for your API. You might create a dependency function that validates a token and provides user information:

```python
from fastapi import Depends, HTTPException, status
from .auth import verify_token, get_current_user

def get_current_user(token: str Depends(oauth2_scheme)):
  user verify_token(token)
  if user is None:
    raise HTTPException(
      status_codestatus.HTTP_401_UNAUTHORIZED,
      detail"Invalid authentication credentials",
    )
```

```
    return user
```

In this function, `oauth2_scheme` represents the OAuth2 token scheme used to extract the token from the request. The `verify_token` function is responsible for validating the token and retrieving the user associated with it. If the token is invalid, an `HTTPException` is raised.

You can then use this authentication dependency in your route handlers:

```python
@app.get("/users/me")
def read_current_user(current_user: User Depends(get_current_user)):
    return current_user
```

In this example, the `current_user` parameter is populated using the `get_current_user` dependency. FastAPI ensures that the user is authenticated before processing the request.

In addition to functional dependencies, FastAPI also supports class-based dependencies. This approach allows you to create reusable components with stateful behavior. For example, you might define a caching class that can be injected into your route handlers:

```python
from typing import Dict

class Cache:
    def __init__(self):
        self.store: Dict[str, str] {}

    def get(self, key: str) -> str:
        return self.store.get(key, "")

    def set(self, key: str, value: str) -> None:
```

```
        self.store[key] value

Dependency function for Cache
def get_cache() -> Cache:
    return Cache()

@app.get("/cache/{key}")
def read_cache(key: str, cache: Cache Depends(get_cache)):
    return {"value": cache.get(key)}
```

In this example, the `Cache` class is used to manage a simple key-value store. The `get_cache` function provides an instance of `Cache` to the route handler, allowing you to use caching within your API.

Through effective use of dependency injection, you can significantly enhance the modularity and maintainability of your FastAPI application. By defining dependencies for common tasks and injecting them into your endpoints, you create a more organized and testable codebase.

When utilizing dependency injection for handling authentication, you can leverage FastAPI's system to ensure that only authorized users can access specific endpoints. This is achieved by defining a dependency that checks user credentials and verifies permissions. For example, consider a scenario where you need a dependency that authenticates users based on a token:

```python
from fastapi import Depends, HTTPException, status
from typing import Optional

class User:
    def __init__(self, username: str):
        self.username username

def get_current_user(token: str) -> User:
```

```
    if token ! "valid-token":
        raise HTTPException(status_codestatus.HTTP_401_UNAUTHORIZED, detail"Invalid Token")
    return User(username"authenticated_user")
```

In this code snippet, `get_current_user` is a dependency function that checks the validity of a token and returns a `User` object if the token is valid. If the token is invalid, it raises an `HTTPException` to indicate unauthorized access. The `User` class represents a simple user model, and this example assumes a token validation mechanism that would typically involve more complex logic, such as checking against a database or an authentication service.

You can use this dependency in your route handlers to protect endpoints that require authentication:

```python
@app.get("/protected-data")
def get_protected_data(user: User Depends(get_current_user)):
    return {"data": "This is protected data", "user": user.username}
```

Here, the `Depends` function ensures that the `get_current_user` dependency is resolved before the endpoint logic executes. If the token is invalid, the request will be denied with an appropriate error message. Otherwise, the endpoint will proceed, and the authenticated user's information will be available for use.

Similarly, dependency injection can be employed to manage caching mechanisms. Suppose you want to implement caching for frequently accessed data to improve performance. You can define a caching dependency that handles retrieving data from a cache or fetching it from the source if it is not present in the cache. Here is an example of a simple caching mechanism:

```python
from fastapi import Depends
from cachetools import LRUCache

cache  LRUCache(maxsize100)

def get_data_from_cache(key: str) -> Optional[str]:
  return cache.get(key)

def cache_data(key: str, data: str):
  cache[key]  data

def get_cached_data(key: str) -> str:
  data  get_data_from_cache(key)
  if data is None:
    data  fetch_data_from_source(key)
    cache_data(key, data)
  return data
```

In this example, `get_data_from_cache` retrieves data from an in-memory cache, `cache_data` stores data in the cache, and `get_cached_data` checks the cache and fetches data from the source if it is not available in the cache. This caching approach can be applied to endpoints where performance optimization is crucial.

To use caching in your endpoints, define a dependency that provides the cached data:

```python
@app.get("/items/{item_id}")
def get_item(item_id: str, cache_key: str  Depends(lambda:
f"item_{item_id}")) -> str:
  data  get_cached_data(cache_key)
  return {"item_id": item_id, "data": data}
```

In this endpoint, the `cache_key` dependency generates a key based on the `item_id`. The `get_cached_data` function is then used to retrieve the data, either from the cache or by fetching it from the source if it's not available in the cache.

By leveraging FastAPI's dependency injection system, you can efficiently manage and inject various components, such as authentication mechanisms, database connections, and caching systems, into your endpoints. This approach not only enhances the modularity of your application but also ensures that your components are reusable and maintainable. Through careful design and implementation of these dependencies, you can build a robust and scalable API that effectively handles a wide range of tasks and scenarios.

To further explore dependency injection in FastAPI, consider implementing a more advanced use case involving database transactions. In complex applications, managing database transactions efficiently is crucial. FastAPI's dependency injection system allows for a clean and effective way to handle transactions, ensuring that database operations are performed consistently and reliably.

To manage database transactions, you can create a dependency that starts and commits a transaction, or rolls it back in case of errors. Here's how you might structure such a dependency:

```python
from fastapi import Depends, HTTPException
from sqlalchemy.orm import Session
from sqlalchemy.exc import SQLAlchemyError
from .database import SessionLocal

def get_db() -> Session:
    db SessionLocal()
    try:
```

```
    yield db
    db.commit()
  except SQLAlchemyError:
    db.rollback()
        raise HTTPException(status_code500, detail"Database
transaction error")
  finally:
    db.close()
```

In this example, `get_db` is a dependency function that initializes a database session and ensures that it is properly committed or rolled back depending on the outcome of the transaction. If an error occurs during the transaction, the session is rolled back, and an `HTTPException` is raised to indicate a server error. This approach ensures that database operations are atomic, consistent, and isolated.

When using this dependency in your route handlers, it will handle the transaction management automatically:

```python
@app.post("/create-item")
def create_item(item: Item, db: Session  Depends(get_db)):
  db.add(item)
  return {"status": "item created"}
```

In this route handler, the `Depends` function ensures that `get_db` is invoked to provide a database session. The session is used to add a new item to the database. If the transaction is successful, it is committed automatically; if any error occurs, it is rolled back, maintaining data integrity.

Furthermore, dependency injection in FastAPI also supports more complex scenarios involving multiple dependencies. You can combine dependencies to create composite functionalities. For example, suppose you have a service that requires both user authentication and database access. You can define a composite dependency that encapsulates both functionalities:

```python
def get_user_and_db(token: str, db: Session Depends(get_db)):
  user get_current_user(token)
  return user, db
```

This function uses `Depends` to inject both the `get_current_user` and `get_db` dependencies. The `get_user_and_db` function returns both the user object and the database session, which can then be used in your route handlers:

```python
@app.get("/user-data")
def get_user_data(token: str, user_and_db: tuple Depends(get_user_and_db)):
  user, db user_and_db
  data db.query(UserData).filter(UserData.user_id user.id).all()
  return {"data": data}
```

In this route handler, `Depends` resolves `get_user_and_db`, providing both the user object and the database session. This approach consolidates the necessary dependencies and ensures that both authentication and data access are handled seamlessly.

In summary, FastAPI's dependency injection system is a powerful tool that supports a range of functionalities, from simple parameter injection to complex scenarios involving authentication, database management, and caching. By defining and using dependencies effectively, you can build robust, maintainable, and scalable applications with clean and reusable code. This system allows for a modular design where components are loosely coupled, improving the overall quality and flexibility of your FastAPI applications.

CHAPTER 7: HANDLING AUTHENTICATION AND AUTHORIZATION

Implementing robust authentication and authorization mechanisms is essential for securing APIs. In FastAPI, we have several strategies to ensure that only authorized users can access specific resources. This section will explore three common methods for securing endpoints: OAuth2, JSON Web Tokens (JWT), and API key-based authentication. Additionally, we will discuss how to manage user roles and permissions effectively.

OAuth2 is a widely used authorization framework that allows third-party applications to obtain limited access to a user's resources. FastAPI provides built-in support for OAuth2 with password flow and bearer tokens. To implement OAuth2 in FastAPI, you must first configure the authentication flow and set up the necessary endpoints.

Start by defining an OAuth2 scheme using FastAPI's `OAuth2PasswordBearer`:

```python
```

```
from fastapi.security import OAuth2PasswordBearer

oauth2_scheme OAuth2PasswordBearer(tokenUrl"token")
```

The `tokenUrl` specifies the endpoint where the token can be obtained. The `OAuth2PasswordBearer` class will handle the extraction and verification of the token from incoming requests.

Next, you need an endpoint to handle user authentication and token issuance. Typically, this involves validating user credentials and generating a token:

```python
from fastapi import FastAPI, Depends, HTTPException, status
from pydantic import BaseModel
from typing import Union
from datetime import datetime, timedelta
from jose import JWTError, jwt

app FastAPI()
SECRET_KEY "your_secret_key"
ALGORITHM "HS256"
ACCESS_TOKEN_EXPIRE_MINUTES 30

class Token(BaseModel):
  access_token: str
  token_type: str

class TokenData(BaseModel):
  username: str

def create_access_token(data: dict, expires_delta:
Union[timedelta, None] None):
  to_encode data.copy()
  if expires_delta:
    expire datetime.utcnow() + expires_delta
  else:
```

```
    expire datetime.utcnow() + timedelta(minutes15)
  to_encode.update({"exp": expire})
         encoded_jwt    jwt.encode(to_encode,   SECRET_KEY,
algorithmALGORITHM)
  return encoded_jwt

@app.post("/token", response_modelToken)
def       login(form_data:       OAuth2PasswordRequestForm
Depends()):
   Dummy user validation
    if form_data.username  "user" and form_data.password
"password":
                                      access_token_expires
timedelta(minutesACCESS_TOKEN_EXPIRE_MINUTES)
    access_token create_access_token(
                          data{"sub":   form_data.username},
expires_deltaaccess_token_expires
    )
         return {"access_token": access_token, "token_type":
"bearer"}
  else:
    raise HTTPException(
      status_codestatus.HTTP_401_UNAUTHORIZED,
      detail"Incorrect username or password",
      headers{"WWW-Authenticate": "Bearer"},
    )
```

In this code, `create_access_token` generates a JWT with an expiration time. The `/token` endpoint authenticates users and returns a token if the credentials are valid. You must replace the dummy user validation logic with actual authentication against a database or another authentication system.

For securing endpoints using the issued JWT, you need to define a dependency that verifies the token and extracts user information:

```python
from fastapi import Depends
from jose import JWTError, jwt
from .schemas import TokenData

def get_current_user(token: str  Depends(oauth2_scheme)) ->
TokenData:
  credentials_exception  HTTPException(
    status_codestatus.HTTP_401_UNAUTHORIZED,
    detail"Could not validate credentials",
    headers{"WWW-Authenticate": "Bearer"},
  )
  try:
                payload    jwt.decode(token,   SECRET_KEY,
algorithms[ALGORITHM])
    username: str  payload.get("sub")
    if username is None:
      raise credentials_exception
    token_data  TokenData(usernameusername)
  except JWTError:
    raise credentials_exception
  return token_data
```

The `get_current_user` function extracts and validates the token. If the token is invalid or expired, it raises an exception. Otherwise, it returns the decoded user information, which can be used to secure your API endpoints.

Next, let's examine JSON Web Tokens (JWT) more closely. JWT is a compact, URL-safe token format that encodes claims about a user. JWTs are used extensively for authentication because they are stateless and self-contained, meaning they carry all necessary information about the user within the token itself. This can be advantageous for scalability, as the server does not need to maintain session state.

The `create_access_token` function demonstrated earlier encodes user data into a JWT, which can then be verified and decoded by the server. JWTs consist of three parts: the header, payload, and signature. The header typically specifies the algorithm used to sign the token, while the payload contains the claims. The signature is generated using the header and payload, signed with a secret key.

For API key-based authentication, the process is straightforward. Each client receives a unique API key that must be included in the request headers. FastAPI makes it easy to implement this by defining a dependency that checks for the presence and validity of the API key:

```python
from fastapi import Header, HTTPException, Security

API_KEY "your_api_key"

def api_key_auth(api_key: str Header(...)) -> str:
  if api_key ! API_KEY:
    raise HTTPException(
      status_codestatus.HTTP_401_UNAUTHORIZED,
      detail"Invalid API Key",
      headers{"WWW-Authenticate": "Bearer"},
    )
  return api_key
```

The `api_key_auth` function verifies the API key against a predefined value. If the key is incorrect or missing, it raises an `HTTPException`. This approach is simple and effective for basic API security needs.

To manage user roles and permissions, you can integrate role-based access control into your authentication system. This involves assigning roles to users and restricting access to resources based on those roles. Typically, you would encode role information into the JWT payload or store it in a database, then use this information to authorize user actions.

For example, if a user's role is stored in the JWT payload:

```python
def get_current_user(token: str  Depends(oauth2_scheme)) ->
TokenData:
  credentials_exception  HTTPException(
    status_codestatus.HTTP_401_UNAUTHORIZED,
    detail"Could not validate credentials",
    headers{"WWW-Authenticate": "Bearer"},
  )
  try:
                    payload     jwt.decode(token,    SECRET_KEY,
algorithms[ALGORITHM])
    username: str  payload.get("sub")
    role: str  payload.get("role")
    if username is None or role is None:
      raise credentials_exception
    token_data  TokenData(usernameusername, rolerole)
  except JWTError:
    raise credentials_exception
  return token_data
```

By incorporating roles into the token, you can check user permissions in your route handlers and enforce access control policies effectively.

Securing APIs with authentication and authorization is a critical aspect of modern web development. FastAPI's flexible and powerful dependency injection system provides robust mechanisms to implement these security features, enabling you to build secure and reliable applications.

Continuing with the implementation of authentication and

authorization methods, let's delve deeper into JSON Web Tokens (JWT), a common approach used alongside OAuth2 for managing user sessions and securing APIs. JWTs provide a compact, URL-safe means of representing claims to be transferred between two parties. They are particularly useful for stateless authentication where the server does not need to maintain session information.

To integrate JWT into FastAPI, you should first ensure you have a method for creating and validating tokens. This involves encoding a payload with claims and a secret key, which will be used to verify the token's integrity on subsequent requests. Here's a more comprehensive example of creating and validating JWT tokens:

```
```python
from jose import JWTError, jwt

SECRET_KEY "your_secret_key"
ALGORITHM "HS256"

def create_access_token(data: dict, expires_delta: timedelta
None):
  to_encode data.copy()
  if expires_delta:
    expire datetime.utcnow() + expires_delta
  else:
    expire datetime.utcnow() + timedelta(minutes15)
  to_encode.update({"exp": expire})
        encoded_jwt    jwt.encode(to_encode,    SECRET_KEY,
algorithmALGORITHM)
  return encoded_jwt

def verify_token(token: str, credentials_exception):
  try:
                  payload    jwt.decode(token,    SECRET_KEY,
algorithms[ALGORITHM])
    username: str payload.get("sub")
```
```

```
        if username is None:
            raise credentials_exception
        return TokenData(usernameusername)
    except JWTError:
        raise credentials_exception
```

In the example above, `create_access_token` generates a JWT by encoding the provided data along with an expiration time. `verify_token` is used to decode the token and retrieve the user's identity. This function also handles any potential errors, such as an invalid or expired token.

When using JWTs, it is crucial to secure your endpoints by enforcing authentication. FastAPI's dependency injection system allows you to easily enforce token validation in your route handlers. You can create a dependency that extracts and verifies the JWT from the request header:

```python
from fastapi import Depends, HTTPException, status
from fastapi.security import OAuth2PasswordBearer

oauth2_scheme OAuth2PasswordBearer(tokenUrl"token")

def get_current_user(token: str Depends(oauth2_scheme)):
    credentials_exception HTTPException(
        status_codestatus.HTTP_401_UNAUTHORIZED,
        detail"Could not validate credentials",
        headers{"WWW-Authenticate": "Bearer"},
    )
    return verify_token(token, credentials_exception)

@app.get("/users/me", response_modelUser)
def read_users_me(current_user: TokenData Depends(get_current_user)):
    return current_user
```

In this example, the `get_current_user` function uses the `oauth2_scheme` dependency to extract the token from the request header and then verifies it. The `read_users_me` endpoint requires this verification and will only return user information if the token is valid.

In addition to JWT and OAuth2, another method for securing APIs is API key-based authentication. This is a straightforward approach where the client includes a unique API key in the request headers. While less complex than OAuth2 or JWT, API key authentication is suitable for simpler use cases and internal services.

To implement API key-based authentication in FastAPI, you would define a dependency that checks for the presence and validity of the API key. Here's how you can set this up:

```python
from fastapi import Header, HTTPException

API_KEY "your_api_key"

def api_key_auth(api_key: str Header(...)):
  if api_key ! API_KEY:
    raise HTTPException(
      status_codestatus.HTTP_403_FORBIDDEN,
      detail"Invalid API Key"
    )

@app.get("/items/")
def read_items(api_key: str Depends(api_key_auth)):
  return {"items": ["item1", "item2", "item3"]}
```

In this setup, the `api_key_auth` function checks if the API key in the request headers matches the expected value. If not, it raises a `403 Forbidden` error. This ensures that only requests with the correct API key can access the endpoint.

Lastly, managing user roles and permissions is another critical aspect of securing your API. FastAPI does not provide built-in role management, but you can extend your application's functionality by incorporating role checks within your authentication logic. For instance, you could modify your JWT claims to include user roles and then implement additional checks in your route handlers based on these roles:

```python
def verify_token(token: str, credentials_exception):
  try:
    payload jwt.decode(token, SECRET_KEY, algorithms[ALGORITHM])
    username: str payload.get("sub")
    roles: list payload.get("roles", [])
    if username is None:
      raise credentials_exception
    return TokenData(usernameusername, rolesroles)
  except JWTError:
    raise credentials_exception

def role_required(role: str):
  def role_checker(current_user: TokenData Depends(get_current_user)):
    if role not in current_user.roles:
      raise HTTPException(
        status_codestatus.HTTP_403_FORBIDDEN,
        detail"Insufficient permissions"
      )
    return current_user
  return role_checker

@app.get("/admin/", response_modelAdminData)
def read_admin_data(current_user: TokenData Depends(role_required("admin"))):
  return {"admin_data": "sensitive data"}
```

In this example, the `role_required` function creates a dependency that checks if the current user has the required role to access the endpoint. The `read_admin_data` endpoint enforces that only users with the "admin" role can access it.

By understanding and implementing these authentication and authorization mechanisms, you can ensure that your FastAPI application is secure and properly manages access to its resources.

When integrating OAuth2 for authentication, FastAPI provides built-in support that simplifies the process. OAuth2 is a protocol that allows users to grant third-party applications access to their resources without exposing their credentials. The protocol involves several flows, with the Authorization Code Flow being one of the most commonly used for server-side applications.

To implement OAuth2 with FastAPI, you will first need to configure your OAuth2 provider, which could be services like Google, Facebook, or any other OAuth2-compliant service. FastAPI uses `OAuth2PasswordBearer` for handling token-based authentication, but for OAuth2 flows, you'll often use the `OAuth2AuthorizationCodeBearer` or similar implementations.

Here's an example of how to integrate OAuth2 using `OAuth2AuthorizationCodeBearer`:

```python
from fastapi import FastAPI, Depends, HTTPException
from fastapi.security import OAuth2AuthorizationCodeBearer
from typing import Optional
from pydantic import BaseModel

app FastAPI()
```

```
oauth2_scheme OAuth2AuthorizationCodeBearer(
            authorizationUrl"https://your-auth-provider.com/
authorize",
  tokenUrl"https://your-auth-provider.com/token",
)

class User(BaseModel):
  username: str

def get_current_user(token: str Depends(oauth2_scheme)):
  try:
     Verify the token and fetch user info from OAuth2 provider
    user_info fetch_user_info_from_token(token)
    return User(usernameuser_info["username"])
  except Exception:
    raise HTTPException(
      status_code401,
      detail"Invalid authentication credentials",
    )

@app.get("/users/me", response_modelUser)
def read_users_me(current_user: User
Depends(get_current_user)):
  return current_user

def fetch_user_info_from_token(token: str):
   Simulate fetching user info from OAuth2 provider
      In practice, you would make an HTTP request to the
provider's user info endpoint
  return {"username": "example_user"}
```

In this setup, `OAuth2AuthorizationCodeBearer` is configured with the authorization and token URLs provided by your OAuth2 provider. The `get_current_user` function handles the extraction and validation of the OAuth2 token, which involves making requests to the OAuth2 provider's user info endpoint. The `fetch_user_info_from_token` function simulates this request, but you would need to implement it according to the actual provider's API.

For API key-based authentication, FastAPI allows you to secure endpoints using a simple dependency that validates the presence and correctness of an API key. This method is often used for simpler use cases or when a lightweight authentication mechanism is sufficient.

Here's an example of implementing API key-based authentication:

```python
from fastapi import Header, HTTPException

API_KEY "your_secret_api_key"

def api_key_auth(api_key: str Header(...)):
  if api_key ! API_KEY:
    raise HTTPException(
      status_code403,
      detail"Invalid API key"
    )

@app.get("/secure-data")
def read_secure_data(api_key: str Depends(api_key_auth)):
  return {"data": "This is protected data"}
```

In this example, the `api_key_auth` dependency checks the `api_key` provided in the request header against a predefined secret key. If the key is incorrect, it raises an HTTP exception with a 403 status code.

Managing user roles is another crucial aspect of authorization, ensuring that different users have appropriate access levels to various parts of your API. FastAPI allows you to define role-based access control (RBAC) using custom dependencies.

For example, you could create a dependency to check if a user has the appropriate role before allowing access to certain endpoints:

```python
from typing import List

def require_roles(roles: List[str]):
    def role_checker(current_user: User
Depends(get_current_user)):
        if current_user.username not in roles:
            raise HTTPException(
                status_code403,
                detail"Insufficient permissions"
            )
        return current_user
    return role_checker

@app.get("/admin-data")
def read_admin_data(current_user: User
Depends(require_roles(["admin"]))):
    return {"data": "This is admin data"}
```

In this example, the `require_roles` function creates a dependency that verifies if the current user has one of the required roles. The roles are checked against the user's data, and if the user does not have the required role, an HTTP exception is raised.

Securing APIs through these methods ensures that your application is not only functional but also protected against unauthorized access. Each method—OAuth2, JWT, API keys, and role-based access control—serves different purposes and can be selected based on your application's security requirements. Combining these strategies effectively will provide a robust security framework for your FastAPI application.

CHAPTER 8: INTEGRATING WITH DATABASES

When integrating FastAPI with databases, you must understand both SQL and NoSQL databases' distinct characteristics and interactions. FastAPI supports various databases, including SQL databases using ORMs (Object-Relational Mappers) like SQLAlchemy and NoSQL databases such as MongoDB. Each approach involves different techniques and tools for data persistence, querying, and transaction management.

Integrating with SQL Databases Using SQLAlchemy

SQLAlchemy is a powerful and flexible ORM that allows you to interact with SQL databases using Python objects. This approach abstracts the SQL queries into Python methods, simplifying database interactions and making code more maintainable.

To begin using SQLAlchemy with FastAPI, you first need to install the necessary packages. Typically, you would install `SQLAlchemy` and `databases` for asynchronous support, alongside `asyncpg` for PostgreSQL or `aiomysql` for MySQL, depending on your database.

Here's a step-by-step guide for setting up SQLAlchemy with FastAPI:

1. Install Dependencies:

```bash
pip install sqlalchemy databases asyncpg
```

2. Define Your Database Models:

Using SQLAlchemy, you define database tables as Python classes. Each class corresponds to a table, and attributes represent columns.

```python
from sqlalchemy import create_engine, Column, Integer, String
from sqlalchemy.ext.declarative import declarative_base
from sqlalchemy.orm import sessionmaker

SQLALCHEMY_DATABASE_URL "postgresql+asyncpg://user:password@localhost/dbname"

engine create_engine(SQLALCHEMY_DATABASE_URL, echoTrue)
SessionLocal sessionmaker(autocommitFalse, autoflushFalse, bindengine)
Base declarative_base()

class User(Base):
  __tablename__ "users"

  id Column(Integer, primary_keyTrue, indexTrue)
  username Column(String, uniqueTrue, indexTrue)
  email Column(String, uniqueTrue, indexTrue)
```

3. Create Database Tables:

You need to create tables based on your models. You can achieve this using SQLAlchemy's `Base.metadata.create_all()` method.

```python
from sqlalchemy.ext.asyncio import AsyncEngine, AsyncSession
from sqlalchemy.future import select

async def init_db():
    async with engine.begin() as conn:
        await conn.run_sync(Base.metadata.create_all)
```

4. Create a Dependency for the Database Session:

In FastAPI, you typically use dependency injection to manage database sessions. Here's an example of how to create a session dependency:

```python
from fastapi import Depends, FastAPI
from sqlalchemy.orm import Session

def get_db():
    db SessionLocal()
    try:
        yield db
    finally:
        db.close()
```

5. Perform CRUD Operations:

With your models and session set up, you can now define your CRUD operations. Here's an example of how to create and read a user:

```python
from fastapi import HTTPException

app FastAPI()

@app.post("/users/", response_modelUser)
```

```
async def create_user(user: User, db: Session
Depends(get_db)):
    db.add(user)
    db.commit()
    db.refresh(user)
    return user

@app.get("/users/{user_id}", response_modelUser)
async def read_user(user_id: int, db: Session
Depends(get_db)):
    user db.query(User).filter(User.id user_id).first()
    if user is None:
        raise HTTPException(status_code404, detail"User not
found")
    return user
```

Integrating with NoSQL Databases Using MongoDB

MongoDB is a popular NoSQL database known for its flexibility and scalability. Unlike SQL databases, MongoDB stores data in BSON (Binary JSON) format, allowing for a more schema-less approach to data storage.

FastAPI can work with MongoDB using libraries such as `pymongo` or `motor` for asynchronous operations. Here's a basic example of how to integrate MongoDB with FastAPI using `motor`.

1. Install Dependencies:

```bash
pip install motor
```

2. Set Up MongoDB Connection:

Define your MongoDB client and database settings.

```python
```

```
from motor.motor_asyncio import AsyncIOMotorClient
from pymongo import MongoClient
from fastapi import FastAPI

app FastAPI()
client AsyncIOMotorClient("mongodb://localhost:27017")
db client.my_database
```

3. Define Your Data Model:

MongoDB collections do not require a predefined schema, but it's useful to define your data model for validation and consistency.

```python
from pydantic import BaseModel

class User(BaseModel):
    username: str
    email: str
```

4. Create CRUD Operations:

You can perform operations using the `motor` client. Here's how you might define an endpoint to create and read documents in MongoDB:

```python
@app.post("/users/")
async def create_user(user: User):
    user_dict user.dict()
    result await db.users.insert_one(user_dict)
    return {"id": str(result.inserted_id)}

@app.get("/users/{user_id}")
async def read_user(user_id: str):
    user await db.users.find_one({"_id": user_id})
    if user is None:
```

```
        raise HTTPException(status_code404, detail"User not
found")
    return user
```

When integrating with databases, whether SQL or NoSQL, managing connections efficiently and ensuring data consistency are paramount. SQLAlchemy provides a structured approach for SQL databases, while `motor` offers an asynchronous solution for MongoDB. Each database integration approach requires careful consideration of connection management, error handling, and efficient querying to ensure robust and scalable applications.

When working with SQLAlchemy in FastAPI, it is essential to manage database sessions properly to ensure that transactions are handled correctly and resources are efficiently used. This entails creating and closing sessions appropriately, which can be done using dependency injection to provide a session lifecycle for each request. This approach ensures that sessions are correctly scoped to the lifetime of a request, helping to avoid issues with uncommitted transactions or stale data.

In FastAPI, you can define a dependency that provides a database session to your route handlers. The dependency handles session creation, management, and closure. Here is an example of how to set up such a dependency:

```python
from sqlalchemy.orm import Session
from fastapi import Depends, FastAPI
from .database import SessionLocal, engine, Base

app FastAPI()

def get_db():
    db SessionLocal()
    try:
```

```
    yield db
  finally:
    db.close()

@app.post("/users/")
async def create_user(user: UserCreate, db: Session
Depends(get_db)):
  db_user User(usernameuser.username, emailuser.email)
  db.add(db_user)
  db.commit()
  db.refresh(db_user)
  return db_user
```

In this example, `get_db` is a dependency that provides a database session to the endpoint function. The session is created when the request starts and closed when the request ends, ensuring that each request operates in its transaction scope.

Integrating with NoSQL Databases Using MongoDB

For NoSQL databases such as MongoDB, FastAPI provides a different integration approach. MongoDB is a document-oriented database that stores data in flexible, JSON-like documents, which can be queried in a variety of ways.

To work with MongoDB in FastAPI, you often use the `motor` library, an asynchronous MongoDB driver for Python. The `pymongo` library is another option but lacks asynchronous support, which is crucial for high-performance applications.

Here's how to set up a MongoDB connection and interact with it using FastAPI:

1. Install Dependencies:

```bash
pip install motor
```

`` ``` ``

2. Set Up the Database Connection:

Establish a connection to MongoDB and define the database and collection. This setup typically happens in a module or function that initializes the database connection.

```python
from motor.motor_asyncio import AsyncIOMotorClient
from fastapi import FastAPI

app FastAPI()

 MongoDB connection setup
MONGO_DETAILS "mongodb://localhost:27017"
client AsyncIOMotorClient(MONGO_DETAILS)
database client.mydatabase
collection database.mycollection
```

3. Create and Query Documents:

Define functions for interacting with MongoDB, such as inserting and querying documents. These functions use the asynchronous methods provided by `motor` for non-blocking operations.

```python
async def create_user(user: dict):
    result await collection.insert_one(user)
    return str(result.inserted_id)

async def get_user(user_id: str):
    user await collection.find_one({"_id": user_id})
    return user
```

4. Integrate with FastAPI Endpoints:

Use the asynchronous functions within your FastAPI route

handlers to interact with the MongoDB database.

```python
@app.post("/users/")
async def create_user_endpoint(user: dict):
    user_id  await create_user(user)
    return {"user_id": user_id}

@app.get("/users/{user_id}")
async def read_user_endpoint(user_id: str):
    user  await get_user(user_id)
    if user is None:
        raise HTTPException(status_code404, detail"User not found")
    return user
```

Transaction Management in Databases

Handling transactions is crucial for ensuring data integrity, especially when dealing with multiple operations that need to be atomic. In SQL databases, transactions are managed using commit and rollback operations. SQLAlchemy abstracts these details and allows you to manage transactions using the session object.

In MongoDB, transactions are less common but are supported for operations that span multiple documents or collections. MongoDB supports multi-document transactions with ACID properties starting from version 4.0. When using transactions with MongoDB, you would need to use a session object to handle the transaction lifecycle.

In SQLAlchemy:

```python
async def create_user_with_transaction(user: UserCreate, db: Session):
  async with db.begin():   Starts a transaction block
```

```
    db_user User(usernameuser.username, emailuser.email)
    db.add(db_user)
    await db.commit()
    db.refresh(db_user)
  return db_user
```

In MongoDB with `motor`:

```python
async def create_user_with_transaction(user: dict):
  async with client.start_session() as session:
    async with session.start_transaction():
      result await collection.insert_one(user, sessionsession)
      return str(result.inserted_id)
```

By carefully managing database connections, sessions, and transactions, you can ensure that your FastAPI application interacts with databases efficiently and reliably, whether using SQL or NoSQL solutions. This approach not only helps in maintaining data consistency but also contributes to the overall performance and scalability of your application.

Continuing with the MongoDB integration, once the connection is established, the next step is to define the operations for interacting with the database. MongoDB's document model differs significantly from the relational model used in SQL databases. Data is organized into collections, which are analogous to tables in SQL databases, but documents within a collection do not need to adhere to a fixed schema. This flexibility allows for more dynamic and scalable data storage solutions.

For working with MongoDB in FastAPI, you should define CRUD (Create, Read, Update, Delete) operations that utilize the `motor` library's asynchronous methods. Here is how you can structure these operations:

Setting Up MongoDB Connection

First, ensure that the MongoDB client is properly initialized. This involves setting up the connection and configuring your database and collection. Typically, this setup occurs in a separate module:

```python
from motor.motor_asyncio import AsyncIOMotorClient
from pymongo import ReturnDocument

client AsyncIOMotorClient("mongodb://localhost:27017")
db client.mydatabase
collection db.mycollection
```

In this code, `AsyncIOMotorClient` is used to create a client instance that connects to MongoDB. The `db` object represents the database, and `collection` is the MongoDB collection where documents are stored.

Creating a Document

To insert a new document into MongoDB, use the `insert_one` method provided by the `motor` library. Here's how you can define a route to create a new document:

```python
from fastapi import FastAPI, HTTPException
from pydantic import BaseModel

app FastAPI()

class Item(BaseModel):
  name: str
  description: str

@app.post("/items/")
async def create_item(item: Item):
  result await collection.insert_one(item.dict())
```

```
    if result.inserted_id:
        return {"id": str(result.inserted_id), "item": item}
    else:
        raise HTTPException(status_code500, detail"Item could not be created")
```

In this route, `insert_one` inserts the document into the collection, and `item.dict()` converts the Pydantic model instance into a dictionary suitable for MongoDB insertion. The response includes the ID of the newly created document.

Reading Documents

To retrieve documents, you use methods like `find_one` or `find`. Here's an example of how to implement a route that reads a document by its ID:

```python
from bson import ObjectId

@app.get("/items/{item_id}")
async def read_item(item_id: str):
    document await collection.find_one({"_id": ObjectId(item_id)})
    if document:
        return document
    else:
        raise HTTPException(status_code404, detail"Item not found")
```

In this route, `find_one` is used to query the collection for a document with a specific ID. `ObjectId` converts the string ID to a format MongoDB can use.

Updating Documents

Updating a document involves finding the document by its ID

and then applying the changes. You can use the `update_one` method as shown here:

```python
@app.put("/items/{item_id}")
async def update_item(item_id: str, item: Item):
  result await collection.update_one({"_id": ObjectId(item_id)},
{"$set": item.dict()})
  if result.modified_count:
    return {"detail": "Item updated"}
  else:
        raise HTTPException(status_code404, detail"Item not
found or no changes made")
```

In this example, `$set` is used to specify the fields that should be updated in the document.

Deleting Documents

To delete a document, use the `delete_one` method:

```python
@app.delete("/items/{item_id}")
async def delete_item(item_id: str):
  result await collection.delete_one({"_id": ObjectId(item_id)})
  if result.deleted_count:
    return {"detail": "Item deleted"}
  else:
        raise HTTPException(status_code404, detail"Item not
found")
```

This route removes a document from the collection based on its ID and returns a confirmation message if the deletion is successful.

Transactions and Error Handling

MongoDB supports multi-document transactions which are useful for ensuring consistency in operations that affect multiple documents. Transactions can be managed through `motor` using the `start_session` method. However, for simpler use cases, such as single document operations, transactions are generally not required.

Error handling is crucial in database operations. Ensure that you catch exceptions and provide meaningful error messages to the client. For MongoDB operations, this often involves handling specific exceptions such as `pymongo.errors.OperationFailure` or general exceptions where appropriate.

By integrating FastAPI with both SQL and NoSQL databases, you leverage the strengths of each database type, allowing for robust, scalable, and flexible applications. Whether you choose SQLAlchemy for relational data or `motor` for document-oriented data, understanding these integrations will help you build effective and efficient APIs.

CHAPTER 9: VALIDATING AND PARSING DATA

In the realm of API development, ensuring that the data flowing through your application is both valid and correctly formatted is crucial for maintaining the integrity and reliability of your services. FastAPI leverages Pydantic, a powerful data validation library, to facilitate this process, allowing you to define clear schemas for your data and automatically handle validation and parsing. This ensures that your API can enforce data integrity and provide meaningful feedback when errors occur.

To begin, FastAPI's integration with Pydantic allows you to define data models that act as schemas for request and response data. These models are instantiated as Python classes and utilize Pydantic's type annotations to enforce data constraints. Let's explore how to define and use these models to validate incoming data.

Defining Data Models with Pydantic

To create a Pydantic model, you derive a class from `pydantic.BaseModel`. Attributes of this class are defined using Python's type annotations, which specify the expected data types. Here's an example of a simple Pydantic model for a user profile:

```python
from pydantic import BaseModel, EmailStr, constr

class UserProfile(BaseModel):
  username: constr(min_length3, max_length50)
  email: EmailStr
  age: int
```

In this model, `username` must be a string with a length between 3 and 50 characters, `email` must be a valid email address, and `age` must be an integer. Pydantic automatically enforces these constraints when the model is instantiated.

Using Models for Request Validation

When defining API endpoints that require request bodies, you can specify the data model as a parameter in your endpoint functions. FastAPI automatically parses and validates the request data against the model. Here's how you might create an endpoint that accepts user profile data:

```python
from fastapi import FastAPI, HTTPException

app FastAPI()

@app.post("/users/")
async def create_user(user: UserProfile):
   The user parameter is automatically validated and parsed
   You can use the validated data here
     return {"username": user.username, "email": user.email,
"age": user.age}
```

In this example, FastAPI validates the incoming JSON payload against the `UserProfile` model. If the data does not conform to the schema, FastAPI automatically returns a 422 Unprocessable Entity response, including details about the validation errors.

Custom Validation

While Pydantic provides robust built-in validation, you might encounter scenarios where you need custom validation logic. Pydantic allows for this through its `@validator` decorators. These decorators enable you to define additional validation rules for your model fields.

For instance, consider a scenario where you want to ensure that a user's age is within a specific range:

```python
from pydantic import BaseModel, validator

class UserProfile(BaseModel):
  username: constr(min_length3, max_length50)
  email: EmailStr
  age: int

   @validator('age')
  def age_must_be_positive(cls, value):
    if value < 0:
      raise ValueError('Age must be a positive integer')
    return value
```

In this example, the `age_must_be_positive` method ensures that the `age` field is not only an integer but also a positive value. If the `age` field is negative, Pydantic raises a validation error.

Handling Validation Errors

FastAPI automatically handles and formats validation errors returned by Pydantic. When a request payload fails validation, FastAPI responds with a 422 status code and includes a JSON body detailing the errors. However, you might want to customize this behavior or handle errors in a specific way.

You can define an exception handler to manage validation errors globally. FastAPI allows you to define custom exception handlers using its `exception_handler` decorator. For example, to customize the response for validation errors, you can do the following:

```python
from fastapi import Request, FastAPI
from fastapi.responses import JSONResponse
from pydantic import ValidationError

app  FastAPI()

@app.exception_handler(ValidationError)
async def validation_exception_handler(request: Request, exc:
ValidationError):
  return JSONResponse(
    status_code422,
    content{"detail": exc.errors()},
  )
```

In this handler, we catch `ValidationError` exceptions, which are raised by Pydantic, and return a custom JSON response. This can be particularly useful for providing a more user-friendly error message or logging additional details about the validation failures.

Parsing Data with Path and Query Parameters

In addition to request bodies, FastAPI also validates and parses data from path and query parameters. Path parameters are used within the URL of a request and are defined directly in the route path. Query parameters are passed in the URL query string and can be included in the endpoint function signature. FastAPI uses type annotations to validate and convert these parameters as well.

For instance, to validate a query parameter, you might use:

```python
from fastapi import FastAPI, Query

app FastAPI()

@app.get("/items/")
async def read_items(skip: int  Query(0, ge0), limit: int
Query(10, le100)):
  return {"skip": skip, "limit": limit}
```

In this example, `skip` and `limit` are query parameters. `Query` is used to specify constraints: `skip` must be a non-negative integer, and `limit` must be between 1 and 100.

By integrating these practices, you ensure that your FastAPI application handles data robustly, maintaining high standards of data integrity and usability. This foundational approach to validation and parsing helps build resilient and reliable APIs.

To further explore data validation and parsing in FastAPI, it is essential to delve into custom validation mechanisms and error handling. While Pydantic models provide a robust foundation for validating basic constraints, there are often scenarios where more complex validation logic is required. Custom validation methods in Pydantic allow you to define additional rules and constraints that go beyond the default validation capabilities.

Custom Validation with Pydantic

Pydantic models support custom validation methods that can be defined using the `@validator` decorator. This decorator allows you to create methods within your model that perform additional checks on the data. For example, suppose you need to validate that a user's age falls within a specific range, or you want to ensure that a username does not contain prohibited characters.

Here's an example of how to implement custom validation using Pydantic:

```python
from pydantic import BaseModel, EmailStr, validator
from typing import Optional

class UserProfile(BaseModel):
    username: str
    email: EmailStr
    age: Optional[int] None

    @validator('username')
    def username_must_not_contain_prohibited_characters(cls, v):
        prohibited_chars {'$', '%', '^', '&', ''}
        if any(char in v for char in prohibited_chars):
            raise ValueError('Username contains prohibited characters')
        return v

    @validator('age')
    def age_must_be_reasonable(cls, v):
        if v is not None and (v < 0 or v > 150):
            raise ValueError('Age must be between 0 and 150')
        return v
```

In this example, the `username_must_not_contain_prohibited_characters` validator checks that the username does not include any of the specified prohibited characters. The `age_must_be_reasonable` validator ensures that the age, if provided, falls within a reasonable range. These custom validation methods are invoked automatically during model instantiation.

Handling Validation Errors

When validation fails, FastAPI provides a structured way to handle errors and return meaningful feedback to clients. By default, FastAPI generates detailed error responses when validation errors occur. These responses include information about the validation issues, making it easier for clients to understand what went wrong.

However, you might want to customize the error handling behavior to better suit your application's needs. FastAPI allows you to define custom exception handlers for various types of errors. To handle validation errors specifically, you can create a custom exception handler that processes `RequestValidationError` exceptions. Here's an example of how to set this up:

```python
from fastapi import FastAPI, Request
from fastapi.exceptions import RequestValidationError
from fastapi.responses import JSONResponse
from pydantic import BaseModel, ValidationError

app FastAPI()

@app.exception_handler(RequestValidationError)
async def validation_exception_handler(request: Request, exc:
RequestValidationError):
  return JSONResponse(
    status_code400,
    content{
      "detail": "Invalid data provided",
      "errors": exc.errors()
    },
  )
```

In this custom exception handler, we capture

`RequestValidationError` exceptions and return a `JSONResponse` with a status code of 400. The response includes a custom message and details about the validation errors. This approach provides a user-friendly error message while also giving clients detailed information about what went wrong.

Parsing and Transforming Data

Beyond validation, FastAPI also supports data parsing and transformation. For instance, you may need to convert date strings into `datetime` objects or format numbers in a specific way. FastAPI, through Pydantic, allows for these transformations using its built-in features.

Consider a scenario where you need to parse a date string and ensure it adheres to a specific format. You can define a model with a `datetime` field, and Pydantic will automatically handle the parsing for you:

```python
from pydantic import BaseModel
from datetime import datetime

class Event(BaseModel):
  event_name: str
  event_date: datetime

@app.post("/events/")
async def create_event(event: Event):
   Pydantic parses the date string into a datetime object
      return {"event_name": event.event_name, "event_date": event.event_date.isoformat()}
```

In this example, the `event_date` field expects a date string that Pydantic will parse into a `datetime` object. FastAPI handles the conversion automatically, allowing you to work with native Python objects rather than raw strings.

Additionally, you can use custom data types and parsers if you need more control over how data is processed. FastAPI's flexibility in data handling ensures that you can tailor the data validation and parsing process to meet your application's specific requirements.

Summary

Effective data validation and parsing are foundational to building robust and reliable APIs. FastAPI, with its integration of Pydantic, provides powerful tools for defining data schemas, implementing custom validation logic, handling validation errors gracefully, and transforming data. By leveraging these features, you can ensure that your API maintains data integrity and provides clear, actionable feedback to clients.

In addressing validation errors, it is beneficial to understand how to customize the responses to better fit the needs of your application. FastAPI's default error handling provides a detailed JSON response that includes the location of the error, the error type, and a description. This is typically sufficient for most use cases, but there are scenarios where you may want to provide more user-friendly or context-specific error messages.

To customize validation error responses, FastAPI allows for the integration of custom exception handlers. These handlers let you intercept exceptions thrown during request processing and return a tailored response. For instance, you can define a custom exception handler to provide more specific error messages or additional details based on the type of validation error encountered.

Here's an example of how to create and register a custom exception handler:

```python
from fastapi import FastAPI, Request, HTTPException
```

```
from fastapi.responses import JSONResponse
from pydantic import ValidationError

app FastAPI()

@app.exception_handler(ValidationError)
async def validation_exception_handler(request: Request, exc:
ValidationError):
  return JSONResponse(
    status_code400,
    content{
      "detail": [
        {
          "loc": error["loc"],
          "msg": error["msg"],
          "type": error["type"]
        } for error in exc.errors()
      ],
      "error_type": "ValidationError"
    }
  )
```

In this custom handler, any `ValidationError` raised by Pydantic models will be caught, and a JSON response with a status code of 400 is returned. The response includes the location (`loc`), message (`msg`), and type (`type`) of each error, along with a custom `"error_type"` field for additional context. This approach can be expanded or adapted to fit different error handling requirements.

Integrating Validation with Query Parameters

FastAPI also allows for validation and parsing of query parameters. When you define query parameters in your path operation functions, FastAPI automatically parses and validates them based on the types specified. If you need to enforce additional constraints on query parameters, you can use Pydantic's `BaseModel` for complex query validation.

Consider an endpoint that filters user profiles based on various criteria. You might want to validate and parse these criteria to ensure they are within acceptable ranges or formats. Here's an example of how to handle such validations:

```python
from typing import Optional
from fastapi import FastAPI, Query, HTTPException
from pydantic import BaseModel, constr

app FastAPI()

class QueryParams(BaseModel):
  age_min: Optional[int] Query(None, ge0)
  age_max: Optional[int] Query(None, le150)
    username: Optional[constr(min_length3, max_length20)]
None

@app.get("/users/")
async def get_users(params: QueryParams):
  Assume a function fetch_users that filters users based on the
provided criteria
          users     fetch_users(age_minparams.age_min,
age_maxparams.age_max, usernameparams.username)
  return {"users": users}
```

In this example, the `QueryParams` model is used to define and validate query parameters. The `age_min` and `age_max` parameters use constraints to ensure they fall within the valid range, while `username` is validated to ensure it meets the length requirements. FastAPI automatically parses query parameters and applies these constraints before passing the validated data to the endpoint function.

Handling Data Parsing and Validation in Responses

Lastly, validation and parsing are not limited to incoming requests; they are equally important for outgoing responses. When constructing responses, especially those involving complex data structures or derived from database queries, it is critical to ensure that the data conforms to the expected schema.

FastAPI supports response models similar to request models, allowing you to define the structure and constraints of the response data. For example:

```python
from typing import List
from pydantic import BaseModel

class User(BaseModel):
  username: str
  email: str
  age: Optional[int]

class UserListResponse(BaseModel):
  users: List[User]

@app.get("/users/", response_modelUserListResponse)
async def list_users():
  users get_all_users()  Fetches all users from the database
  return {"users": users}
```

In this scenario, the `UserListResponse` model ensures that the response conforms to the expected structure, containing a list of `User` objects. FastAPI performs serialization and validation on the response data before sending it to the client, ensuring that it adheres to the defined schema.

By leveraging these techniques for validation and parsing, you can ensure the integrity and consistency of data throughout the lifecycle of your FastAPI application, providing a robust and reliable API experience for users.

CHAPTER 10: ERROR HANDLING AND EXCEPTION MANAGEMENT

Managing errors and exceptions is a fundamental aspect of developing robust applications. In FastAPI, effective error handling is not only crucial for providing a smooth user experience but also essential for maintaining and debugging your API. This discussion delves into the mechanisms provided by FastAPI for managing exceptions, creating custom handlers, and ensuring that errors are both meaningful and well-documented.

FastAPI's design philosophy incorporates extensive support for handling exceptions in a manner that ensures clear and informative feedback to clients. By default, FastAPI provides structured responses for a variety of common error scenarios. However, in many real-world applications, you will need to customize this behavior to fit specific needs and scenarios, particularly to enhance user experience and streamline debugging processes.

When an exception is raised in FastAPI, it is typically handled by the built-in exception handlers which return a JSON response detailing the error. For instance, if a request fails due to validation errors, FastAPI responds with a structured error message that includes the location of the error, the type of error, and a descriptive message. While this default behavior is helpful, there are situations where additional customization is beneficial.

Creating Custom Exception Handlers

FastAPI allows you to define custom exception handlers that can be used to modify the default error responses. Custom exception handlers provide a means to deliver more user-friendly error messages or to incorporate additional logging and monitoring capabilities. To create a custom exception handler, you define a function that takes an exception and a request object as parameters and returns a `JSONResponse` or another type of response.

Here is an example of how to implement a custom exception handler for generic application errors:

```python
from fastapi import FastAPI, Request, HTTPException
from fastapi.responses import JSONResponse

app FastAPI()

class CustomException(Exception):
  def __init__(self, name: str):
    self.name name

@app.exception_handler(CustomException)
async def custom_exception_handler(request: Request, exc: CustomException):
  return JSONResponse(
    status_code500,
    content{
      "detail": f"An error occurred: {exc.name}",
      "error_type": "CustomException"
    }
  )
```

```

In this example, `CustomException` is a user-defined exception. The custom exception handler function, `custom_exception_handler`, captures instances of `CustomException` and returns a response with a status code of 500, indicating a server error. The response body includes a custom message and error type, providing more context to the client about the nature of the error.

Returning Meaningful Error Messages

When designing custom error messages, it's important to strike a balance between providing sufficient information for debugging and avoiding the exposure of sensitive details. Error messages should be clear and helpful, allowing users to understand what went wrong and how they might correct it. At the same time, messages should not disclose internal implementation details or other sensitive information that could compromise security.

Consider a situation where a database connection fails. A generic error message such as "Database error" is often more appropriate than exposing internal database details. Here's an example of handling such scenarios:

```python
@app.exception_handler(HTTPException)
async def http_exception_handler(request: Request, exc: HTTPException):
  return JSONResponse(
    status_codeexc.status_code,
    content{
      "detail": exc.detail,
      "error_type": "HTTPException"
    }
  )
```
```

In this example, the `http_exception_handler` captures HTTP exceptions, providing the client with the status code and the detail message while specifying that the error type is `HTTPException`. This ensures that clients receive relevant information without exposing internal workings.

Logging and Monitoring Errors

Effective error handling also involves logging and monitoring errors to ensure they are tracked and can be addressed. FastAPI does not include built-in logging or monitoring capabilities, but it integrates seamlessly with Python's logging module, allowing you to record error details and track issues.

To implement logging, you configure the logging module and integrate it into your exception handlers. Here's a basic example of how to set up logging for your FastAPI application:

```python
import logging
from fastapi import FastAPI, Request, HTTPException
from fastapi.responses import JSONResponse

Set up logging configuration
logging.basicConfig(levellogging.INFO, format'%(asctime)s - %(levelname)s - %(message)s')
logger logging.getLogger(__name__)

app FastAPI()

@app.exception_handler(Exception)
async def general_exception_handler(request: Request, exc: Exception):
        logger.error(f"Unhandled error occurred: {exc}", exc_infoTrue)
  return JSONResponse(
    status_code500,
    content{
```

```
        "detail": "An unexpected error occurred. Please try again later.",
        "error_type": "UnhandledException"
    }
  )
```

In this configuration, any unhandled exceptions are logged with detailed information, including the traceback (`exc_infoTrue`), which is invaluable for debugging. The client receives a generic error message, ensuring that sensitive details are not exposed.

In summary, effective error handling in FastAPI involves customizing exception responses to improve user experience, logging and monitoring errors for better maintainability, and balancing transparency with security. By leveraging FastAPI's capabilities for exception handling and combining them with robust logging practices, you can build resilient and user-friendly APIs.

When dealing with error handling in FastAPI, it's essential to understand how to manage exceptions in a way that not only provides clarity to the client but also aids in debugging and maintaining the application. Building upon the custom exception handler discussed earlier, we need to explore additional strategies for managing exceptions effectively and ensuring that they integrate smoothly with your application's overall architecture.

Handling Validation Errors

Validation errors are among the most common exceptions encountered in APIs. FastAPI provides built-in support for handling validation errors using Pydantic models. When a request payload fails to meet the requirements defined by the Pydantic model, FastAPI automatically generates a detailed error response. This response includes information on which fields are invalid and why, which is crucial for both client-side error handling and debugging.

However, you might need to customize the validation error responses to better fit your application's requirements or to provide more user-friendly messages. To achieve this, you can create a custom exception handler specifically for validation errors. This handler can format the error messages to be more readable or include additional context that is relevant to your application.

Here's an example of how to create a custom handler for validation errors:

```python
from fastapi.exceptions import RequestValidationError
from fastapi.responses import JSONResponse

@app.exception_handler(RequestValidationError)
async def validation_exception_handler(request: Request, exc:
RequestValidationError):
  errors exc.errors()
  error_details [f"Field '{e['loc'][-1]}' - {e['msg']}" for e in errors]
  return JSONResponse(
    status_code422,
        content{"detail": "Validation error occurred", "errors":
error_details}
  )
```

In this example, the `validation_exception_handler` function formats the validation errors into a more user-friendly format, extracting specific field errors and providing a clearer message to the client.

Logging and Monitoring Exceptions

Effective error management extends beyond handling exceptions and includes robust logging and monitoring.

Logging provides a detailed record of errors that occur in your application, which is invaluable for debugging and analyzing issues. Monitoring, on the other hand, involves tracking the frequency and types of errors to identify patterns or recurring issues.

FastAPI does not provide built-in logging or monitoring features, but it integrates seamlessly with Python's logging module and third-party monitoring tools. By configuring Python's logging module, you can capture and store error logs, which can be crucial for diagnosing issues that arise in production environments.

To set up logging in a FastAPI application, you configure the logging module and then use it within your exception handlers to record errors. Here's how you can configure logging and use it in your custom exception handler:

```python
import logging
from fastapi import FastAPI, Request
from fastapi.responses import JSONResponse

Configure logging
logging.basicConfig(levellogging.INFO, format"%(asctime)s - %(levelname)s - %(message)s")
logger logging.getLogger(__name__)

app FastAPI()

@app.exception_handler(Exception)
async def general_exception_handler(request: Request, exc: Exception):
    logger.error(f"Unexpected error occurred: {exc}", exc_infoTrue)
  return JSONResponse(
    status_code500,
    content{"detail": "An unexpected error occurred"}
```

```
)
```

In this setup, the `general_exception_handler` function logs the error message along with a traceback (`exc_infoTrue`), which provides detailed context for the error. This logging information is crucial for debugging and understanding the root cause of issues in production.

For more advanced monitoring, you might integrate with external services like Sentry, Datadog, or Prometheus. These tools provide sophisticated monitoring capabilities, including real-time error tracking, performance metrics, and alerting features. Integration usually involves installing an SDK provided by the monitoring service and configuring it to capture and report errors from your application.

Returning Meaningful Error Messages

When crafting error responses, it's important to ensure that the messages are not only clear but also actionable. Clients interacting with your API should receive responses that help them understand what went wrong and how to correct their requests. This includes providing:

1. Clear Descriptions: Use descriptive error messages that explain what went wrong. Avoid vague messages like "An error occurred"; instead, specify whether it was a validation error, an authentication issue, or something else.

2. Error Codes: Include error codes in your responses that can be referenced in documentation or support tickets. These codes should be consistent and meaningful, helping clients quickly identify the nature of the error.

3. Actionable Information: Whenever possible, provide guidance on how the client can resolve the issue. For example, if a request fails due to invalid data, include details on the expected format or valid values.

By adhering to these principles, you ensure that your API is not only robust but also user-friendly, providing a better experience for clients and simplifying the debugging and maintenance processes for developers.

When dealing with the broader aspects of error handling and exception management in FastAPI, one crucial area is the integration of exception handling with logging and monitoring systems. These tools not only help in tracking errors but also in improving the reliability and maintainability of your application.

Advanced Exception Handling

While the custom exception handlers we've discussed cover many common scenarios, you might encounter more complex situations that require specialized handling. For instance, you may need to deal with exceptions that arise from external services or systems, such as database errors or third-party API failures. In such cases, it is important to create custom exception handlers tailored to these specific types of errors.

For example, consider a scenario where your application interacts with an external API. If the external API is down or returns an unexpected response, you need to handle this gracefully. You can define a custom exception and create a handler for it:

```python
from fastapi import HTTPException

class ExternalAPIException(Exception):
  def __init__(self, detail: str):
    self.detail detail

@app.exception_handler(ExternalAPIException)
async def external_api_exception_handler(request: Request, exc: ExternalAPIException):
```

```
  return JSONResponse(
    status_code503,
    content{"detail": exc.detail}
  )
```

In this example, `ExternalAPIException` is a custom exception used to indicate problems with external APIs. The `external_api_exception_handler` ensures that a meaningful response is sent to the client, indicating the service is unavailable.

Integrating Logging

Integrating logging into your FastAPI application involves configuring Python's `logging` module to capture and store logs of various levels, such as DEBUG, INFO, WARNING, ERROR, and CRITICAL. Properly setting up logging helps in diagnosing issues and understanding the application's behavior over time.

Here is a basic setup for logging in a FastAPI application:

```python
import logging

Configure the logger
logging.basicConfig(levellogging.INFO, format'%(asctime)s - %(name)s - %(levelname)s - %(message)s')

logger logging.getLogger(__name__)

@app.exception_handler(Exception)
async def global_exception_handler(request: Request, exc: Exception):
        logger.error(f"Unhandled error occurred: {exc}", exc_infoTrue)
  return JSONResponse(
    status_code500,
```

```
    content{"detail": "An unexpected error occurred"}
  )
```

In this setup, the logger captures all unhandled exceptions and logs them with a severity level of ERROR. The `exc_infoTrue` parameter ensures that the traceback is included in the logs, which provides detailed information about the error.

Monitoring and Alerts

While logging provides insights into errors after they occur, monitoring tools can proactively alert you about issues. Tools such as Prometheus, Grafana, Sentry, or New Relic can be integrated with FastAPI to monitor the health of your application and track error rates.

To integrate a monitoring tool like Sentry, you first need to install the Sentry SDK and configure it:

```bash
pip install sentry-sdk
```

Next, configure Sentry in your FastAPI application:

```python
import sentry_sdk
from sentry_sdk.integrations.asgi import SentryAsgiMiddleware

sentry_sdk.init(
  dsn"your_sentry_dsn_here",
  traces_sample_rate1.0
)

app FastAPI()
app.add_middleware(SentryAsgiMiddleware)
```

This configuration sends all exceptions to Sentry, where they are aggregated and displayed on the Sentry dashboard. You can set up alerts to notify you via email or other channels when errors occur, providing immediate awareness of issues in production.

Graceful Error Responses

An important aspect of error handling is ensuring that your API returns consistent and meaningful error responses. Beyond just logging errors, providing users with clear and actionable information is key. Custom error responses should adhere to a standard format, including a clear status code, an error message, and optionally additional details.

Consider the following example of a custom error response for a resource not found scenario:

```python
from fastapi.responses import JSONResponse

@app.exception_handler(HTTPException)
async def http_exception_handler(request: Request, exc: HTTPException):
  return JSONResponse(
    status_codeexc.status_code,
    content{"error": exc.detail}
  )
```

This handler ensures that HTTP errors, such as 404 Not Found, return a consistent format, improving the client-side experience and making error handling on the client side more straightforward.

Testing Error Handling

Finally, testing is an integral part of managing exceptions effectively. Writing unit tests and integration tests that simulate error conditions helps ensure that your exception handlers and logging mechanisms work as expected. You can use testing frameworks like `pytest` to create tests that validate how your application handles various error scenarios.

For example, you might write a test to verify that a specific exception is logged correctly:

```python
def test_internal_server_error_logging(client: TestClient, caplog):
    with caplog.at_level(logging.ERROR):
        response client.get("/endpoint_that_triggers_error")
        assert response.status_code 500
        assert "Unhandled error occurred" in caplog.text
```

In this test, `caplog` captures the log output, allowing you to assert that the error was logged correctly.

By combining well-defined exception handling, robust logging, effective monitoring, and thorough testing, you create a resilient and maintainable API that provides a reliable user experience and facilitates efficient debugging and issue resolution.

CHAPTER 11: BUILDING AND DOCUMENTING APIS

FastAPI stands out not only for its performance and ease of use but also for its robust support for building and documenting APIs. The framework automatically generates interactive API documentation through Swagger UI and ReDoc, which significantly enhances the developer experience. However, beyond the out-of-the-box functionality, there are several ways to customize and enhance this documentation to better serve your API's users.

To begin, FastAPI provides a straightforward way to include documentation using its built-in features. By default, when you create an API with FastAPI, it automatically integrates Swagger UI and ReDoc. These tools offer interactive documentation where users can explore and test the API endpoints directly from the browser. Swagger UI provides a user-friendly interface that displays API endpoints, their parameters, and responses. ReDoc, on the other hand, presents the API documentation in a more structured and comprehensive manner.

However, to truly leverage the power of FastAPI's documentation capabilities, it's crucial to customize it to fit your API's specific needs. Customizing the documentation involves several aspects, such as adding metadata, modifying documentation settings, and providing more detailed descriptions for endpoints.

Customizing Metadata

Metadata plays a crucial role in API documentation as it provides essential information about the API, such as its title, description, and version. FastAPI allows you to customize this metadata by providing parameters to the `FastAPI` class when creating an instance of the application. This customization not only helps in making the API documentation more informative but also improves the overall user experience.

Here's how you can set up basic metadata for your FastAPI application:

```python
from fastapi import FastAPI

app FastAPI(
  title"My API",
  description"This is a detailed description of my API.",
  version"1.0.0",
  terms_of_service"https://myapi.com/terms/",
  contact{
    "name": "API Support",
    "url": "https://myapi.com/support",
    "email": "support@myapi.com",
  },
  license_info{
    "name": "MIT License",
    "url": "https://opensource.org/licenses/MIT",
  }
)
```

In this setup, the `title`, `description`, and `version`

parameters provide a basic introduction to the API. The `terms_of_service`, `contact`, and `license_info` parameters offer additional details that can be useful for API consumers, helping them understand the terms under which the API is provided and how to get support.

Enhancing Endpoint Descriptions

To further enrich the API documentation, FastAPI allows you to add detailed descriptions to your endpoints. You can specify these descriptions directly in the route decorators. This includes providing summaries, descriptions, and detailed information about the parameters and responses.

Consider the following example where we add descriptions to an endpoint:

```python
from fastapi import FastAPI, HTTPException
from pydantic import BaseModel

app FastAPI()

class Item(BaseModel):
  name: str
  description: str  None
  price: float
  tax: float  None

@app.post("/items/", summary"Create an Item", description"Create an item with the provided details.")
async def create_item(item: Item):
  """
  Create an item with the provided details.


    - name: The name of the item.
  - description: A description of the item (optional).
  - price: The price of the item.
```

```
    - tax: The tax applicable to the item (optional).
    """
    return item
```

In this example, the `summary` provides a brief overview of what the endpoint does, while the `description` offers a more detailed explanation. Additionally, the docstring inside the function provides even more context about the parameters.

Customizing Documentation Appearance

While FastAPI's default documentation styles are functional, you might want to customize their appearance to better fit your branding or to provide additional functionalities. FastAPI allows you to do this by configuring the `docs_url` and `redoc_url` parameters when creating the `FastAPI` instance.

For example, if you want to change the default URLs for the Swagger UI and ReDoc documentation, you can configure them like this:

```python
app FastAPI(
    docs_url"/api/docs",
    redoc_url"/api/redoc",
)
```

This configuration changes the URLs for accessing the Swagger UI and ReDoc documentation. By setting `docs_url` to `/api/docs` and `redoc_url` to `/api/redoc`, you customize where these documents can be accessed, which might be useful for avoiding conflicts with other routes or integrating with existing systems.

Moreover, if you need to apply further customizations to Swagger UI or ReDoc, such as modifying their appearance or functionality, you would typically do this by serving custom HTML or JavaScript files. However, this level of customization often requires a deeper understanding of how these tools are built and their specific configuration options.

By leveraging FastAPI's comprehensive documentation capabilities, you can ensure that your API is not only functional but also easy to understand and use. This approach not only benefits external developers who interact with your API but also contributes to better maintenance and evolution of the API over time.

Continuing from the initial setup, it is essential to delve deeper into customizing the documentation of your API to enhance clarity and usability. FastAPI's flexibility in documentation allows for detailed descriptions, examples, and more nuanced control over how your API is presented. This is not only useful for improving developer experience but also for ensuring that the API is self-explanatory and easy to use.

Customizing Endpoints Documentation

Each endpoint in your FastAPI application can be individually customized to provide specific details about its functionality. This is achieved through the use of parameters like `summary`, `description`, and `response_model`. For instance, you can use the `summary` parameter to provide a brief overview of what an endpoint does, while the `description` parameter allows for a more detailed explanation. This can be particularly helpful when the endpoint performs complex operations or has nuanced behavior.

Consider the following example where an endpoint is defined with comprehensive documentation:

```python
from fastapi import FastAPI, HTTPException
```

```
from pydantic import BaseModel

app FastAPI()

class Item(BaseModel):
  name: str
  description: str None
  price: float
  tax: float None

@app.post("/items/", summary"Create an item",
description"Create a new item with a name, description, price,
and optional tax.")
async def create_item(item: Item):
  """
  Create an item endpoint.


    - name: Name of the item (required).
  - description: Description of the item (optional).
  - price: Price of the item (required).
  - tax: Tax on the item (optional).
  """
  if item.price < 0:
    raise HTTPException(status_code400, detail"Price must be
greater than 0")
  return {"item": item}
```

In this example, the `summary` provides a concise overview, while the `description` gives a more detailed account of what the endpoint does. The docstring within the function further elaborates on the parameters, which can help users understand the data requirements and behavior of the endpoint more thoroughly.

Adding Examples

Providing examples is another important aspect of effective

API documentation. FastAPI allows you to include examples in both request bodies and responses. This feature is particularly useful for illustrating how to use an endpoint and what kind of responses to expect. To add examples, you use the `example` parameter in the Pydantic model or within the endpoint definition.

Here's how you might include examples in the Pydantic model:

```python
from typing import Optional
from pydantic import BaseModel

class Item(BaseModel):
  name: str
  description: Optional[str]  None
  price: float
  tax: Optional[float]  None

    class Config:
     schema_extra {
       "example": {
         "name": "Sample Item",
         "description": "This is a sample item for demonstration
purposes.",
         "price": 29.99,
         "tax": 2.5
       }
    }
```

In this code, the `schema_extra` configuration is used to provide an example of what a valid `Item` might look like. This example will appear in the Swagger UI and ReDoc documentation, helping users understand how to format their requests.

Customizing Responses

Alongside request examples, it is beneficial to customize response examples to illustrate what users can expect from the API. FastAPI supports this by allowing you to define response models with examples. Here's an example of how to provide a response example:

```python
from fastapi import FastAPI
from pydantic import BaseModel

app  FastAPI()

class Item(BaseModel):
  name: str
  description: str  None
  price: float
  tax: float  None

class ResponseModel(BaseModel):
  item: Item
  message: str

@app.get("/items/{item_id}", response_modelResponseModel)
async def read_item(item_id: int):
  """
  Retrieve an item by its ID.


    - item_id: The ID of the item to retrieve.
  """
   Example data
  example_item  Item(name"Example Item", price19.99)
    return {"item": example_item, "message": "Item retrieved successfully"}
```

Here, the `ResponseModel` class defines the structure of the response, and the example response is automatically included in the documentation. Users can see what a typical response looks like and understand how the data is structured.

Securing Documentation

While documenting your API, consider the security implications of exposing certain endpoints and data. FastAPI allows for customization of documentation visibility based on the security and authentication of endpoints. For instance, you can restrict access to sensitive API endpoints or use different documentation configurations based on user roles.

To secure documentation, you can use FastAPI's dependency injection system to enforce authentication and authorization before accessing specific documentation features. This approach ensures that only authorized users can view or interact with sensitive parts of the API documentation.

By carefully customizing and enhancing your API documentation with these techniques, you provide a clearer and more user-friendly interface for developers interacting with your API. This not only improves their experience but also contributes to more effective API usage and integration.

To further enhance API documentation in FastAPI, it is imperative to explore advanced customization options and how they can be leveraged to create a more intuitive and informative interface for users. This section will address how to fine-tune API documentation using metadata, custom tags, and more elaborate examples, as well as methods for integrating additional documentation tools if needed.

Adding Metadata to API Documentation

Metadata in FastAPI documentation plays a significant role in providing contextual information about the API. Metadata can include details like versioning, contact information, license, and terms of service. This information is crucial for users who need to understand the context in which the API operates, its governance, and how to contact the maintainers for support or inquiries.

Here is an example of how to add metadata to the FastAPI app:

```python
from fastapi import FastAPI

app FastAPI(
  title"Sample API",
  description"A sample API to demonstrate FastAPI documentation customization.",
  version"1.0.0",
  contact{
    "name": "API Support",
    "url": "http://example.com/support",
    "email": "support@example.com",
  },
  license_info{
    "name": "MIT License",
    "url": "https://opensource.org/licenses/MIT",
  }
)
```

In this example, `title`, `description`, `version`, `contact`, and `license_info` parameters are used to provide detailed metadata about the API. This information appears in the automatically generated Swagger UI and ReDoc documentation, making it easier for users to find essential details about the API's functionality and support options.

Using Custom Tags

Custom tags are a powerful feature that allows you to group and organize endpoints in the documentation. Tags help users navigate through different sections of the API documentation, making it easier to locate specific functionality or related endpoints.

Here's how you can use tags to categorize endpoints:

```python
from fastapi import FastAPI

app FastAPI()

@app.get("/items/", tags["items"])
async def get_items():
    """
    Retrieve a list of items.
    """
    return {"items": ["item1", "item2", "item3"]}

@app.post("/items/", tags["items"])
async def create_item(item: dict):
    """
    Create a new item.
    """
    return {"item": item}

@app.get("/users/", tags["users"])
async def get_users():
    """
    Retrieve a list of users.
    """
    return {"users": ["user1", "user2", "user3"]}
```

In this setup, endpoints are tagged with `"items"` or `"users"`, which organizes them under respective sections in the documentation. This categorization improves readability and helps users understand the API's structure better.

Providing Detailed Examples

Examples can make the documentation more actionable by showing users precisely how to use the API. FastAPI supports including examples directly in the request and response schemas. These examples are visible in Swagger UI and ReDoc, helping users understand the format and structure of the data expected by or returned from the API.

Here's an illustration of how to include examples in request and response schemas:

```python
from typing import List
from pydantic import BaseModel, Field

class Item(BaseModel):
    name: str  Field(..., example"Sample Item")
     description: str  Field(None, example"This is a sample item description")
    price: float  Field(..., example19.99)
    tax: float  Field(None, example1.99)

@app.post("/items/", response_modelItem, responses{201: {"model": Item}})
async def create_item(item: Item):
    """
    Create a new item.


      Example request body:
    {
     "name": "Sample Item",
     "description": "This is a sample item description",
     "price": 19.99,
     "tax": 1.99
    }


      Example response body:
    {
     "name": "Sample Item",
```

```
    "description": "This is a sample item description",
    "price": 19.99,
    "tax": 1.99
  }
  """
  return item
```

In this example, the `Field` function from Pydantic is used to include examples directly in the schema. The documentation will show these examples in the interactive API documentation, making it clear to users what a valid request and response should look like.

Integrating Additional Documentation Tools

While FastAPI provides robust documentation tools out of the box, there might be scenarios where additional tools or integrations are necessary. For instance, you may want to integrate API documentation with external tools or services for enhanced analytics or custom reporting.

One way to achieve this is by using middleware or external documentation services that can complement FastAPI's built-in features. For example, integrating with tools like Redocly or SwaggerHub can provide additional capabilities such as collaborative documentation, advanced versioning, and interactive API design.

To integrate an external documentation tool, you would typically set up your FastAPI application to expose a Swagger or ReDoc specification file, which can then be imported into the external tool. FastAPI makes this straightforward by providing an OpenAPI specification that can be accessed and used by various external services for additional documentation and analytics purposes.

By following these practices, you can significantly improve the usability and quality of your API documentation, making it a valuable resource for developers and users alike.

CHAPTER 12: TESTING FASTAPI APPLICATIONS

Testing is a fundamental aspect of software development that ensures the reliability, performance, and correctness of an application. For FastAPI applications, thorough testing involves writing unit tests, integration tests, and employing robust testing tools such as Pytest. This section will delve into the methodologies for testing FastAPI applications, focusing on strategies for endpoint testing, validating functionality, and adhering to best practices.

Unit tests are essential for validating the smallest testable parts of your application in isolation. For FastAPI applications, this means testing individual components such as utility functions, service layers, and business logic separately from the API routes. Pytest, a popular testing framework in Python, provides a simple and effective way to write unit tests.

To illustrate unit testing in a FastAPI application, consider a scenario where we have a function that performs a simple calculation. Here's a sample function and its corresponding unit test:

```python
app/utils.py
def calculate_total(price: float, quantity: int) -> float:
  return price  quantity
```

```
tests/test_utils.py
from app.utils import calculate_total

def test_calculate_total():
    assert calculate_total(10.0, 2) 20.0
    assert calculate_total(5.5, 3) 16.5
    assert calculate_total(0, 100) 0.0
```

In this example, the `calculate_total` function is tested with various inputs to ensure it behaves as expected. Pytest will execute this test and verify that the function produces the correct outputs.

Integration tests, on the other hand, focus on verifying that different parts of the application work together correctly. For FastAPI applications, this often involves testing API endpoints to ensure that they interact with the underlying database or other services as expected. These tests validate that the complete workflow from request to response functions correctly.

FastAPI provides a test client through `fastapi.testclient`, which is a wrapper around the popular `requests` library. This client allows you to simulate HTTP requests to your API and inspect the responses. Here is an example of how to write integration tests for FastAPI endpoints:

```python
tests/test_api.py
from fastapi.testclient import TestClient
from app.main import app

client TestClient(app)

def test_read_items():
    response client.get("/items/")
    assert response.status_code 200
```

```
  assert response.json() {"items": ["item1", "item2", "item3"]}

def test_create_item():
  response client.post("/items/", json{"name": "item4"})
  assert response.status_code 201
  assert response.json() {"name": "item4", "status": "created"}
```

In this example, the `TestClient` is used to send HTTP requests to the API endpoints and validate that the responses meet expectations. The tests check both the status codes and the content of the responses.

Effective testing also requires managing test dependencies and isolating test environments. For FastAPI applications, you might need to set up a test database or mock external services. FastAPI supports dependency overrides, which allow you to replace real dependencies with test-specific versions. This approach is particularly useful when you want to avoid using production databases or services during testing.

Here's an example of how to override a dependency for testing purposes:

```python
app/dependencies.py
from fastapi import Depends

def get_database():
   Production database connection
  pass

app/main.py
from fastapi import FastAPI, Depends
from app.dependencies import get_database

app FastAPI()

@app.get("/items/")
async def read_items(dbDepends(get_database)):
```

```
     Endpoint implementation
   pass

tests/conftest.py
import pytest
from fastapi.testclient import TestClient
from app.main import app
from app.dependencies import get_database

@pytest.fixture
def override_dependencies():
   def mock_get_database():
      Return a mock database connection
      pass

     app.dependency_overrides[get_database]
mock_get_database
   yield
   app.dependency_overrides  {}

@pytest.fixture
def client(override_dependencies):
   return TestClient(app)
```

In this setup, the `override_dependencies` fixture replaces the `get_database` dependency with a mock implementation during tests. This allows the tests to run in isolation without affecting the production environment.

Best practices for testing FastAPI applications include writing clear and concise test cases, covering a range of scenarios including edge cases and error conditions, and ensuring that tests are automated and run regularly. Additionally, incorporating continuous integration (CI) tools to run tests automatically on code changes helps maintain application quality over time.

By employing these testing strategies and leveraging tools

such as Pytest, you can ensure that your FastAPI application is robust, reliable, and ready for production deployment.

To further delve into integration testing for FastAPI applications, it's imperative to understand how to effectively utilize FastAPI's `TestClient` for simulating HTTP requests and validating responses. This approach allows you to test the end-to-end functionality of your application, ensuring that your API routes interact correctly with other components such as the database or external services.

Let us expand on the earlier example by incorporating more sophisticated tests. Suppose we have an API endpoint that creates a new user and returns the user's data. To test this endpoint, we need to set up the `TestClient`, make requests to the endpoint, and assert that the responses match our expectations.

Consider the following FastAPI route for creating a user:

```python
app/main.py
from fastapi import FastAPI, HTTPException
from pydantic import BaseModel

app  FastAPI()

class User(BaseModel):
  username: str
  email: str

In-memory "database" for demonstration purposes
fake_db  []

@app.post("/users/", response_modelUser)
def create_user(user: User):
  if any(u['email']  user.email for u in fake_db):
    raise HTTPException(status_code400, detail"Email already
registered")
```

```
    fake_db.append(user.dict())
    return user
```

For this endpoint, the corresponding integration test would look like this:

```python
tests/test_api.py
from fastapi.testclient import TestClient
from app.main import app

client  TestClient(app)

def test_create_user():
    response  client.post("/users/", json{"username": "testuser", "email": "test@example.com"})
    assert response.status_code  200
    assert response.json()  {"username": "testuser", "email": "test@example.com"}

    Test for email duplication
    response  client.post("/users/", json{"username": "anotheruser", "email": "test@example.com"})
    assert response.status_code  400
    assert response.json()  {"detail": "Email already registered"}
```

In this test, we first verify that the endpoint correctly creates a user and returns the expected JSON response. We then test the scenario where an attempt is made to create a user with an email that already exists in the "database," ensuring that the application handles this case as intended by returning a 400 error and the appropriate error message.

Integration testing also includes scenarios involving more complex interactions, such as database operations. To test such cases, you may need to set up a test database environment or use mocking techniques to simulate database operations.

FastAPI's `TestClient` does not handle database setup directly, so integrating with databases in tests typically involves creating and tearing down test-specific data or configurations.

For scenarios where you need to test interactions with a real database, you might use a separate test database. This setup ensures that tests do not interfere with the production data. For instance, using SQLAlchemy with FastAPI, you can configure a different database URL for testing and apply migrations accordingly. Here is a simplified approach for testing with SQLAlchemy:

```python
tests/conftest.py
import pytest
from sqlalchemy import create_engine
from sqlalchemy.orm import sessionmaker
from app.main import app
from fastapi.testclient import TestClient
from app.database import Base, get_db

Create a test database engine
SQLALCHEMY_DATABASE_URL "sqlite:///./test.db"
engine create_engine(SQLALCHEMY_DATABASE_URL)
TestingSessionLocal sessionmaker(autocommitFalse,
autoflushFalse, bindengine)

Create all tables in the test database
Base.metadata.create_all(bindengine)

Override the dependency to use the test database
def override_get_db():
  db TestingSessionLocal()
  try:
    yield db
  finally:
    db.close()
```

```
app.dependency_overrides[get_db] override_get_db

client TestClient(app)

@pytest.fixture(scope"module", autouseTrue)
def setup_and_teardown():
   Code to run before any tests
  yield
   Code to run after all tests
  Base.metadata.drop_all(bindengine)
```

In this setup, `conftest.py` configures a separate SQLite database for testing purposes, ensuring that tests do not affect the production database. The `setup_and_teardown` fixture ensures that the database schema is created before tests run and dropped afterward, maintaining a clean state.

Testing asynchronous code, such as API endpoints that perform asynchronous operations, also requires special consideration. Pytest can handle async tests with the `pytest-asyncio` plugin, which allows you to write asynchronous test functions. An example test for an asynchronous endpoint might look like this:

```python
tests/test_api_async.py
import pytest
from fastapi.testclient import TestClient
from app.main import app

client TestClient(app)

@pytest.mark.asyncio
async def test_async_endpoint():
  response await client.get("/async-endpoint/")
  assert response.status_code 200
      assert response.json() {"message": "Async operation
```

```
completed"}
```

In this example, `pytest.mark.asyncio` enables support for asynchronous testing, and the `await` keyword is used to handle asynchronous requests.

In summary, testing FastAPI applications involves a range of strategies, from unit tests of individual components to integration tests of complete workflows. Effective use of tools like Pytest and understanding testing strategies, including database interactions and asynchronous operations, ensures that your application functions correctly and remains reliable throughout its lifecycle.

As we continue exploring testing strategies for FastAPI applications, it becomes evident that proper management of test environments and dependencies is crucial for maintaining the integrity and effectiveness of tests. Ensuring that tests are isolated and repeatable often involves setting up dedicated testing configurations, using mock objects, and managing state effectively. This section delves into these aspects, focusing on how to manage test databases and environment configurations.

When performing integration testing, especially with database interactions, it is essential to avoid affecting your production or development databases. A common practice is to use a separate test database or an in-memory database to run tests. This setup ensures that tests do not alter or rely on production data and that they can be run multiple times without interference.

For example, when using SQLAlchemy with FastAPI, you can configure a test database that is distinct from your production database. Here's how you might set up a test configuration using SQLAlchemy:

```python
app/db.py
from sqlalchemy import create_engine
from sqlalchemy.orm import sessionmaker
from sqlalchemy.ext.declarative import DeclarativeMeta,
declarative_base

DATABASE_URL "sqlite:///./test.db"  Using SQLite for testing

engine create_engine(DATABASE_URL,
connect_args{"check_same_thread": False})
SessionLocal sessionmaker(autocommitFalse, autoflushFalse,
bindengine)
Base: DeclarativeMeta declarative_base()

def get_db():
  db SessionLocal()
  try:
    yield db
  finally:
    db.close()
```

In your test setup, you would then use this test database configuration to isolate test runs:

```python
tests/conftest.py
import pytest
from app.db import engine, Base, SessionLocal

@pytest.fixture(scope"module")
def setup_db():
   Base.metadata.create_all(bindengine)  Create tables in test
database
  yield
  Base.metadata.drop_all(bindengine)  Clean up after tests
```

```
@pytest.fixture
def db_session(setup_db):
  db SessionLocal()
  try:
    yield db
  finally:
    db.close()
```

In this setup, `setup_db` is a fixture that creates the database schema before any tests are run and drops it after all tests have completed. The `db_session` fixture provides a database session for individual tests, ensuring that each test operates in isolation with a fresh state.

Another essential aspect of testing is managing external dependencies and ensuring that your tests are not dependent on live external services. This is where mocking comes into play. Mocking allows you to simulate the behavior of external services or components, ensuring that tests are not only faster but also more reliable and isolated.

For example, suppose your FastAPI application relies on an external API to fetch user data. You can use a mocking library such as `pytest-mock` or `unittest.mock` to simulate responses from this API without making actual network requests. Here's a simple example using `pytest-mock`:

```python
tests/test_api.py
from fastapi.testclient import TestClient
from app.main import app
from unittest.mock import patch

client TestClient(app)

@patch("app.main.some_external_service")
def test_external_service(mock_service):
```

```
    mock_service.return_value {"data": "mocked data"}
    response client.get("/some-endpoint/")
    assert response.status_code 200
    assert response.json() {"data": "mocked data"}
```

In this example, `@patch` is used to replace the `some_external_service` function with a mock object. This mock object is configured to return predefined data, allowing you to test how your application handles this data without relying on the actual external service.

Finally, monitoring and logging during testing is critical for diagnosing issues and understanding test failures. FastAPI applications often integrate with logging frameworks like Python's built-in `logging` module. During tests, ensuring that logs are properly captured and examined can provide insights into why certain tests fail or how the application behaves under test conditions.

Consider configuring a logging setup that writes logs to a file or a console during tests, and ensure that your tests assert not only on the returned results but also on the logs generated if necessary. This practice helps in maintaining visibility into the application's behavior and aids in debugging complex issues.

By managing test databases, employing mocks for external dependencies, and integrating logging, you can create a robust testing framework for your FastAPI application. This approach ensures that your application remains reliable, maintainable, and ready for production deployment, with a comprehensive understanding of its functionality and behavior under various scenarios.

CHAPTER 13: IMPLEMENTING ASYNCHRONOUS ENDPOINTS

FastAPI's support for asynchronous programming is pivotal in constructing scalable and efficient web applications. Asynchronous endpoints leverage Python's `async` and `await` keywords to allow concurrent execution of tasks, making it possible to handle multiple requests simultaneously without blocking the server. This capability is particularly important when dealing with I/O-bound operations such as database queries, file operations, or external API calls.

To start with asynchronous endpoints in FastAPI, you need to define your route functions with the `async def` syntax. This distinction allows FastAPI to recognize the endpoint as asynchronous, enabling it to handle requests in a non-blocking manner. For example, an asynchronous endpoint for fetching user data might look like this:

```python
from fastapi import FastAPI
from typing import List

app FastAPI()

@app.get("/users/", response_modelList[User])
```

```
async def read_users():
    users await fetch_users_from_database() Asynchronous
database call
  return users
```

In this snippet, `fetch_users_from_database` is an asynchronous function that performs the database operation. By using `await`, you allow the event loop to continue executing other tasks while waiting for the database query to complete. This non-blocking behavior improves the application's responsiveness and throughput.

Handling asynchronous database queries requires using asynchronous database libraries. For instance, if you use SQLAlchemy, the `asyncio` extension provides async capabilities. You need to ensure that your database setup and query functions are compatible with asynchronous operations. Here's an example of how to set up asynchronous database interaction with SQLAlchemy:

```python
from sqlalchemy.ext.asyncio import AsyncSession,
create_async_engine
from sqlalchemy.orm import sessionmaker

DATABASE_URL "postgresql+asyncpg://
user:password@localhost/dbname"

engine create_async_engine(DATABASE_URL, echoTrue)
AsyncSessionLocal sessionmaker(autocommitFalse,
autoflushFalse, bindengine, class_AsyncSession)

async def get_db() -> AsyncSession:
  async with AsyncSessionLocal() as session:
    yield session
```

In this configuration, `create_async_engine` establishes an

asynchronous engine for connecting to the PostgreSQL database, and `AsyncSessionLocal` is a session factory that produces asynchronous sessions. The `get_db` function provides an asynchronous context manager for managing database sessions.

When defining an asynchronous database query, you must ensure that the ORM or database client you use supports asynchronous operations. For instance, when using `SQLAlchemy`, your query functions need to be declared with `async def` and utilize `await` for executing queries:

```python
from sqlalchemy.future import select

async def fetch_users_from_database(db: AsyncSession):
  async with db.begin():
    result await db.execute(select(User))
    users result.scalars().all()
  return users
```

In this function, `db.execute` performs an asynchronous query, allowing the event loop to handle other operations while the query is being processed. The `scalars().all()` method retrieves all rows from the result set in a non-blocking manner.

Managing concurrency effectively in asynchronous programming involves understanding how to handle simultaneous operations and their potential impact on system resources. For instance, when dealing with high traffic, properly managing connections to external services, optimizing database queries, and using efficient data structures can significantly affect performance.

FastAPI's `BackgroundTasks` can be employed for offloading tasks that do not need to be executed in the request-response cycle. This can be particularly useful for long-running operations like sending emails or processing large files:

```python
from fastapi import BackgroundTasks

@app.post("/send-email/")
async def send_email(background_tasks: BackgroundTasks,
email: Email):
  background_tasks.add_task(send_email_task, email)
  return {"message": "Email is being sent in the background"}

async def send_email_task(email: Email):
   Simulate a long-running email sending process
  await asyncio.sleep(10)
  print(f"Email sent to {email.recipient}")
```

In this example, `send_email_task` is scheduled to run in the background, allowing the endpoint to respond immediately while the task continues to execute asynchronously. This approach helps in preventing endpoint delays and ensures that the API remains responsive under load.

Lastly, when working with asynchronous programming, it's crucial to be aware of common pitfalls such as blocking operations within asynchronous functions, which can negate the benefits of asynchronous execution. Avoid using synchronous calls within async functions and ensure that all I/O operations are handled asynchronously.

In summary, implementing asynchronous endpoints in FastAPI allows for enhanced scalability and responsiveness by enabling concurrent task execution. Proper use of async/await syntax, asynchronous database operations, and background tasks are essential for building efficient and high-performance APIs. By adhering to these practices and carefully managing concurrency, you can significantly improve the performance and reliability of your FastAPI applications.

When designing asynchronous endpoints in FastAPI, it's essential to grasp how concurrency management works in this context. Asynchronous endpoints leverage Python's asynchronous features, enabling the handling of numerous tasks simultaneously without blocking the event loop. This approach is particularly advantageous for I/O-bound operations, such as interacting with databases or calling external APIs, which often involve waiting periods that would otherwise block the server if handled synchronously.

Let us delve deeper into asynchronous database queries. To properly execute asynchronous queries, you need to use an asynchronous ORM (Object-Relational Mapping) library or a database driver. For instance, if you opt for SQLAlchemy, the `sqlalchemy.ext.asyncio` module provides support for asynchronous operations. This module allows you to define asynchronous database sessions and queries, which can significantly enhance performance when dealing with multiple concurrent requests.

In an asynchronous setup with SQLAlchemy, it is crucial to set up your database connection and session management correctly. The following code illustrates how to configure an asynchronous database engine and session:

```python
from sqlalchemy.ext.asyncio import create_async_engine, AsyncSession
from sqlalchemy.orm import sessionmaker

DATABASE_URL "postgresql+asyncpg://user:password@localhost/mydatabase"

engine create_async_engine(DATABASE_URL, echoTrue)
AsyncSessionLocal sessionmaker(autocommitFalse, autoflushFalse, bindengine, class_AsyncSession)
```

```
async def get_db() -> AsyncSession:
    async with AsyncSessionLocal() as session:
        yield session
```

Here, `create_async_engine` is used to create an asynchronous engine connected to your PostgreSQL database. The `AsyncSessionLocal` sessionmaker instance is configured to generate asynchronous sessions. The `get_db` function demonstrates how to create and manage an asynchronous session context, which you can inject into your endpoints.

An important consideration in asynchronous programming is managing concurrency effectively. FastAPI's asynchronous capabilities are built on top of Python's `asyncio` library, which provides an event loop that handles multiple tasks concurrently. When writing asynchronous code, you must ensure that tasks are properly awaited to avoid creating bottlenecks or introducing bugs due to unhandled concurrent operations.

Let's consider an example where an endpoint needs to perform multiple I/O-bound operations concurrently. Suppose you need to fetch data from multiple external APIs and combine the results. Using asynchronous programming, you can execute these operations concurrently and aggregate their results efficiently:

```python
import httpx
from fastapi import FastAPI

app  FastAPI()

async def fetch_from_api(url: str) -> dict:
    async with httpx.AsyncClient() as client:
        response  await client.get(url)
```

```
    response.raise_for_status()
    return response.json()

@app.get("/aggregate/")
async def aggregate_data():
        urls     ["https://api.example.com/data1",    "https://
api.example.com/data2"]
  results  await asyncio.gather((fetch_from_api(url) for url in
urls))
  combined_result  {"data1": results[0], "data2": results[1]}
  return combined_result
```

In this code snippet, `httpx.AsyncClient` is used to perform asynchronous HTTP requests. The `fetch_from_api` function asynchronously fetches data from a specified URL. The `aggregate_data` endpoint uses `asyncio.gather` to run multiple `fetch_from_api` tasks concurrently. By gathering the results of these tasks, you can return a combined response to the client.

Handling concurrency also involves dealing with potential issues such as race conditions and deadlocks. Although asynchronous programming improves performance, it requires careful consideration of these issues. For example, when dealing with shared resources or states, ensure that your code correctly manages access to prevent conflicts. This might involve using locks or other synchronization mechanisms if needed.

Another aspect of asynchronous programming is testing asynchronous endpoints. Testing asynchronous code involves using testing frameworks that support async operations. Pytest, for instance, provides support for asynchronous testing through plugins like `pytest-asyncio`. When writing tests for asynchronous endpoints, you should ensure that you properly handle the event loop and await asynchronous calls as needed.

In summary, implementing asynchronous endpoints in FastAPI enables you to build high-performance applications capable of handling many concurrent operations efficiently. By leveraging Python's asynchronous features and using asynchronous libraries for database and I/O operations, you can create scalable applications that remain responsive under load. Properly managing concurrency and testing asynchronous code are also crucial for maintaining the reliability and robustness of your application.

To fully grasp asynchronous programming in FastAPI, it's crucial to understand how asynchronous endpoints function within the framework. Asynchronous endpoints are defined using `async def`, which marks the endpoint handler as asynchronous. This allows FastAPI to utilize Python's `asyncio` to handle multiple requests concurrently without blocking the server. The ability to handle numerous requests in parallel enhances scalability and performance, particularly for I/O-bound operations.

Consider a scenario where your application needs to call several external APIs to gather data before responding to a client. If these API calls are handled synchronously, the server would block on each request, resulting in significant delays. However, by using asynchronous programming, these calls can be performed concurrently, significantly reducing the response time.

Here's how you can define an asynchronous endpoint that performs multiple concurrent operations:

```python
from fastapi import FastAPI
import httpx

app FastAPI()
```

```
async def fetch_data_from_api(url: str):
  async with httpx.AsyncClient() as client:
    response await client.get(url)
    return response.json()

@app.get("/combined-data")
async def get_combined_data():
  urls [
    "https://api.example.com/data1",
    "https://api.example.com/data2",
    "https://api.example.com/data3"
  ]
    responses await asyncio.gather([fetch_data_from_api(url)
for url in urls])
    combined_data {f"data{i+1}": response for i, response in
enumerate(responses)}
  return combined_data
```

In this example, the `fetch_data_from_api` function performs an asynchronous HTTP GET request using `httpx.AsyncClient`. The `get_combined_data` endpoint uses `asyncio.gather` to run multiple `fetch_data_from_api` calls concurrently. This approach allows the server to wait for all API calls to complete in parallel, optimizing the overall performance of the endpoint.

Asynchronous programming also requires careful handling of errors and exceptions. In asynchronous functions, exceptions can propagate differently compared to synchronous functions. FastAPI handles exceptions in asynchronous endpoints similarly to synchronous ones, but you should be aware of how they can affect your code flow. Implementing robust error handling and logging is essential to maintain the stability and reliability of your application.

To illustrate, consider an updated version of the asynchronous endpoint that includes error handling:

```python
from fastapi import HTTPException

@app.get("/combined-data")
async def get_combined_data():
  urls [
    "https://api.example.com/data1",
    "https://api.example.com/data2",
    "https://api.example.com/data3"
  ]
  try:
    responses  await asyncio.gather([fetch_data_from_api(url) for url in urls])
      combined_data  {f"data{i+1}": response for i, response in enumerate(responses)}
    return combined_data
  except httpx.HTTPStatusError as exc:
    raise HTTPException(status_codeexc.response.status_code, detailstr(exc))
  except Exception as exc:
    raise HTTPException(status_code500, detail"An unexpected error occurred")
```

In this code, exceptions related to HTTP errors are caught and translated into appropriate HTTP responses using FastAPI's `HTTPException`. General exceptions are also caught to prevent the application from failing silently.

Finally, while asynchronous endpoints can significantly improve performance, they can also introduce complexity. It's essential to ensure that your use of asynchronous programming is appropriate for your use case. For example, if your application primarily handles CPU-bound tasks, asynchronous programming might not offer significant benefits. On the other hand, for I/O-bound tasks, such as network or file operations, asynchronous endpoints can offer considerable performance improvements.

In summary, implementing asynchronous endpoints in FastAPI involves defining endpoint handlers with `async def`, using asynchronous libraries and functions, and managing concurrency and errors effectively. This approach enhances scalability and performance by allowing the server to handle multiple operations concurrently, particularly for I/O-bound tasks. Proper error handling and understanding when to use asynchronous programming are critical to ensuring the reliability and efficiency of your FastAPI application.

CHAPTER 14: DEPLOYING FASTAPI APPLICATIONS

Deploying a FastAPI application involves several steps that ensure your application runs reliably in production environments. This final phase is crucial as it determines how your application will handle real-world traffic, security, and scalability. In this section, I will cover the essential strategies for deploying FastAPI applications, including configuring Uvicorn with various servers, deploying to cloud platforms such as AWS and Heroku, and managing configurations for different environments.

Firstly, Uvicorn serves as the ASGI server for FastAPI applications. It is designed for high performance and supports asynchronous communication, making it well-suited for handling high-throughput applications. When deploying FastAPI with Uvicorn, it's important to choose the right server and configuration based on your deployment environment.

Uvicorn can be run directly from the command line or integrated with a process manager like Gunicorn or Docker. Running Uvicorn directly is straightforward for development purposes but may not be suitable for production due to limitations in process management and scalability. For production deployments, integrating Uvicorn with Gunicorn is a common practice. Gunicorn is a WSGI server that can manage multiple worker processes, improving the application's ability to handle concurrent requests. To run Uvicorn with Gunicorn, you would use the following command:

```bash
gunicorn -w 4 -k uvicorn.workers.UvicornWorker myapp:app
```

In this command, `-w 4` specifies the number of worker processes, and `-k uvicorn.workers.UvicornWorker` tells Gunicorn to use Uvicorn's worker class.

For containerized deployments, Docker provides an effective solution. Docker allows you to package your FastAPI application along with its dependencies into a container, ensuring consistency across different environments. To deploy a FastAPI application using Docker, you will need to create a `Dockerfile`. Here is a basic example of a Dockerfile for a FastAPI application:

```dockerfile
FROM python:3.9

Set environment variables
ENV PYTHONDONTWRITEBYTECODE 1
ENV PYTHONUNBUFFERED 1

Set working directory
WORKDIR /app

Install dependencies
COPY requirements.txt /app/
RUN pip install --no-cache-dir -r requirements.txt

Copy project files
COPY . /app/

Expose port
EXPOSE 8000
```

```
Run the application
CMD ["uvicorn", "myapp:app", "--host", "0.0.0.0", "--port", "8000"]
```

This Dockerfile starts with a Python base image, sets environment variables, installs dependencies from `requirements.txt`, and sets the working directory. It then copies the application files into the container, exposes port 8000, and specifies the command to run Uvicorn.

Deploying to cloud platforms like AWS and Heroku involves additional steps. On AWS, you can use Elastic Beanstalk or ECS (Elastic Container Service) to deploy Docker containers. Elastic Beanstalk simplifies the deployment process by managing the underlying infrastructure, while ECS provides more control over container orchestration.

To deploy with Elastic Beanstalk, you need to prepare a configuration file (`.ebextensions`) and a `Dockerrun.aws.json` file that defines the Docker container setup. After configuring your application, you can use the Elastic Beanstalk CLI to deploy:

```bash
eb init -p docker my-fastapi-app
eb create my-fastapi-env
eb deploy
```

Heroku, on the other hand, is known for its simplicity and ease of use. To deploy a FastAPI application on Heroku, you need to create a `Procfile`, which tells Heroku how to run your application. The `Procfile` might look like this:

```procfile
web: uvicorn myapp:app --host 0.0.0.0 --port $PORT
```

This configuration instructs Heroku to run Uvicorn and bind it to the port provided by the environment variable `$PORT`.

For both AWS and Heroku, you must manage environment variables and secrets securely. In AWS, this can be done using AWS Secrets Manager or Parameter Store. On Heroku, you can set environment variables using the Heroku CLI:

```bash
heroku config:set MY_ENV_VARvalue
```

Configuring your deployment for different environments is critical. For development, staging, and production environments, you will typically have different configurations and settings. Using environment variables allows you to manage these differences without modifying your codebase. FastAPI's settings management can be accomplished using `pydantic` settings, which can dynamically load configuration based on the environment.

Finally, it's important to monitor your application after deployment. Monitoring tools such as Prometheus, Grafana, or cloud-native solutions like AWS CloudWatch and Heroku Metrics can help you track performance, error rates, and other critical metrics.

Deploying FastAPI applications requires careful planning and configuration to ensure optimal performance and reliability. By using the right server configurations, containerization, cloud platforms, and environment management strategies, you can successfully bring your FastAPI applications into production and maintain their performance and stability.

The next phase in deploying your FastAPI application involves setting up and configuring deployment to various cloud platforms. Cloud services like AWS and Heroku offer scalable and flexible environments for hosting applications.

Understanding how to deploy to these platforms effectively will ensure that your application is robust, maintainable, and scalable.

Starting with AWS, one of the most widely used cloud services, the deployment process involves several components. Amazon Web Services (AWS) provides a range of services such as EC2 (Elastic Compute Cloud) for hosting virtual servers and ECS (Elastic Container Service) for managing Docker containers. When deploying a FastAPI application on AWS EC2, you will typically follow these steps:

1. Provisioning an EC2 Instance: First, you need to launch an EC2 instance from the AWS Management Console. Choose an appropriate instance type based on your application's resource requirements. For a simple FastAPI application, a t2.micro or t3.micro instance might be sufficient. After selecting an instance type, configure the security group to allow HTTP (port 80) and HTTPS (port 443) traffic.

2. Setting Up the Environment: Once your instance is up and running, SSH into it to set up your application environment. Install necessary packages such as Python, pip, and any other dependencies required by your FastAPI application. You can use a script to automate the installation of these dependencies. For instance, you might use the following commands to install Python and Uvicorn:

```bash
sudo apt update
sudo apt install python3-pip
pip3 install uvicorn fastapi
```

3. Deploying Your Application: Transfer your FastAPI application code to the EC2 instance. You can use SCP (Secure Copy Protocol) or Git to clone your repository directly onto the server. Once the code is on the server, you need to install any

additional dependencies specified in your `requirements.txt` file:

```bash
pip3 install -r requirements.txt
```

4. Configuring Uvicorn: Start your FastAPI application using Uvicorn. You can run Uvicorn directly from the command line or set it up as a service. For a production setup, it's advisable to use a process manager such as `systemd` or `supervisor` to manage the application. Here is an example of how to create a `systemd` service unit file for Uvicorn:

```ini
[Unit]
DescriptionUvicorn instance to serve FastAPI application
Afternetwork.target

[Service]
Userubuntu
Groupubuntu
WorkingDirectory/home/ubuntu/myapp
ExecStart/usr/local/bin/uvicorn myapp:app --host 0.0.0.0 --
port 8000
Restartalways

[Install]
WantedBymulti-user.target
```

Save this file as `/etc/systemd/system/myapp.service`, then enable and start the service with the following commands:

```bash
sudo systemctl enable myapp
sudo systemctl start myapp
```

5. Setting Up a Reverse Proxy: For better performance and security, you should set up a reverse proxy using Nginx or Apache. Nginx is a popular choice due to its efficiency and ease of configuration. Here's a basic Nginx configuration for proxying requests to Uvicorn:

```nginx
server {
  listen 80;
  server_name your_domain_or_ip;

    location / {
    proxy_pass http://127.0.0.1:8000;
    proxy_set_header Host $host;
    proxy_set_header X-Real-IP $remote_addr;
                    proxy_set_header   X-Forwarded-For
$proxy_add_x_forwarded_for;
    proxy_set_header X-Forwarded-Proto $scheme;
  }
}
```

Save this configuration file in `/etc/nginx/sites-available/`, then create a symbolic link to enable it and restart Nginx:

```bash
sudo ln -s /etc/nginx/sites-available/myapp /etc/nginx/sites-
enabled/
sudo systemctl restart nginx
```

Heroku is another popular platform for deploying FastAPI applications, particularly if you want a simpler deployment process with less configuration. Deploying a FastAPI application to Heroku involves:

1. Creating a Heroku Account: Sign up for a Heroku account and install the Heroku CLI (Command Line Interface) on your

local machine.

2. Preparing Your Application: Ensure your FastAPI application has a `Procfile`, which tells Heroku how to run your application. A simple `Procfile` for a FastAPI application might look like this:

```
web: uvicorn myapp:app --host 0.0.0.0 --port ${PORT}
```

Heroku automatically sets the `PORT` environment variable, so you don't need to specify it manually.

3. Deploying to Heroku: Initialize a Git repository in your project directory if you haven't already:

```bash
git init
```

Add your files to the repository and commit:

```bash
git add .
git commit -m "Initial commit"
```

Create a new Heroku application:

```bash
heroku create
```

Deploy your code to Heroku:

```bash
git push heroku master
```

Heroku will automatically build and deploy your

application, and you can open it in your browser with:

```bash
heroku open
```

In both AWS and Heroku deployments, it is crucial to manage your application's configuration for different environments, such as development, staging, and production. This typically involves setting up environment variables and configuring settings such as database URLs, API keys, and logging levels. For AWS, you might use AWS Secrets Manager or SSM (Systems Manager Parameter Store) to manage sensitive configuration. For Heroku, you can set environment variables using the Heroku CLI:

```bash
heroku config:set KEYvalue
```

Ensuring that your FastAPI application is properly deployed and configured will help you maintain a stable, scalable, and secure application in production environments.

When deploying FastAPI applications on cloud platforms, attention must be paid to managing deployment configurations for different environments, ensuring reliability and scalability. Beyond AWS EC2, platforms like Heroku offer an alternative approach that simplifies deployment but also requires specific steps to ensure that the application runs smoothly.

Deploying to Heroku involves several straightforward steps. Heroku abstracts much of the underlying infrastructure management, making it easier to deploy and scale applications. Here is a detailed guide to deploying a FastAPI application on Heroku:

First, ensure that you have the Heroku CLI installed on

your local development machine. This command-line tool is essential for interacting with Heroku and managing your deployments. If you haven't installed it yet, you can download it from the Heroku website.

Begin by preparing your FastAPI application for deployment. Heroku uses a `Procfile` to determine how to run your application. Create a `Procfile` in the root directory of your project if it does not already exist. This file should specify the command Heroku should use to start your FastAPI app. For a typical FastAPI application using Uvicorn, the `Procfile` might look like this:

```
web: uvicorn main:app --host0.0.0.0 --port${PORT}
```

In this `Procfile`, `main` refers to the Python file containing your FastAPI application, and `app` refers to the FastAPI instance within that file. The `${PORT}` environment variable is automatically set by Heroku to the port on which your application should listen.

Next, you need a `requirements.txt` file that lists all the dependencies your application needs. Heroku will use this file to install the necessary Python packages. You can generate this file by running the following command in your development environment:

```
pip freeze > requirements.txt
```

Another important file is `runtime.txt`, which specifies the Python version your application should use. Create a `runtime.txt` file in your project root with the desired Python version, such as:

```
```

```
python-3.9.6
```

With these files in place, you can now proceed with deploying your FastAPI application to Heroku. Initialize a Git repository if you haven't already, and commit your code and configuration files. Then, use the Heroku CLI to create a new Heroku application and push your code:

```
heroku create
git push heroku master
```

Heroku will automatically detect the Python environment, install dependencies, and start your application based on the configuration in your `Procfile`. After deployment, Heroku will provide a URL where your application is accessible. You can open this URL in a web browser to verify that your application is running as expected.

Managing deployment configurations for different environments is crucial to ensure that your application behaves correctly across development, staging, and production environments. Environment-specific settings often include database connection strings, API keys, and other configuration variables that should not be hard-coded into your application. Instead, use environment variables to manage these settings securely.

In FastAPI, you can access environment variables using Python's `os` module. For example, if you need to access a database URL, you can retrieve it with:

```python
import os

DATABASE_URL os.getenv('DATABASE_URL')
```

In Heroku, you can set environment variables through the Heroku Dashboard or by using the Heroku CLI. To set an environment variable using the CLI, you can use:

```
heroku config:set DATABASE_URLyour_database_url
```

For more advanced deployments, you might also consider using Docker to containerize your FastAPI application. Docker allows you to package your application along with its dependencies into a container, which can then be deployed across various environments with consistent behavior. To deploy a Dockerized FastAPI application, you would need to create a `Dockerfile` specifying the build instructions and a `docker-compose.yml` file if you're managing multi-container applications.

Once your Docker container is built, you can push it to a container registry such as Docker Hub or Amazon ECR (Elastic Container Registry). From there, you can deploy it to container orchestration platforms like AWS ECS or Kubernetes. Both of these platforms offer powerful tools for managing containerized applications, including scaling and load balancing.

In conclusion, deploying a FastAPI application involves selecting the appropriate infrastructure and configuring it correctly. Whether using traditional virtual servers like AWS EC2 or cloud platforms like Heroku, attention to detail in configuration files, environment variables, and deployment strategies ensures that your application is reliable, scalable, and ready for production. This process, while intricate, lays the foundation for successful application deployment and management.

CHAPTER 15: ADVANCED DEPENDENCY INJECTION TECHNIQUES

Dependency injection in FastAPI extends beyond basic usage, offering a robust framework for managing complex dependencies efficiently. This section explores advanced techniques that leverage FastAPI's dependency injection system to streamline the architecture of your application, enhance code maintainability, and facilitate the management of services and configurations.

In FastAPI, dependency injection is typically used to provide dependencies to path operations, but its potential extends much further. One of the primary advantages of dependency injection is the decoupling of components, which fosters a modular and maintainable codebase. For complex applications, where dependencies might involve services, configurations, or other reusable components, the advanced features of FastAPI's dependency injection system become crucial.

To begin, consider the management of services that your application might depend on. Services are often implemented as classes that encapsulate business logic or interact with external systems. For instance, if you have a service responsible for sending emails, you can inject this service into your path operations rather than instantiating it within each operation. This approach not only centralizes the service management but also allows you to configure it in a single place.

Here's an example of how you might define and inject such a service. Suppose you have an `EmailService` class that sends emails:

```python
class EmailService:
  def __init__(self, smtp_server: str):
    self.smtp_server  smtp_server

   def send_email(self, to: str, subject: str, body: str):
     Implementation for sending email
    pass
```

To inject this service, you can use FastAPI's dependency injection system. Define a dependency that provides an instance of `EmailService`:

```python
from fastapi import Depends

def get_email_service() -> EmailService:
      smtp_server   "smtp.example.com"    Configuration or
environment variable
  return EmailService(smtp_serversmtp_server)
```

In your path operation, you can now use this dependency:

```python
from fastapi import FastAPI
```

```
app FastAPI()

@app.post("/send/")
async def send_email(to: str, subject: str, body: str,
email_service: EmailService Depends(get_email_service)):
  email_service.send_email(toto, subjectsubject, bodybody)
  return {"message": "Email sent"}
```

This technique ensures that `EmailService` is configured in a single place and injected wherever needed, promoting a clean and maintainable architecture.

Moving beyond services, dependency injection can also handle configurations efficiently. Configuration settings often vary between development, testing, and production environments. Instead of hardcoding these configurations, you can inject them as dependencies. For example, consider a scenario where you need to inject different configurations based on the environment:

```python
from typing import Dict

class Config:
  def __init__(self, settings: Dict[str, str]):
    self.settings settings

def get_config() -> Config:
  environment "production"  Or determine dynamically
  settings {
    "api_key": "prod_api_key" if environment "production" else
"dev_api_key"
  }
  return Config(settingssettings)
```

In your path operations, you can now inject this configuration:

```python
@app.get("/config/")
async def get_configuration(config: Config
Depends(get_config)):
  return {"settings": config.settings}
```

This approach abstracts away the configuration details from your application logic, making it easier to manage and change configurations without altering your core code.

Another advanced technique involves using reusable components or objects that require initialization. For instance, if your application uses a database connection pool, you might want to manage this pool as a dependency:

```python
from sqlalchemy import create_engine
from sqlalchemy.orm import sessionmaker

class DatabaseSession:
  def __init__(self, database_url: str):
    self.engine create_engine(database_url)
    self.Session sessionmaker(bindself.engine)

   def get_session(self):
    return self.Session()

def get_database_session() -> DatabaseSession:
      database_url "sqlite:///./test.db" Configuration or
environment variable
  return DatabaseSession(database_urldatabase_url)
```

In your path operations, you inject the `DatabaseSession`:

```python
@app.get("/items/")
async def read_items(db: DatabaseSession
```

```
Depends(get_database_session)):
  session db.get_session()
   Perform database operations using the session
  return {"message": "Database session used"}
```

This pattern ensures that your database connections are managed efficiently and consistently across your application.

Lastly, consider the use of dependency overrides for testing purposes. FastAPI allows you to override dependencies for testing scenarios, which is useful when you need to inject mock or alternative implementations during testing. By leveraging dependency overrides, you can inject test doubles or stubs instead of real implementations:

```python
from fastapi.testclient import TestClient

def override_get_email_service() -> EmailService:
    return MockEmailService()   A mock implementation for
testing

app.dependency_overrides[get_email_service]
override_get_email_service

client TestClient(app)
response client.post("/send/", json{"to": "test@example.com",
"subject": "Test", "body": "Test body"})
assert response.json() {"message": "Email sent"}
```

This flexibility in testing ensures that you can test your application thoroughly without relying on real services or configurations.

By mastering these advanced dependency injection techniques, you can create more modular, maintainable, and testable FastAPI applications. These techniques leverage

FastAPI's powerful dependency injection system to manage complex dependencies effectively, ensuring your application remains robust and adaptable to changing requirements.

When dealing with advanced dependency injection in FastAPI, it's also crucial to consider how to manage configurations and environment-specific settings. Often, these configurations are not static but need to vary depending on the environment, such as development, testing, or production. To handle this effectively, you can inject configuration settings into your application using dependency injection.

First, define a configuration class that holds your settings. This class can be instantiated with settings from environment variables, configuration files, or other sources. For example:

```python
from typing import Any
import os

class Config:
  def __init__(self):
            self.database_url: str   os.getenv("DATABASE_URL",
"sqlite:///./test.db")
    self.debug: bool  os.getenv("DEBUG", "false").lower()  "true"

def get_config() -> Config:
  return Config()
```

The `Config` class encapsulates all necessary settings, which you can then inject into your services or path operations. Using a dependency provider function like `get_config`, you can supply this configuration to various parts of your application:

```python
from fastapi import Depends, FastAPI
```

```
app FastAPI()

@app.get("/settings/")
async def read_settings(config: Config Depends(get_config)):
  return {
    "database_url": config.database_url,
    "debug": config.debug
  }
```

This approach ensures that all components that need configuration settings get their values from a single source of truth, thus maintaining consistency and simplifying the management of environment-specific configurations.

Another advanced technique involves the use of dependency injection to handle reusable components. For instance, consider a scenario where your application needs to interact with an external API, such as a payment gateway. Instead of creating a new client instance in each endpoint, you can create a reusable component that gets injected where needed.

Define the API client as a class:

```python
class PaymentGatewayClient:
  def __init__(self, api_key: str):
    self.api_key api_key

   def process_payment(self, amount: float, currency: str) ->
Any:
     Implementation for processing payment
    pass
```

You can then create a dependency that provides an instance of this client:

```python
```

```
def get_payment_gateway_client() -> PaymentGatewayClient:
  api_key os.getenv("PAYMENT_API_KEY", "default_key")
  return PaymentGatewayClient(api_keyapi_key)
```

And inject it into your path operations:

```python
@app.post("/pay/")
async def make_payment(amount: float, currency: str, client:
PaymentGatewayClient
Depends(get_payment_gateway_client)):
  result client.process_payment(amount, currency)
  return {"result": result}
```

By doing this, you ensure that the payment gateway client is only instantiated once per request, reducing overhead and improving efficiency.

Managing dependencies across large applications also benefits from hierarchical dependency injection. In complex systems, you may have several layers of dependencies. For instance, an endpoint might need a service that itself requires a repository, and the repository might need a configuration object. FastAPI's dependency injection system supports this by allowing nested dependencies.

Consider a scenario where you have a user service that depends on a user repository, and the user repository needs access to configuration settings. You can define these dependencies hierarchically:

```python
from fastapi import Depends

class UserRepository:
  def __init__(self, config: Config):
    self.config config
```

```
    def get_user(self, user_id: int) -> Any:
     Implementation to get a user
     pass

def get_user_repository(config: Config  Depends(get_config)) -
> UserRepository:
  return UserRepository(configconfig)

class UserService:
  def __init__(self, user_repository: UserRepository):
    self.user_repository  user_repository

   def find_user(self, user_id: int) -> Any:
    return self.user_repository.get_user(user_id)

def get_user_service(user_repository: UserRepository
Depends(get_user_repository)) -> UserService:
  return UserService(user_repositoryuser_repository)

@app.get("/user/{user_id}")
async def read_user(user_id: int, user_service: UserService
Depends(get_user_service)):
  user  user_service.find_user(user_id)
  return {"user": user}
```

This hierarchical dependency injection allows each component to focus on its specific responsibility while relying on FastAPI's dependency management system to handle the construction and provision of dependencies.

In summary, leveraging advanced dependency injection techniques in FastAPI involves not only injecting services and configurations but also managing complex, nested dependencies effectively. By using these techniques, you can ensure that your application remains modular, maintainable, and scalable, accommodating the complexities of real-world software systems.

To further explore advanced dependency injection techniques in FastAPI, it's important to address the concept of dependency overrides. Dependency overrides allow you to replace the default dependency with a different implementation, which is particularly useful in testing scenarios or when dealing with multiple environments.

FastAPI's dependency injection system supports overrides through the `dependency_overrides` attribute of the `FastAPI` class. This allows you to substitute a real dependency with a mock or a different implementation dynamically. For instance, consider a scenario where you have a real service that interacts with an external API but want to use a mock service for testing purposes.

First, you define your real service as follows:

```python
class RealService:
  def perform_action(self) -> str:
    return "Real action performed"
```

In your FastAPI application, you might use this service as a dependency:

```python
from fastapi import Depends, FastAPI

app FastAPI()

def get_service() -> RealService:
  return RealService()

@app.get("/perform/")
async def perform_action(service: RealService
Depends(get_service)):
  return {"result": service.perform_action()}
```

For testing, you might create a mock service that simulates the behavior of `RealService` but does not perform actual operations:

```python
class MockService:
  def perform_action(self) -> str:
    return "Mock action performed"
```

You can then override the dependency in your test setup:

```python
def test_override_dependency():
            app.dependency_overrides[get_service]        lambda:
MockService()


    client  TestClient(app)
  response  client.get("/perform/")
  assert response.json()  {"result": "Mock action performed"}
```

By overriding the `get_service` function with a lambda that returns an instance of `MockService`, you can test your application without relying on the real implementation. This technique is invaluable for unit testing, where you want to isolate the components of your application and control their behavior.

In addition to dependency overrides, another advanced technique involves the use of dependency injection for managing database transactions. For instance, if your application requires a database session for handling multiple requests, you can inject a database session into your dependencies and manage transactions effectively.

Here's how you can set up a database session dependency

using SQLAlchemy:

```python
from sqlalchemy.orm import sessionmaker, Session
from sqlalchemy import create_engine
from fastapi import Depends

SQLALCHEMY_DATABASE_URL "sqlite:///./test.db"
engine create_engine(SQLALCHEMY_DATABASE_URL)
SessionLocal sessionmaker(autocommitFalse, autoflushFalse,
bindengine)

def get_db() -> Session:
  db SessionLocal()
  try:
    yield db
  finally:
    db.close()
```

This dependency, `get_db`, provides a new database session for each request and ensures it is closed after the request is processed. You can then use this session in your path operations:

```python
@app.get("/items/{item_id}")
async def read_item(item_id: int, db: Session
Depends(get_db)):
  item db.query(Item).filter(Item.id item_id).first()
  return {"item": item}
```

In this example, the `db` dependency is automatically injected into the `read_item` function, which allows for database operations to be performed within the context of a session.

Managing complex dependencies through FastAPI's injection

system enables the separation of concerns, making your codebase more modular and maintainable. By effectively using dependency injection, you can handle configurations, services, and reusable components with ease, enhancing the scalability and testability of your application.

Moreover, leveraging dependency overrides and session management techniques ensures that your application remains robust, flexible, and easy to test. These practices not only streamline the architecture of your application but also significantly improve code maintainability and developer productivity. As you apply these advanced dependency injection techniques, you will find that they provide a solid foundation for building high-quality, scalable FastAPI applications.

CHAPTER 16: WORKING WITH BACKGROUND TASKS

FastAPI's ability to handle background tasks allows you to perform operations asynchronously, improving the responsiveness of your application by offloading long-running tasks from the main request-response cycle. This feature is particularly useful for scenarios where you need to execute time-consuming operations such as sending emails, processing data, or interacting with external services without delaying the response to the client.

To begin with, FastAPI provides built-in support for background tasks through its `BackgroundTasks` class. This class can be utilized to schedule tasks that will be executed after the response has been sent to the client. The implementation of background tasks is straightforward and integrates seamlessly into your FastAPI application.

Consider a scenario where you need to send a confirmation email after a user registers on your platform. This operation can be handled as a background task to ensure that the registration process is not delayed. Below is an example of how to set up and use background tasks in FastAPI:

First, you need to define the function that performs the background task. For instance, the function responsible for sending an email might look like this:

```python
from typing import Optional
import time

def send_email(email_address: str, subject: str, body: str) ->
None:
    Simulate a time-consuming email sending process
   time.sleep(5)
       print(f"Sending email to {email_address} with subject
'{subject}' and body '{body}'")
```

Next, integrate this function into a FastAPI endpoint by using the `BackgroundTasks` class. The `BackgroundTasks` class allows you to add tasks to be executed after the response is sent. Here's how you can define an endpoint that utilizes this functionality:

```python
from fastapi import FastAPI, BackgroundTasks

app FastAPI()

@app.post("/register/")
async def register_user(email: str, background_tasks:
BackgroundTasks):
    Register the user (logic not shown here)
    Add the email sending task to the background tasks
    background_tasks.add_task(send_email, email, "Welcome!",
"Thank you for registering.")
   return {"message": "User registered successfully"}
```

In the above example, the `register_user` endpoint receives an email address as input and adds the `send_email` function to the background tasks. When a user registers, they receive an immediate response confirming their registration, while the email is sent asynchronously in the background. This ensures that the registration process is not held up by the time-consuming email sending operation.

FastAPI's background tasks are managed by the `starlette` library, which FastAPI is built upon. The `BackgroundTasks` class handles the execution of these tasks using a worker thread. As a result, tasks added to the background do not block the execution of other requests.

It is also worth noting that background tasks are not suitable for very long-running tasks or tasks that require significant resources. For such tasks, it might be more appropriate to use a dedicated task queue system such as Celery, which provides advanced features for task scheduling, retrying, and managing distributed tasks.

In cases where you have multiple background tasks to manage, you can create more complex task management scenarios. For example, you might want to schedule tasks that need to be executed periodically or handle tasks that require complex workflows. FastAPI does not provide built-in support for these advanced scheduling needs, so you would typically rely on external libraries or services.

For example, you might integrate FastAPI with Celery to handle distributed background tasks. Celery is a powerful distributed task queue that can manage tasks across multiple worker nodes. It provides robust features for scheduling, retries, and task prioritization. To use Celery with FastAPI, you need to set up a Celery instance and configure it to work with your application.

Here's a basic outline of how you might integrate Celery with FastAPI:

1. Install Celery and a message broker: Celery requires a message broker to handle task queues. Redis and RabbitMQ are popular choices. You can install Celery with pip:

```bash
pip install celery[redis]
```

2. Configure Celery: Create a Celery configuration file and define your Celery instance. For example, you can create a `celery.py` file:

```python
from celery import Celery

celery_app Celery(
'tasks',
broker'redis://localhost:6379/0',
backend'redis://localhost:6379/0'
)
```

3. Define Celery tasks: Create tasks that you want to run asynchronously with Celery. For instance:

```python
@celery_app.task
def send_email_task(email_address: str, subject: str, body: str) -> None:
Simulate a time-consuming email sending process
time.sleep(5)
print(f"Sending email to {email_address} with subject '{subject}' and body '{body}'")
```

4. Integrate Celery with FastAPI: Use the Celery tasks in your FastAPI endpoints. For instance:

```python
from fastapi import FastAPI
from celery import Celery
from .celery import celery_app
```

```
app FastAPI()

@app.post("/register/")
async def register_user(email: str):
    Register the user (logic not shown here)
    Add the email sending task to Celery
    send_email_task.delay(email, "Welcome!", "Thank you for registering.")
    return {"message": "User registered successfully"}
```

In this integration, the `send_email_task.delay` method schedules the task to be executed by the Celery worker, allowing your FastAPI application to offload the email sending process.

By using background tasks and integrating with external task queues like Celery, you can effectively manage long-running operations and ensure that your FastAPI application remains responsive and efficient.

To effectively utilize background tasks in FastAPI, it is essential to understand how they are managed and the impact they can have on your application's performance and architecture. Background tasks in FastAPI are designed to handle operations that can be executed independently of the primary request-response cycle. This means that while the main thread is handling incoming requests and responding to clients, background tasks can be processed in parallel, ensuring that time-consuming operations do not hinder the responsiveness of your API.

Beyond the basic use of `BackgroundTasks`, there are several considerations and techniques to effectively manage background tasks. One important aspect is ensuring that the background tasks are idempotent. Idempotency means that the task can be executed multiple times without changing the result beyond the initial application. This is crucial for tasks like sending emails or updating records to avoid duplicate operations in case of retries or failures.

Another consideration is the management of exceptions within background tasks. By default, exceptions thrown in a background task do not affect the response of the main request. However, it is important to handle exceptions within the background task itself to ensure that any errors are logged or addressed properly. Here is an extended example where error handling is incorporated into the background task:

```
```python
from fastapi import FastAPI, BackgroundTasks
import logging

app FastAPI()
logging.basicConfig(levellogging.INFO)

def send_email(email_address: str, subject: str, body: str) ->
None:
  try:
     Simulate email sending process
    if email_address "fail@example.com":
      raise ValueError("Simulated failure")
     Simulate sending email
        print(f"Sending email to {email_address} with subject
'{subject}' and body '{body}'")
  except Exception as e:
       logging.error(f"Failed to send email to {email_address}:
{e}")

@app.post("/register/")
async def register_user(email: str, background_tasks:
BackgroundTasks):
   background_tasks.add_task(send_email, email, "Welcome!",
"Thank you for registering.")
  return {"message": "User registered successfully"}
```
```

` ` `

In this example, if the `send_email` function encounters an error (e.g., if the email address is `"fail@example.com"`), the error is logged using Python's `logging` module. This ensures that any issues with the background task are recorded and can be reviewed later.

Managing background tasks also involves understanding how to scale them effectively. For applications with a high volume of background tasks, it may be necessary to use a more robust task queue system, such as Celery or Redis Queue. These systems provide advanced features for managing task distribution, retry mechanisms, and monitoring.

Celery, for instance, is a powerful distributed task queue that integrates well with FastAPI. It supports various brokers and backends for task management and results storage. Here's a brief overview of how to set up Celery with FastAPI:

1. Install Celery and a message broker, such as Redis:

```bash
pip install celery[redis]
```

2. Configure Celery in a separate module (e.g., `celery_config.py`):

```python
from celery import Celery

app Celery('tasks', broker'redis://localhost:6379/0', backend'redis://localhost:6379/0')

@app.task
def send_email_task(email_address: str, subject: str, body: str) -> None:
    Simulate email sending process
        print(f"Sending email to {email_address} with subject
```

```
'{subject}' and body '{body}'")
```

3. Update your FastAPI application to use Celery tasks:

```python
from fastapi import FastAPI
from celery_config import send_email_task

app FastAPI()

@app.post("/register/")
async def register_user(email: str):
    send_email_task.delay(email, "Welcome!", "Thank you for registering.")
    return {"message": "User registered successfully"}
```

In this setup, `send_email_task.delay()` schedules the email task to be executed by Celery workers. This approach allows your FastAPI application to delegate the task management to Celery, which can handle the load more efficiently.

Moreover, monitoring background tasks is a key aspect of maintaining the health of your application. With tools like Celery, you can leverage Flower, a real-time monitoring tool, to track task progress and performance metrics. For simpler setups, logging can provide sufficient insight into task execution and issues.

Asynchronous task execution can also be applied to other operations, such as data processing or interacting with external APIs. It is crucial to test and profile these tasks to ensure they do not inadvertently become performance bottlenecks. Optimizing the efficiency of background tasks involves tuning task parameters, ensuring efficient use of resources, and handling edge cases effectively.

Understanding and implementing these strategies will

enable you to build more resilient and performant FastAPI applications, leveraging background tasks to enhance functionality while keeping the main application responsive.

When utilizing background tasks in FastAPI, it's crucial to manage resources effectively and ensure that the tasks integrate seamlessly with your application's workflow. Beyond handling exceptions and logging, another important aspect to consider is the management of task execution time and concurrency. As background tasks can potentially run for extended periods, you must design them to be resilient and performant under varying loads.

One effective way to manage long-running tasks is by utilizing task queues. FastAPI itself does not provide a built-in task queue mechanism, but it can be integrated with external libraries and services designed for this purpose. Celery is one of the most popular task queue libraries that work well with FastAPI. It allows you to distribute tasks across worker nodes, manage task retries, and monitor task status.

To integrate Celery with FastAPI, follow these steps:

1. Install Celery and Redis: Celery requires a message broker to handle task distribution. Redis is a popular choice for this. Install Celery and Redis using pip:

```bash
pip install celery[redis]
```

2. Configure Celery: Create a `celery.py` file in your project. This file will configure your Celery instance and connect it to Redis.

```python
from celery import Celery

app Celery('myapp', broker'redis://localhost:6379/0')

@app.task
```

```
def send_email(email_address: str, subject: str, body: str) ->
None:
    Simulate email sending process
        print(f"Sending email to {email_address} with subject
'{subject}' and body '{body}'")
```

3. Update FastAPI Application: Modify your FastAPI application to use Celery for background tasks.

```python
from fastapi import FastAPI
from celery import Celery
from celery.result import AsyncResult
from .celery import send_email

app FastAPI()

@app.post("/register/")
async def register_user(email: str):
        send_email.delay(email, "Welcome!", "Thank you for
registering.")
    return {"message": "User registered successfully"}
```

4. Run Celery Worker: Start the Celery worker process to handle the tasks.

```bash
celery -A celery worker --loglevelinfo
```

By using Celery, you can effectively manage task execution, handle retries, and ensure that your FastAPI application remains responsive even under high load. Celery also provides robust tools for monitoring and managing tasks, which can be integrated with web-based tools like Flower for real-time task monitoring.

Another consideration for background tasks is the

management of database operations. When a background task involves database interactions, it's crucial to ensure that these operations do not lead to issues such as connection leaks or data inconsistencies. For example, if your background task needs to perform database queries or updates, it should be designed to handle database connections properly. Using context managers or dedicated database connection pools can help manage database interactions more effectively.

For instance, if you are using SQLAlchemy with FastAPI, ensure that each background task establishes its own database session and closes it properly after the task completes. Here's an example demonstrating this approach:

```python
from sqlalchemy.orm import Session
from fastapi import FastAPI, BackgroundTasks
from .database import SessionLocal, engine
from .models import User
import logging

app FastAPI()
logging.basicConfig(levellogging.INFO)

def get_db():
  db SessionLocal()
  try:
    yield db
  finally:
    db.close()

def process_user_data(user_id: int, db: Session) -> None:
  try:
    user db.query(User).filter(User.id user_id).first()
     Simulate data processing
    print(f"Processing data for user: {user.name}")
  except Exception as e:
      logging.error(f"Error processing data for user {user_id}:
```

```
{e}")

@app.post("/process/")
async def process_user(user_id: int, background_tasks: BackgroundTasks):
    db SessionLocal()
    background_tasks.add_task(process_user_data, user_id, db)
    return {"message": "Data processing started"}
```

In this example, `process_user_data` is a background task that processes user data using a database session. It's crucial to handle the database session within the task to ensure proper management of resources.

When implementing background tasks, consider the scalability of your solution. Depending on the volume and complexity of tasks, you may need to adjust your architecture to handle high throughput. This might involve scaling your worker processes, optimizing task execution, or using distributed systems to manage background tasks more efficiently.

Finally, always keep in mind the security implications of running background tasks. Ensure that any sensitive information processed by background tasks is handled securely and that access controls are in place to prevent unauthorized operations. Proper validation and sanitization of inputs to background tasks are essential to protect against security vulnerabilities.

By effectively managing background tasks in FastAPI, you can build scalable and efficient applications that handle complex operations without compromising performance or user experience.

CHAPTER 17: HANDLING FILE UPLOADS AND DOWNLOADS

In the realm of web development, handling file uploads and downloads is a common requirement, particularly for applications that involve user-generated content or data exchange. FastAPI provides a straightforward and efficient way to manage file uploads and downloads, but understanding the intricacies of handling files securely and effectively requires attention to detail. This discussion will cover the mechanisms for managing file uploads, validating file types and sizes, and implementing file storage. Additionally, we will explore the process for handling file downloads and streaming large files.

To begin, handling file uploads in FastAPI involves using the `File` and `UploadFile` classes provided by the framework. These classes enable you to receive files from clients, manage their content, and validate their properties. The `UploadFile` class is particularly useful because it provides an interface for handling files asynchronously, which is beneficial for processing large files without blocking the main thread.

When defining an endpoint that accepts file uploads, you will typically use the `UploadFile` class within a form request. For example, to create an endpoint that allows users to upload a profile picture, you might define the endpoint as follows:

```python
from fastapi import FastAPI, File, UploadFile
from typing import List

app FastAPI()

@app.post("/uploadfile/")
async def upload_file(file: UploadFile File(...)):
    contents await file.read()
    with open(f"uploaded_files/{file.filename}", "wb") as f:
        f.write(contents)
    return {"filename": file.filename}
```

In this example, the `upload_file` function accepts an `UploadFile` object, which is then read asynchronously. The contents of the file are written to a specified directory on the server. This basic implementation handles file uploads, but there are several important considerations to ensure the functionality is both secure and efficient.

One critical aspect is file validation. Ensuring that files meet specific criteria, such as size limits and acceptable types, helps prevent malicious files from being uploaded and consuming unnecessary resources. FastAPI makes it possible to implement these validations by checking the file's properties before processing it. For example, to validate that the uploaded file is an image and does not exceed a certain size, you might update the endpoint as follows:

```python
from fastapi import HTTPException
from starlette.status import HTTP_400_BAD_REQUEST

@app.post("/uploadfile/")
async def upload_file(file: UploadFile File(...)):
```

```
  if file.content_type not in ["image/jpeg", "image/png"]:
    raise HTTPException(
      status_codeHTTP_400_BAD_REQUEST,
        detail"Invalid file type. Only JPEG and PNG images are
allowed."
    )


   if file.spool_max_size > 10  1024  1024:  10 MB limit
    raise HTTPException(
      status_codeHTTP_400_BAD_REQUEST,
      detail"File size exceeds limit of 10 MB."
    )


   contents  await file.read()
  with open(f"uploaded_files/{file.filename}", "wb") as f:
    f.write(contents)
  return {"filename": file.filename}
```

In this updated example, we check the file's MIME type and size before processing it. If the file does not meet the criteria, an HTTP exception is raised, providing feedback to the client.

Handling file downloads and streaming large files are equally important. FastAPI supports file downloads through response objects, which can be used to serve files from the server to the client. For example, to provide a downloadable file, you can use the `FileResponse` class from `starlette.responses`:

```python
from fastapi import FastAPI
from starlette.responses import FileResponse

app  FastAPI()

@app.get("/downloadfile/{filename}")
async def download_file(filename: str):
```

```
    file_path f"uploaded_files/{filename}"
    return FileResponse(pathfile_path, filenamefilename)
```

This endpoint returns a file from the server for download. The `FileResponse` class handles the file streaming efficiently, allowing clients to download large files without overloading the server's memory.

Streaming large files is crucial when dealing with sizable data, as it prevents the server from loading the entire file into memory. FastAPI's `FileResponse` class is well-suited for this purpose. When using `FileResponse`, the file is streamed in chunks, which reduces memory usage and enhances performance.

In addition to `FileResponse`, you can use the `StreamingResponse` class to handle more complex streaming scenarios. This class allows you to stream content from any iterable or generator, making it possible to stream data dynamically. For instance, to stream a large dataset or generate a file on the fly, you might use:

```python
from fastapi import FastAPI
from starlette.responses import StreamingResponse
import io

app FastAPI()

@app.get("/streamfile/")
async def stream_file():
    def generate_large_file():
        for i in range(1000000):  Simulate a large file
            yield f"Line {i}\n"

    file_like io.StringIO()
    response StreamingResponse(generate_large_file(), media_type"text/plain")
```

```
    response.headers["Content-Disposition"]  "attachment;
filenamelargefile.txt"
  return response
```

This example demonstrates how to stream content dynamically using a generator function. The `StreamingResponse` class efficiently handles large data streams without consuming excessive memory.

By carefully managing file uploads, validations, downloads, and streaming, you can build robust and scalable file-handling capabilities into your FastAPI applications. Understanding and implementing these techniques will help ensure that your application can efficiently handle file operations while maintaining high performance and security.

When implementing file uploads, an essential consideration is how to handle and validate the uploaded files effectively to maintain both performance and security. To this end, FastAPI provides robust mechanisms for validating file types and sizes, which can be integrated seamlessly into your endpoint logic.

In the context of file size validation, it is often necessary to set limits on the maximum allowed file size to avoid excessive memory consumption and potential denial-of-service attacks. FastAPI does not enforce file size limits natively, so this must be managed within your endpoint logic. For instance, you can inspect the size of the file and raise an HTTP exception if it exceeds a predefined limit:

```python
from fastapi import FastAPI, File, UploadFile, HTTPException
from starlette.status import HTTP_400_BAD_REQUEST

app  FastAPI()

MAX_FILE_SIZE  5  1024  1024   5 MB
```

```
@app.post("/uploadfile/")
async def upload_file(file: UploadFile  File(...)):
  if file.spool_max_size > MAX_FILE_SIZE:
                                                          raise
HTTPException(status_codeHTTP_400_BAD_REQUEST,
detail"File size exceeds limit")


    contents  await file.read()
  with open(f"uploaded_files/{file.filename}", "wb") as f:
    f.write(contents)
  return {"filename": file.filename}
```

In this code snippet, the `spool_max_size` attribute, which should be checked against `MAX_FILE_SIZE`, determines if the file exceeds the specified limit. If it does, an `HTTPException` is raised to indicate that the file size is too large.

Additionally, validating the file type is crucial to ensure that only acceptable file formats are processed. This can be achieved by examining the file's MIME type or its extension. Here is an example of how you might validate that only image files are accepted:

```python
from fastapi import FastAPI, File, UploadFile, HTTPException
import mimetypes
from starlette.status import HTTP_400_BAD_REQUEST

app  FastAPI()

ALLOWED_EXTENSIONS  {'jpg', 'jpeg', 'png'}

def allowed_file(filename: str) -> bool:
  extension  filename.rsplit('.', 1)[1].lower()
  return extension in ALLOWED_EXTENSIONS
```

```
@app.post("/uploadfile/")
async def upload_file(file: UploadFile  File(...)):
  if not allowed_file(file.filename):
                                                                    raise
HTTPException(status_codeHTTP_400_BAD_REQUEST,
detail"Invalid file type")

    contents  await file.read()
  with open(f"uploaded_files/{file.filename}", "wb") as f:
    f.write(contents)
  return {"filename": file.filename}
```

Here, the `allowed_file` function checks the file extension to ensure it is one of the allowed types. If the file does not match the allowed extensions, the endpoint raises an `HTTPException` to reject the upload.

Handling file storage efficiently is another crucial aspect. FastAPI's ability to integrate with various storage solutions—such as local filesystems, cloud storage services like AWS S3, or distributed storage systems—makes it versatile. For local file storage, the code provided earlier demonstrates a simple approach to saving files to a specified directory on the server. However, for larger-scale applications, or when dealing with files that need to be accessed across multiple instances of your application, using a cloud storage solution is often more appropriate.

To upload files to AWS S3, for example, you can use the `boto3` library, which provides a Python interface to AWS services. Here's how you could modify the file upload logic to store files in an S3 bucket:

```python
import boto3
```

```
from fastapi import FastAPI, File, UploadFile, HTTPException
from starlette.status import HTTP_400_BAD_REQUEST

app FastAPI()
s3_client boto3.client('s3', region_name'your-region')

BUCKET_NAME 'your-bucket-name'
ALLOWED_EXTENSIONS {'jpg', 'jpeg', 'png'}

def allowed_file(filename: str) -> bool:
  extension filename.rsplit('.', 1)[1].lower()
  return extension in ALLOWED_EXTENSIONS

@app.post("/uploadfile/")
async def upload_file(file: UploadFile File(...)):
  if not allowed_file(file.filename):
                                                                raise
HTTPException(status_codeHTTP_400_BAD_REQUEST,
detail"Invalid file type")

    file_content await file.read()
  s3_client.put_object(
    BucketBUCKET_NAME,
    Keyfile.filename,
    Bodyfile_content,
    ContentTypefile.content_type
  )
  return {"filename": file.filename}
```

In this code, `boto3` is used to interact with S3. The `put_object` method uploads the file to the specified bucket. The `ContentType` parameter helps ensure that the file is stored with the correct MIME type.

Managing file downloads and streaming is similarly important, particularly for large files that might not be practical to load entirely into memory. FastAPI supports streaming responses, which allows you to serve files efficiently without needing to read the entire file into memory. Here's how you might implement a file download endpoint using streaming:

```python
from fastapi import FastAPI, HTTPException
from fastapi.responses import StreamingResponse
import os

app FastAPI()

@app.get("/downloadfile/{filename}")
async def download_file(filename: str):
  file_path f"uploaded_files/{filename}"
  if not os.path.exists(file_path):
        raise HTTPException(status_code404, detail"File not found")


    file_like open(file_path, mode"rb")
        return StreamingResponse(file_like, media_type"application/octet-stream")
```

In this endpoint, `StreamingResponse` is used to stream the file from the filesystem directly to the client. This approach helps manage memory usage efficiently, as the file is read in chunks rather than being loaded all at once.

By integrating these techniques, you can manage file uploads and downloads in FastAPI with robust validation, secure storage, and efficient data handling. This setup ensures that your application can handle file operations effectively while maintaining good performance and security practices.

When it comes to handling file downloads in FastAPI, the approach differs slightly from uploads but involves its own set of considerations for efficiency and usability. Downloading files, especially large ones, requires careful handling to ensure that the server can deliver files without unnecessary memory overhead and to maintain a responsive application. FastAPI provides mechanisms to facilitate file downloads through the use of `FileResponse`, which is designed to stream files efficiently from disk to the client.

To begin with, `FileResponse` is part of FastAPI's response system and is tailored for serving files from the filesystem. It allows you to send files in response to HTTP requests, leveraging streaming to handle large files gracefully. Here's a basic example of how to implement a file download endpoint:

```python
from fastapi import FastAPI
from fastapi.responses import FileResponse
import os

app FastAPI()

@app.get("/download/{filename}")
async def download_file(filename: str):
  file_path f"files/{filename}"
  if os.path.exists(file_path):
    return FileResponse(pathfile_path, filenamefilename)
  else:
        raise HTTPException(status_code404, detail"File not
found")
```

In this example, the `download_file` function constructs the path to the requested file and uses `FileResponse` to stream it to the client. The `filename` parameter in the URL is used to locate the file, and `FileResponse` takes care of streaming the file content in a memory-efficient manner. The server sends the file in chunks, avoiding loading the entire file into memory, which is particularly important for handling large files.

Another crucial aspect when dealing with file downloads

is ensuring proper handling of errors and edge cases. For instance, if a user requests a file that does not exist, the server should return a `404 Not Found` response. This is handled by checking the file's existence using `os.path.exists()`, and raising an `HTTPException` if the file is not found.

Streaming for large files can also be handled using a more manual approach if necessary. This approach involves reading the file in chunks and yielding these chunks as the response is being sent. Here's an example of how to implement manual streaming:

```python
from fastapi import FastAPI, HTTPException
from fastapi.responses import StreamingResponse
import os

app FastAPI()

@app.get("/stream/{filename}")
async def stream_file(filename: str):
  file_path f"files/{filename}"
  if os.path.exists(file_path):
    def iter_file():
      with open(file_path, "rb") as f:
        while chunk : f.read(1024):
          yield chunk
                              return    StreamingResponse(iter_file(),
media_type"application/octet-stream")
  else:
        raise HTTPException(status_code404, detail"File not
found")
```

In this code, `StreamingResponse` is used to stream the file contents in chunks to the client. The `iter_file` function reads the file in 1024-byte chunks and yields each chunk, allowing the file to be streamed efficiently. This approach is particularly useful when dealing with very large files that may not fit comfortably into memory all at once.

Handling file uploads and downloads effectively also involves considerations around security and performance. For file uploads, always ensure that you validate the file content to prevent uploading of malicious files, and use a secure method to handle file storage. When implementing file downloads, consider setting appropriate content types and handling large file transfers efficiently to provide a smooth experience for users.

In summary, managing file uploads and downloads in FastAPI requires careful attention to validation, security, and performance considerations. By leveraging FastAPI's built-in functionalities such as `FileResponse` and `StreamingResponse`, along with implementing proper error handling and streaming techniques, you can build robust and efficient file handling features into your application. This ensures that your API can handle a range of file operations effectively, providing a reliable and user-friendly experience for end users.

CHAPTER 18: CUSTOMIZING MIDDLEWARE

In FastAPI, middleware functions offer a powerful way to implement cross-cutting concerns that are not directly tied to the business logic of an application. By creating and using custom middleware, developers can efficiently handle tasks such as logging, modifying requests and responses, or managing other common concerns that apply globally across the application. This chapter will explore the principles of middleware, guide you through the process of developing your own custom middleware, and illustrate how to integrate it into your FastAPI application to enhance its functionality.

Middleware in FastAPI is designed to operate at a global level, processing requests before they reach the route handlers and processing responses before they are sent to the client. To create custom middleware, one must adhere to specific patterns that FastAPI follows. This involves defining a middleware class that implements a callable `__call__` method, which will be invoked for each request and response cycle.

Firstly, consider the structure of a basic middleware class. The `__call__` method is crucial here, as it must accept three parameters: `scope`, `receive`, and `send`. These parameters are essential for interacting with the ASGI

(Asynchronous Server Gateway Interface) lifecycle of the application. The `scope` parameter provides context about the request, including its type and details about the connection. The `receive` parameter is a callable that allows for receiving messages from the client, while `send` is a callable used to send responses back to the client.

Here is a simple example of a custom middleware class that logs the duration of each request:

```python
import time
from starlette.middleware.base import BaseHTTPMiddleware
from starlette.requests import Request
from starlette.responses import Response

class LoggingMiddleware(BaseHTTPMiddleware):
    async def dispatch(self, request: Request, call_next):
        start_time time.time()
        response: Response  await call_next(request)
        process_time time.time() - start_time
        print(f"Request took {process_time:.4f} seconds")
        return response
```

In this example, `LoggingMiddleware` inherits from `BaseHTTPMiddleware`, a convenience class provided by Starlette (the ASGI framework underlying FastAPI). The `dispatch` method is where the core logic of the middleware is executed. It captures the start time, forwards the request to the next handler in the middleware chain using `call_next`, and then calculates the processing time. Finally, it prints the duration of the request handling.

Integrating this middleware into your FastAPI application involves using the `add_middleware` method provided by the FastAPI app instance. Here's how you can add the `LoggingMiddleware` to your FastAPI app:

```python
from fastapi import FastAPI

app FastAPI()

app.add_middleware(LoggingMiddleware)
```

Once added, the `LoggingMiddleware` will automatically be invoked for every incoming request, allowing you to monitor performance metrics or other cross-cutting concerns globally across the application.

Another common use case for middleware is modifying requests or responses. For instance, you may want to add custom headers to every response. This can be achieved with middleware by intercepting the response and adding the necessary headers before sending it to the client. Here's an example of a middleware class that adds a custom header:

```python
class AddCustomHeaderMiddleware(BaseHTTPMiddleware):
  async def dispatch(self, request: Request, call_next):
    response: Response  await call_next(request)
    response.headers['X-Custom-Header']  'Value'
    return response
```

In this example, the `AddCustomHeaderMiddleware` class intercepts the response and adds an `X-Custom-Header` header with the value `'Value'`. This header will be included in every response sent by the FastAPI application, allowing for custom header management globally.

Moreover, middleware can also be utilized to handle authentication or authorization logic before the request reaches the route handlers. For example, you could implement middleware that checks for a valid token in the request headers and processes requests accordingly. Here's a simplistic example of such middleware:

```python
class AuthenticationMiddleware(BaseHTTPMiddleware):
  async def dispatch(self, request: Request, call_next):
    token request.headers.get('Authorization')
    if token ! 'valid-token':
      return Response('Unauthorized', status_code401)
    response: Response await call_next(request)
    return response
```

In this scenario, `AuthenticationMiddleware` checks for a specific token in the `Authorization` header. If the token is not present or is invalid, it returns a 401 Unauthorized response. Otherwise, it forwards the request to the next handler.

Custom middleware can greatly enhance the capabilities of a FastAPI application, providing a robust mechanism for handling various global concerns. By creating middleware classes that align with the ASGI lifecycle and integrating them into your application, you can ensure that cross-cutting tasks are managed efficiently and consistently across all routes. Whether you are logging performance metrics, modifying responses, or enforcing authentication, middleware offers a flexible and powerful approach to extend the functionality of your FastAPI application.

To further elucidate the concept of middleware in FastAPI, let us delve deeper into how middleware can be utilized to handle a variety of cross-cutting concerns. One essential aspect of custom middleware is its ability to modify both requests and responses. This capability is particularly useful when dealing with tasks such as request validation, authentication, or modifying response headers.

Consider a scenario where you need to add custom headers to every response sent by your application. This can be achieved by extending the previously discussed `LoggingMiddleware` to include header modification. The revised middleware class might look like this:

```python
class HeaderMiddleware(BaseHTTPMiddleware):
  async def dispatch(self, request: Request, call_next):
    response: Response  await call_next(request)
    response.headers['X-Custom-Header'] 'CustomValue'
    return response
```

In this updated example, the `HeaderMiddleware` class appends a custom header to every response. This demonstrates how middleware can be employed to influence the response phase by attaching or modifying headers as needed.

Middleware can also be used to handle authentication and authorization checks. For instance, suppose you want to ensure that certain routes are accessible only to authenticated users. You could implement a middleware class that checks for the presence of a valid authentication token in the request headers. Here's a simplified version of how such middleware might be implemented:

```python
class AuthMiddleware(BaseHTTPMiddleware):
  async def dispatch(self, request: Request, call_next):
    token request.headers.get('Authorization')
    if not token or not self.is_valid_token(token):
      return Response("Unauthorized", status_code401)
    response: Response  await call_next(request)
    return response
```

```
    def is_valid_token(self, token: str) -> bool:
      Implement your token validation logic here
     return token  "valid_token"
```

In this `AuthMiddleware`, the `dispatch` method checks the `Authorization` header for a token. If the token is missing or invalid, the middleware responds with a 401 Unauthorized status. Otherwise, it proceeds to handle the request as usual. This illustrates how middleware can act as a gatekeeper, ensuring that only authenticated users gain access to certain parts of the application.

When integrating custom middleware into a FastAPI application, it is essential to understand how to configure and use it within the application setup. FastAPI provides a convenient way to add middleware to an application using the `add_middleware` method of the `FastAPI` class. This method allows you to specify middleware classes that should be applied globally to all requests and responses.

Here is how you might integrate the `HeaderMiddleware` into your FastAPI application:

```python
from fastapi import FastAPI
from starlette.middleware.base import BaseHTTPMiddleware

app  FastAPI()

app.add_middleware(HeaderMiddleware)
```

By invoking `add_middleware` with your custom middleware class, FastAPI ensures that the middleware is executed for every request and response cycle. This approach allows for a centralized configuration of middleware, simplifying the management of global concerns.

Another important consideration when working with middleware is the order in which multiple middleware classes are applied. Middleware is executed in the order it is added to the application. This means that if you have multiple middleware classes, their effects will be applied sequentially based on their order of addition. For instance, if you have both `LoggingMiddleware` and `HeaderMiddleware`, the logging will occur before the headers are added. The following example illustrates this ordering:

```python
app.add_middleware(LoggingMiddleware)
app.add_middleware(HeaderMiddleware)
```

In this setup, logging information will be printed before the custom header is appended to the response. It is crucial to consider this ordering when designing your middleware to ensure that it behaves as intended.

Furthermore, while developing middleware, it is important to handle exceptions gracefully. Middleware should be robust and capable of managing unexpected errors. For example, if your middleware encounters an exception while processing a request, it should handle it appropriately to prevent the application from crashing. An enhanced version of the `AuthMiddleware` with exception handling might look like this:

```python
class SafeAuthMiddleware(BaseHTTPMiddleware):
    async def dispatch(self, request: Request, call_next):
        try:
            token request.headers.get('Authorization')
            if not token or not self.is_valid_token(token):
                return Response("Unauthorized", status_code401)
            response: Response await call_next(request)
```

```
        return response
    except Exception as e:
        Log the exception and return a generic error message
        print(f"An error occurred: {e}")
        return Response("Internal Server Error", status_code500)
```

In this `SafeAuthMiddleware`, any exceptions that occur during request processing are caught and logged, and a generic error message is returned to the client. This approach ensures that your middleware is resilient to errors and maintains the stability of your application.

Custom middleware in FastAPI provides a flexible mechanism for handling various cross-cutting concerns. By leveraging middleware, developers can efficiently manage tasks that span multiple parts of an application, such as logging, request validation, and response transformation. Understanding how to create, configure, and integrate custom middleware is essential for building robust and maintainable FastAPI applications.

When it comes to integrating custom middleware into a FastAPI application, the process is straightforward yet crucial for ensuring that the middleware functions as intended across the application. FastAPI utilizes the ASGI (Asynchronous Server Gateway Interface) specification, and middleware must be registered correctly to ensure proper execution. The following section will guide you through how to incorporate the middleware classes into your FastAPI application and outline some advanced concepts for customization.

To integrate middleware into your FastAPI application, you need to instantiate your middleware class and add it to the application's middleware stack. FastAPI provides a `Middleware` class that can be used to configure this. This is typically done in the main application setup file where you initialize the `FastAPI` app instance. Here's how you can do it:

```python
from fastapi import FastAPI
from starlette.middleware.base import BaseHTTPMiddleware

app FastAPI()

app.add_middleware(HeaderMiddleware)
app.add_middleware(AuthMiddleware)
```

In this example, the `HeaderMiddleware` and `AuthMiddleware` classes are added to the FastAPI application. The order in which you add middleware matters, as it determines the sequence in which they process requests and responses. Middleware is executed in the order it is added; thus, if you need one piece of middleware to act before another, ensure it is listed first.

Another advanced use of middleware involves managing asynchronous operations. Middleware in FastAPI can perform async operations, allowing you to handle tasks that involve waiting for I/O operations, such as querying a database or calling external APIs. Consider a scenario where you need to log detailed request information to an external logging service. You could implement this functionality asynchronously within a middleware class. Here is an example:

```python
import httpx
from starlette.middleware.base import BaseHTTPMiddleware
from starlette.requests import Request
from starlette.responses import Response

class AsyncLoggingMiddleware(BaseHTTPMiddleware):
  async def dispatch(self, request: Request, call_next):
     Log request details asynchronously
    async with httpx.AsyncClient() as client:
```

```
            await client.post("https://logging-service.com/logs",
json{
            "method": request.method,
            "url": str(request.url),
            "headers": dict(request.headers)
        })
    response: Response  await call_next(request)
    return response
```

In this `AsyncLoggingMiddleware` class, the request details are sent to an external logging service asynchronously. This demonstrates how middleware can be leveraged to handle more complex tasks that involve asynchronous operations, enhancing the overall capability of your FastAPI application.

It is also important to consider error handling within your middleware. In cases where middleware operations may fail, proper error handling ensures that the application remains robust and provides meaningful feedback. For example, if the middleware responsible for logging encounters an error while contacting the external service, you should catch and handle this exception gracefully to avoid disrupting the request-response cycle. Here is an enhanced version of the previous middleware with error handling:

```python
class SafeLoggingMiddleware(BaseHTTPMiddleware):
  async def dispatch(self, request: Request, call_next):
    try:
      async with httpx.AsyncClient() as client:
            await client.post("https://logging-service.com/logs",
json{
            "method": request.method,
            "url": str(request.url),
            "headers": dict(request.headers)
        })
```

```
        except httpx.HTTPStatusError as e:
          print(f"Logging failed: {e}")
        response: Response  await call_next(request)
        return response
```

In this `SafeLoggingMiddleware` class, any exceptions raised by the `httpx.AsyncClient` are caught and logged, ensuring that the middleware handles failures gracefully without impacting the request handling.

Lastly, while integrating middleware into your FastAPI application, it is beneficial to understand its impact on performance. Middleware can introduce additional processing overhead, so it is crucial to ensure that it is optimized and efficient. Performance considerations may include minimizing the time spent in middleware processing and avoiding synchronous blocking operations that could slow down request handling.

By carefully implementing and managing middleware, you can effectively address various cross-cutting concerns within your FastAPI application. Whether it involves logging, authentication, request modification, or response transformation, custom middleware offers a flexible and powerful mechanism to enhance the functionality and maintainability of your application.

CHAPTER 19: OPTIMIZING PERFORMANCE AND SCALABILITY

In the realm of application development, performance optimization is essential for ensuring that your FastAPI application can handle increasing loads efficiently and remain responsive under stress. This discussion will focus on several strategies to enhance the performance and scalability of FastAPI applications. We will explore techniques for optimizing database queries, managing concurrency, leveraging caching mechanisms, and employing profiling and benchmarking to identify and address performance bottlenecks.

To begin with, optimizing database queries is a critical aspect of performance enhancement. Inefficient database interactions can significantly degrade the performance of your application. One approach to optimization is to analyze and refine your queries to minimize their execution time. This includes ensuring that your queries are using appropriate indexes and avoiding unnecessary data retrieval.

In FastAPI, you can employ various libraries for database interactions, such as SQLAlchemy for relational databases or Tortoise-ORM for async support. Regardless of the library used, it is vital to focus on writing efficient queries. For instance, consider using pagination to handle large datasets. Instead of retrieving all records at once, which can lead to memory exhaustion and slow responses, you can fetch data in smaller chunks. Here's a brief example of how pagination can be implemented with SQLAlchemy:

```python
from sqlalchemy.orm import Session
from sqlalchemy import select

def get_items(db: Session, skip: int 0, limit: int 10):
    return db.execute(select(Item).offset(skip).limit(limit)).scalars().all()
```

In this example, `get_items` function retrieves a subset of items based on the provided `skip` and `limit` parameters. This method improves performance by preventing large amounts of data from being loaded into memory all at once.

Managing concurrency is another crucial factor in optimizing FastAPI applications. FastAPI's asynchronous capabilities allow it to handle many concurrent operations efficiently. However, managing concurrency involves ensuring that your application can handle multiple requests simultaneously without causing contention or performance degradation. To achieve this, you should leverage asynchronous programming paradigms and make use of asynchronous libraries where possible.

For example, if your application needs to perform I/O-bound tasks, such as making HTTP requests or accessing a database, you should use asynchronous functions to prevent blocking the event loop. Here's an example of an asynchronous endpoint using FastAPI and `httpx`:

```python
```

```
import httpx
from fastapi import FastAPI

app FastAPI()

@app.get("/external-data")
async def fetch_external_data():
  async with httpx.AsyncClient() as client:
    response await client.get("https://api.example.com/data")
  return response.json()
```

In this example, the `fetch_external_data` endpoint uses `httpx.AsyncClient` to perform non-blocking HTTP requests, allowing other tasks to proceed concurrently.

Leveraging caching mechanisms is another effective strategy for enhancing performance. Caching helps reduce the load on your backend systems by storing frequently accessed data in a fast-access storage layer. This can significantly decrease response times and improve the overall efficiency of your application. FastAPI does not come with built-in caching, but you can integrate caching solutions such as Redis or Memcached with your application.

For instance, you can use `aioredis` to integrate Redis caching into your FastAPI application. Here is a basic example of how to use Redis for caching:

```python
import aioredis
from fastapi import FastAPI
from pydantic import BaseModel

app FastAPI()
redis aioredis.from_url("redis://localhost")

class Item(BaseModel):
  name: str
```

```
  description: str

@app.get("/items/{item_id}")
async def read_item(item_id: int):
  cached_item  await redis.get(f"item:{item_id}")
  if cached_item:
    return cached_item
  item  fetch_item_from_database(item_id)
  await redis.set(f"item:{item_id}", item)
  return item
```

In this example, the `read_item` endpoint first checks if the item is available in the Redis cache. If it is, the cached item is returned. If not, the item is fetched from the database, cached, and then returned. This caching mechanism helps reduce database load and improve response times.

Finally, profiling and benchmarking are indispensable tools for identifying and addressing performance bottlenecks. Profiling involves analyzing the execution of your application to identify which parts are consuming the most resources. This can be achieved using tools such as `cProfile` for CPU profiling or `async-profiler` for asynchronous code. Benchmarking, on the other hand, measures the performance of your application under different conditions to understand how it scales with increasing loads.

For example, you can use `pytest-benchmark` to benchmark your FastAPI application endpoints:

```python
from fastapi.testclient import TestClient
from myapp import app

client  TestClient(app)

def test_read_item(benchmark):
  result  benchmark(client.get, "/items/1")
```

```
    assert result.status_code 200
```

In this test, the `pytest-benchmark` plugin measures the response time of the `/items/1` endpoint, providing insights into how well the endpoint performs under test conditions.

By applying these strategies—optimizing database queries, managing concurrency, leveraging caching mechanisms, and utilizing profiling and benchmarking tools—you can significantly enhance the performance and scalability of your FastAPI application, ensuring it remains robust and responsive as it grows.

When it comes to optimizing performance and scalability in FastAPI, leveraging caching mechanisms can play a pivotal role. Caching allows you to store frequently accessed data temporarily, thus reducing the need to recompute or fetch data repeatedly. By implementing caching strategies, you can alleviate the load on your database or external services, leading to faster response times and a more efficient application.

FastAPI does not provide built-in caching, but it integrates seamlessly with external caching libraries. A popular choice for caching is Redis, an in-memory data structure store. Redis supports various caching strategies, such as time-based expiration and LRU (Least Recently Used) eviction, which can help manage memory usage effectively. To utilize Redis with FastAPI, you can use the `aioredis` library, which offers asynchronous support for Redis operations.

Here's a basic example of how to integrate Redis caching into a FastAPI application using `aioredis`:

```python
import aioredis
from fastapi import FastAPI, Depends
```

```
from pydantic import BaseModel
from typing import Optional

app FastAPI()
redis aioredis.from_url("redis://localhost")

class Item(BaseModel):
  name: str
  description: Optional[str] None

@app.get("/items/{item_id}")
async def get_item(item_id: int, redisDepends(lambda: redis)):
  cache_key f"item:{item_id}"
  cached_item await redis.get(cache_key)


    if cached_item:
     return cached_item

     Simulate database query
  item {"id": item_id, "name": "Item Name", "description": "Item
Description"}
    await redis.set(cache_key, item, ex60)   Cache item for 60
seconds
  return item
```

In this example, the `get_item` endpoint first checks the Redis cache for the requested item. If the item is not found in the cache, it retrieves the data (simulated here as a static dictionary), stores it in the cache, and returns the response. This approach ensures that subsequent requests for the same item within the cache duration are served more quickly.

Another essential aspect of optimizing performance is profiling and benchmarking. These techniques help you identify performance bottlenecks and understand how different parts of your application perform under various conditions. Profiling involves measuring the time taken by different parts of your code, while benchmarking focuses on assessing the overall performance of your application in terms of speed and throughput.

FastAPI applications can be profiled using various tools and techniques. One widely used tool is `cProfile`, a built-in Python module that provides detailed profiling information. To profile a FastAPI application, you would typically run the server with `cProfile` and analyze the generated profiling data to pinpoint slow or inefficient parts of your code. For instance:

```python
import cProfile
from fastapi import FastAPI

app FastAPI()

@app.get("/")
async def read_root():
  return {"Hello": "World"}

if __name__ "__main__":
  cProfile.run("app.run()", "profile_output.prof")
```

In this snippet, `cProfile.run` is used to execute the FastAPI application and generate a profiling output file named `profile_output.prof`. The profiling data can be analyzed using tools like `pstats` or `snakeviz` to gain insights into performance issues.

Benchmarking, on the other hand, assesses how your application performs under load. Tools like `locust` or `k6` are commonly used for load testing. These tools simulate multiple concurrent users interacting with your application to measure its performance and identify potential scalability issues. For example, with `locust`, you can write a test script to simulate user behavior and analyze metrics such as response time and throughput:

```python
from locust import HttpUser, task, between

class WebsiteUser(HttpUser):
  wait_time between(1, 5)

   @task
  def load_main_page(self):
    self.client.get("/")
```

Running this `locust` script will simulate users accessing the root endpoint of your FastAPI application and provide a detailed report on how it handles concurrent requests.

In conclusion, optimizing performance and scalability in FastAPI involves a multifaceted approach. By focusing on efficient database queries, managing concurrency through asynchronous programming, implementing caching mechanisms, and employing profiling and benchmarking techniques, you can significantly enhance your application's responsiveness and ability to handle increased loads. These strategies, when applied thoughtfully, will ensure that your FastAPI application performs optimally in real-world scenarios and scales effectively as demands grow.

To effectively optimize the performance and scalability of a FastAPI application, profiling and benchmarking play crucial roles in identifying and addressing performance bottlenecks. Profiling involves analyzing the application to determine which parts consume the most resources or take the most time to execute. Benchmarking, on the other hand, measures the performance of your application under different conditions and loads to assess its efficiency and scalability.

Profiling can be accomplished using various tools designed to capture and analyze the application's performance metrics.

For Python applications, tools like `cProfile`, `Py-Spy`, and `tracemalloc` are commonly used. Each of these tools provides insights into different aspects of performance. For instance, `cProfile` offers detailed statistics on function call frequency and execution time, while `Py-Spy` provides a sampling profiler that can be run without modifying the codebase.

Here's how you might use `cProfile` to profile a FastAPI application:

1. Create a script to run the FastAPI application and profile it:

```python
import cProfile
from myapp import app
from fastapi import FastAPI
from uvicorn import run

 def profile_app():
  run(app, host"0.0.0.0", port8000)

 if __name__ "__main__":
  cProfile.run("profile_app()", "profile_stats")
```

2. After running the application with this script, analyze the generated `profile_stats` file using `pstats` or a visualization tool like `SnakeViz`:

```bash
python -m pstats profile_stats
```

Profiling helps to pinpoint inefficient code segments, enabling developers to optimize those areas for better performance. For example, if profiling reveals that a particular database query is consuming an excessive amount of time, you might consider optimizing that query or adding indexes to speed up its execution.

Benchmarking involves testing the application's performance under various conditions to understand its behavior and limitations. This process often involves simulating a high load to evaluate how the application handles stress. Tools such as `Locust`, `Apache JMeter`, or `k6` can be used to create load tests that measure response times, throughput, and other performance metrics.

To use `Locust` for benchmarking a FastAPI application, you would follow these steps:

1. Install Locust:

```bash
pip install locust
```

2. Create a `locustfile.py` with the following content:

```python
from locust import HttpUser, task, between

class WebsiteUser(HttpUser):
    wait_time between(1, 5)

    @task
    def load_main_page(self):
        self.client.get("/")

    @task
    def load_item(self):
        self.client.get("/items/1")
```

3. Run Locust and open the web interface to start the load test:

```bash
locust -f locustfile.py
```

By analyzing the results of the load tests, you can identify how your application performs under different levels of stress and where improvements might be necessary. For example, if response times increase significantly with higher load, it might indicate a need for scaling the application or optimizing certain components.

Additionally, adopting best practices for performance optimization is vital. For instance, ensuring that asynchronous operations are used where appropriate can significantly enhance concurrency and reduce response times. FastAPI's asynchronous capabilities allow for non-blocking operations, which are essential for handling a high number of simultaneous requests.

Optimizing data access patterns is another best practice. This involves ensuring that database operations are efficient and that data retrieval and storage are done in a manner that minimizes overhead. For instance, using bulk operations instead of individual transactions can reduce database load and improve performance.

Finally, regular monitoring of application performance is crucial for maintaining optimal performance as the application evolves. Tools like Prometheus and Grafana can be employed to monitor application metrics and visualize performance data. By integrating these tools into your application, you can continuously track performance metrics and address issues proactively.

In summary, optimizing performance and scalability in FastAPI involves a multi-faceted approach, including optimizing database queries, managing concurrency, leveraging caching mechanisms, and employing profiling and benchmarking techniques. By applying these strategies, you can ensure that your FastAPI application performs efficiently and scales effectively to meet growing demands.

CHAPTER 20: WORKING WITH WEBSOCKETS

WebSockets offer a powerful mechanism for establishing a persistent, bidirectional communication channel between clients and servers, enabling real-time data exchange. FastAPI, being a modern web framework built on top of ASGI (Asynchronous Server Gateway Interface), provides robust support for WebSocket connections. This capability is particularly valuable for building interactive applications that require live data updates, such as chat applications, live notifications, or real-time collaboration tools.

To begin working with WebSockets in FastAPI, it is essential to understand the fundamental concepts and the process for setting up WebSocket endpoints. WebSockets are designed to provide a full-duplex communication channel over a single, long-lived connection. This is different from the traditional HTTP request-response model, where each interaction is discrete and stateless. WebSockets maintain an open connection that allows data to be sent and received continuously until either the client or server decides to close it.

FastAPI makes it straightforward to create WebSocket endpoints by defining them in the same way as you would for HTTP endpoints, but with specific WebSocket-related handling. To set up a WebSocket endpoint, you use the `WebSocket` class from the `fastapi` package, which provides methods for accepting connections, receiving messages, and sending responses.

Consider the following example of a basic WebSocket endpoint in FastAPI:

```python
from fastapi import FastAPI, WebSocket

app  FastAPI()

@app.websocket("/ws")
async def websocket_endpoint(websocket: WebSocket):
  await websocket.accept()   Accept the WebSocket connection
  while True:
    data  await websocket.receive_text()   Receive text message from the client
      await websocket.send_text(f"Message text was: {data}")   Send response back to the client
```

In this example, the `websocket_endpoint` function handles incoming WebSocket connections at the `/ws` path. The `await websocket.accept()` call is necessary to accept the WebSocket connection from the client. Once the connection is established, the server enters a loop where it continuously waits for incoming messages using `await websocket.receive_text()`. Upon receiving a message, the server sends a response back to the client using `await websocket.send_text()`.

Handling real-time data updates through WebSockets involves more than just echoing messages. For applications that require broadcasting updates to multiple clients or maintaining state information, you need to manage multiple WebSocket connections and coordinate data distribution.

To handle multiple connections, you can maintain a list or

dictionary of active WebSocket connections and broadcast messages to all connected clients. Here is an example illustrating how to manage and broadcast messages to multiple clients:

```python
from fastapi import FastAPI, WebSocket
from typing import List

app FastAPI()
clients: List[WebSocket] []

@app.websocket("/ws")
async def websocket_endpoint(websocket: WebSocket):
  await websocket.accept()
    clients.append(websocket)   Add the client to the list of
connected clients
  try:
    while True:
      data await websocket.receive_text()
      for client in clients:
        if client is not websocket:
          await client.send_text(f"Message text was: {data}")
  except:
    clients.remove(websocket)  Remove the client from the list
if they disconnect
```

In this revised version, the `clients` list keeps track of all active WebSocket connections. When a message is received from one client, it is broadcasted to all other connected clients. The `try` block ensures that if a client disconnects, it is removed from the list of active connections to prevent sending messages to a non-existent connection.

Managing WebSocket connections also involves handling connection closures and errors gracefully. In the example above, the `except` block handles cases where a client disconnects unexpectedly by removing the client from the list of active connections. This is crucial for maintaining a clean and functional list of WebSocket connections and ensuring that resources are freed appropriately.

WebSockets also allow for more sophisticated interactions beyond simple message exchange. For example, you can implement a chat application where clients can send and receive different types of messages, or a live data feed where updates are pushed to clients in real-time. Implementing these features typically requires more advanced logic, such as message parsing, user authentication, and state management, but the foundational principles remain the same.

In summary, WebSockets enable real-time communication between clients and servers, and FastAPI provides a robust framework for implementing WebSocket endpoints. By understanding how to set up WebSocket connections, handle real-time data updates, and manage multiple connections, you can build interactive applications that require live data updates efficiently and effectively.

When working with WebSockets in FastAPI, managing real-time data updates requires a clear understanding of how to handle multiple concurrent connections and distribute messages to connected clients efficiently. This becomes particularly relevant when building interactive applications where the server needs to push updates to clients in real-time, such as in a live chat application, a collaborative editor, or a real-time dashboard.

A common scenario involves broadcasting messages to all connected clients. To achieve this, you'll need to maintain a list of active WebSocket connections and iterate over this list to send messages to each connection. This approach can be implemented using a global or shared state to keep track of connections. Here's an example that demonstrates how to implement a simple chat server where all messages are broadcasted to every connected client:

```python
from fastapi import FastAPI, WebSocket
from typing import List

app  FastAPI()
clients: List[WebSocket]  []

@app.websocket("/ws/chat")
async def chat(websocket: WebSocket):
  await websocket.accept()
  clients.append(websocket)
  try:
    while True:
      message  await websocket.receive_text()
      for client in clients:
        if client is not websocket:
          await client.send_text(f"New message: {message}")
  except Exception as e:
    print(f"Connection error: {e}")
  finally:
    clients.remove(websocket)
```

In this example, the `clients` list keeps track of all connected WebSocket clients. When a new client connects, it is added to this list. Upon receiving a message from one client, the server iterates through the list of connected clients and sends the message to all clients except the sender. The `try-except-finally` block ensures that the WebSocket connection is removed from the list if an error occurs or if the connection is closed.

Handling WebSocket connections efficiently also involves dealing with connection lifecycle events, such as opening, closing, and errors. It's essential to handle these events to ensure that the server maintains the correct state and cleans up resources as needed. The example provided above uses a `try-except-finally` block to handle errors and ensure that disconnected clients are properly removed from the list. However, more complex scenarios might require additional logic to manage connection state, handle reconnections, or integrate with other services.

Another crucial aspect of working with WebSockets is implementing security measures to protect the communication channel. WebSocket connections, like other network communications, can be vulnerable to various security threats, including unauthorized access and data interception. To secure WebSocket connections, consider implementing authentication and authorization mechanisms.

For example, you can use query parameters or custom headers to pass authentication tokens when initiating a WebSocket connection. On the server side, validate these tokens to ensure that only authorized users can establish a connection. Here's an example demonstrating how to validate an authentication token:

```python
from fastapi import FastAPI, WebSocket, Query, HTTPException

app FastAPI()

@app.websocket("/ws/protected")
async def protected_websocket(websocket: WebSocket, token: str Query(...)):
  if not is_valid_token(token):
    await websocket.close(code4000) Close with a specific code indicating invalid token
    return
  await websocket.accept()
  try:
    while True:
```

```
        message await websocket.receive_text()
        await websocket.send_text(f"Received: {message}")
    except Exception as e:
      print(f"Connection error: {e}")

def is_valid_token(token: str) -> bool:
    Implement your token validation logic here
    return token "valid_token"
```

In this snippet, the `protected_websocket` function requires a valid token to be provided as a query parameter. The `is_valid_token` function is a placeholder for the actual token validation logic. If the token is invalid, the server closes the WebSocket connection with a specific code indicating an authentication issue. This method ensures that only clients with valid tokens can connect to the protected WebSocket endpoint.

Managing WebSocket connections also involves understanding the resource implications. Each open WebSocket connection consumes server resources, such as memory and CPU. Therefore, it is important to implement strategies for managing a large number of connections efficiently. For instance, consider implementing connection limits, optimizing resource usage, and handling connection timeouts to ensure that your server can scale effectively and maintain performance.

In summary, working with WebSockets in FastAPI allows you to build interactive and real-time applications with efficient communication channels. By setting up WebSocket endpoints, handling real-time data updates, managing multiple connections, and implementing security measures, you can create robust applications that deliver live data updates and engage users effectively.

When it comes to managing WebSocket connections, it is

also important to consider security implications. WebSocket connections, due to their persistent nature, can be susceptible to various security risks if not properly managed. Common threats include unauthorized access, data interception, and Denial of Service (DoS) attacks. To mitigate these risks, several best practices should be adhered to.

Firstly, securing WebSocket connections involves implementing authentication and authorization mechanisms. Unlike traditional HTTP requests where authentication is handled on a per-request basis, WebSockets require a persistent authentication strategy. One effective method is to use tokens or cookies for authentication. Upon establishing a WebSocket connection, the server can validate the token or session associated with the request. For instance, consider a scenario where a WebSocket connection is initiated with an authentication token passed in the query parameters or headers:

```python
from fastapi import FastAPI, WebSocket,
WebSocketDisconnect
from fastapi.security import OAuth2PasswordBearer

app FastAPI()
oauth2_scheme OAuth2PasswordBearer(tokenUrl"token")

@app.websocket("/ws/secure")
async def secure_websocket(websocket: WebSocket, token: str
Depends(oauth2_scheme)):
  if not validate_token(token):
    await websocket.close(code4000)
    return
  await websocket.accept()
  try:
    while True:
      data await websocket.receive_text()
```

```
            await websocket.send_text(f"Secure message: {data}")
    except WebSocketDisconnect:
        print("Client disconnected")
```

In this example, the `secure_websocket` function uses the `OAuth2PasswordBearer` dependency to extract and validate the authentication token. If the token is invalid, the connection is closed with a custom code. Proper validation of tokens or credentials ensures that only authorized users can establish a WebSocket connection.

Another important aspect of securing WebSocket connections is handling encryption. WebSocket connections should be established over TLS (Transport Layer Security) to ensure that data transmitted between the client and server is encrypted. This helps protect against eavesdropping and data tampering. To enable TLS for WebSocket connections, ensure that your server is configured to use HTTPS, which will automatically apply to WebSocket connections (wss://).

Finally, rate limiting and monitoring are essential practices to prevent abuse and ensure the stability of your WebSocket server. Rate limiting involves restricting the number of messages or requests that a client can send within a certain timeframe. This helps prevent DoS attacks or excessive resource consumption. Monitoring tools can track WebSocket connections, identify unusual patterns or spikes in activity, and provide insights into performance and security metrics.

FastAPI allows integration with various monitoring and logging tools. For example, you might use a combination of Prometheus for metrics collection and Grafana for visualization. Logging middleware can be employed to capture connection events, message exchanges, and errors, providing valuable data for analyzing and improving the performance and security of your WebSocket server.

In conclusion, WebSocket support in FastAPI provides a robust foundation for building real-time, interactive applications. By setting up WebSocket endpoints, managing real-time data updates, and handling connection lifecycle events effectively, you can create dynamic and responsive applications. Ensuring security through authentication, encryption, and rate limiting, combined with monitoring and logging, will help maintain a secure and performant WebSocket environment. As you continue to develop applications that leverage WebSockets, applying these principles will enable you to build scalable and reliable real-time communication solutions.

CHAPTER 21: INTEGRATING WITH EXTERNAL APIS

In the development of modern applications, integrating with external APIs is a common requirement. FastAPI, with its robust features and efficient design, provides a seamless way to interact with third-party APIs. This section will cover how to integrate FastAPI with external APIs, handle external API requests and responses, and manage API rate limits. By understanding these concepts, you will be able to build robust and reliable integrations for your applications.

To start, integrating FastAPI with external APIs involves making HTTP requests to interact with services provided by other applications. FastAPI does not include built-in functionality for making HTTP requests, but it integrates well with popular libraries such as `httpx` and `requests`. Both of these libraries are designed to handle HTTP requests and responses efficiently. `httpx` is particularly notable for its asynchronous capabilities, which align well with FastAPI's asynchronous nature, allowing for non-blocking I/O operations.

Here's an example of how to use `httpx` to interact with an external API from a FastAPI endpoint. Suppose we want to fetch weather data from a weather API:

```python
```

```
import httpx
from fastapi import FastAPI

app FastAPI()

async def fetch_weather(city: str):
  async with httpx.AsyncClient() as client:
      response await client.get(f"https://api.weatherapi.com/
v1/current.json?keyYOUR_API_KEY&q{city}")
    response.raise_for_status()
    return response.json()

@app.get("/weather/{city}")
async def get_weather(city: str):
  weather_data await fetch_weather(city)
  return weather_data
```

In this example, the `fetch_weather` function uses `httpx.AsyncClient` to perform an asynchronous HTTP GET request to the weather API. The `await` keyword ensures that the request is non-blocking, and the `response.raise_for_status()` method raises an exception if the HTTP request returned an error status code. The `get_weather` endpoint calls `fetch_weather` and returns the weather data to the client.

Handling API responses effectively is crucial for integrating with external services. It is essential to process the responses received from external APIs to ensure they meet your application's needs. For example, handling errors gracefully and ensuring that the response data is in the expected format can prevent potential issues. In the example above, we handle potential errors using `raise_for_status()` which will raise an exception if the API returns an error response. This approach allows you to manage errors by using exception handling mechanisms such as try-except blocks.

Furthermore, managing API rate limits is an important consideration when integrating with external APIs. Many external APIs impose rate limits to prevent abuse and ensure fair usage. Rate limits define the maximum number of API requests that can be made within a specific timeframe, such as per minute or per hour. Exceeding these limits can result in throttling, which may lead to temporary blocks or delays in accessing the API.

To handle rate limits effectively, you should be aware of the rate limits imposed by the API you are integrating with and implement appropriate measures to comply with these limits. This can include implementing retry logic with exponential backoff, using rate limit headers provided by the API to manage request pacing, and caching responses to reduce the number of API calls.

Here's an example of how to implement basic retry logic with exponential backoff using `httpx`:

```python
import httpx
import asyncio
from fastapi import FastAPI

app  FastAPI()

async def fetch_data_with_retries(url: str, retries: int  3):
    for attempt in range(retries):
        try:
            async with httpx.AsyncClient() as client:
                response  await client.get(url)
                response.raise_for_status()
                return response.json()
        except httpx.RequestError as e:
            if attempt < retries - 1:
                wait_time  2  attempt  Exponential backoff
```

```
            await asyncio.sleep(wait_time)
        else:
            raise e

@app.get("/data")
async def get_data():
    url "https://api.example.com/data"
    data await fetch_data_with_retries(url)
    return data
```

In this example, the `fetch_data_with_retries` function attempts to fetch data from the API up to a specified number of retries. If an error occurs, the function waits for an exponentially increasing amount of time before retrying. This strategy helps to handle temporary issues such as network failures or rate limit errors more gracefully.

By integrating these techniques, you can build applications that not only interact with external APIs effectively but also handle errors and rate limits in a robust manner. FastAPI's capabilities combined with these practices will enable you to develop applications that are reliable, responsive, and well-integrated with third-party services.

Handling API responses effectively involves several key practices to ensure data integrity and robustness in your integration. When working with external APIs, it is essential to anticipate and manage various response scenarios, including successful responses, client-side and server-side errors, and unexpected data formats.

To handle successful responses, you should first validate the data you receive from the external API. This can involve checking that the response contains the necessary fields and that the data types are as expected. For instance, if you are expecting a JSON object with specific keys, you should verify that these keys exist and are of the correct type before processing the data.

Consider the following example where we fetch user data from an external API and validate the response:

```python
import httpx
from fastapi import FastAPI, HTTPException

app  FastAPI()

async def fetch_user(user_id: str):
  async with httpx.AsyncClient() as client:
        response   await client.get(f"https://api.example.com/
users/{user_id}")
    response.raise_for_status()
    user_data  response.json()


       Validate response data
    if 'id' not in user_data or 'name' not in user_data:
          raise HTTPException(status_code500, detail"Invalid
response format")


      return user_data

@app.get("/user/{user_id}")
async def get_user(user_id: str):
  try:
    user_data  await fetch_user(user_id)
    return user_data
  except httpx.HTTPStatusError as e:
      raise HTTPException(status_codee.response.status_code,
detail"Error fetching user data")
```

In this example, after fetching the user data, we check if the required keys (`'id'` and `'name'`) are present in the response.

If any key is missing, we raise an `HTTPException` to indicate an internal error. Additionally, if the `httpx` request itself fails due to an HTTP status error, we catch this exception and return a relevant error message to the client.

Dealing with client-side and server-side errors from external APIs also requires thoughtful handling. External APIs may return various HTTP status codes to indicate different types of errors. For example, a 400 Bad Request status might indicate that the request was malformed, while a 500 Internal Server Error suggests an issue on the server side. Properly interpreting these status codes and providing meaningful error messages to the client helps improve the robustness and user experience of your application.

To manage API rate limits effectively, you need to be aware of the rate limiting policies of the external APIs you are integrating with. Many APIs impose limits on the number of requests you can make within a specific time frame to prevent abuse and ensure fair usage. Exceeding these limits often results in the API returning a 429 Too Many Requests status code.

To handle rate limiting, you can implement a strategy to manage request quotas and retry logic. This might involve tracking the number of requests made and implementing exponential backoff or other retry mechanisms. Here's an example of handling rate limiting with `httpx`:

```python
import httpx
import time
from fastapi import FastAPI, HTTPException

app FastAPI()

async def fetch_data_with_retries(url: str, retries: int 3):
  async with httpx.AsyncClient() as client:
```

```
    for attempt in range(retries):
      try:
        response  await client.get(url)
        if response.status_code  429:
          retry_after  int(response.headers.get('Retry-After', 1))
          time.sleep(retry_after)
          continue


            response.raise_for_status()
        return response.json()
      except httpx.HTTPStatusError as e:
        if e.response.status_code in {400, 404, 500}:
                                                    raise
HTTPException(status_codee.response.status_code,
detail"API request failed")
      except httpx.RequestError as e:
          raise HTTPException(status_code500, detail"Request
error occurred")
      break
          raise  HTTPException(status_code503,  detail"Service
unavailable after retries")

@app.get("/data")
async def get_data():
  url  "https://api.example.com/data"
  data  await fetch_data_with_retries(url)
  return data
```

In this example, the `fetch_data_with_retries` function attempts to fetch data from the API with a specified number of retries. If a 429 status code is returned, the function pauses execution based on the `Retry-After` header and retries the request. If after all retries the request still fails, it raises a `HTTPException` to indicate that the service is unavailable.

By understanding and implementing these strategies, you can build integrations with external APIs that are both robust and reliable, ensuring that your application can handle various scenarios gracefully and efficiently.

When integrating with external APIs, managing API rate limits is a crucial aspect of building reliable and resilient applications. Rate limits are imposed by external APIs to control the amount of traffic and prevent abuse. Violating these limits can result in temporary or permanent bans, which can disrupt your application's functionality. To handle rate limits effectively, you must implement strategies to monitor and adhere to these limits.

Firstly, you should familiarize yourself with the rate limiting policies of the external API you are working with. Most APIs provide details about their rate limits in their documentation, including the maximum number of requests allowed per minute, hour, or day. This information is often communicated via HTTP headers in the API responses. Common headers include `X-RateLimit-Limit`, `X-RateLimit-Remaining`, and `X-RateLimit-Reset`.

Here's how you might extract and use these headers in FastAPI when making requests to an external API:

```python
import httpx
from fastapi import FastAPI, HTTPException

app FastAPI()

async def fetch_data_with_rate_limit_handling(url: str):
  async with httpx.AsyncClient() as client:
    response await client.get(url)
    rate_limit response.headers.get('X-RateLimit-Limit')
     rate_limit_remaining response.headers.get('X-RateLimit-
Remaining')
```

```
    rate_limit_reset response.headers.get('X-RateLimit-Reset')

      if response.status_code 429:  Too Many Requests
      reset_time int(rate_limit_reset)
       raise HTTPException(status_code429, detailf"Rate limit exceeded. Try again after {reset_time} seconds.")

      response.raise_for_status()
    return response.json()

@app.get("/data")
async def get_data():
  try:
    data await fetch_data_with_rate_limit_handling("https://api.example.com/data")
    return data
  except httpx.HTTPStatusError as e:
     raise HTTPException(status_codee.response.status_code, detail"Error fetching data")
```

In this example, the `fetch_data_with_rate_limit_handling` function makes a request to an external API and checks for rate limit headers in the response. If the rate limit is exceeded (indicated by a 429 status code), the function raises an HTTPException, advising the client to wait before making further requests. By extracting rate limit information from the headers, you can implement client-side logic to avoid hitting the limit too frequently.

Implementing caching strategies can also help mitigate the impact of rate limits and enhance performance. By caching responses from external APIs, you can reduce the number of requests made to the API and improve response times for your users. FastAPI does not have built-in caching mechanisms, but you can use external libraries like `cachetools` or integrate with caching services such as Redis.

Here's a basic example of how you might implement caching using the `cachetools` library:

```python
import httpx
from fastapi import FastAPI, HTTPException
from cachetools import TTLCache

app FastAPI()
cache TTLCache(maxsize100, ttl300) Cache with a TTL of 5 minutes

async def fetch_data_with_caching(url: str):
  if url in cache:
    return cache[url]


   async with httpx.AsyncClient() as client:
    response await client.get(url)
    response.raise_for_status()
    data response.json()
    cache[url] data
    return data

@app.get("/cached-data")
async def get_cached_data():
  try:
        data await fetch_data_with_caching("https://api.example.com/data")
    return data
  except httpx.HTTPStatusError as e:
     raise HTTPException(status_codee.response.status_code, detail"Error fetching data")
```

In this example, the `fetch_data_with_caching` function uses a `TTLCache` to store responses from the external API. If a request is made for a URL that is already in the cache, the cached response is returned immediately, thus avoiding a new request to the external API.

To summarize, integrating FastAPI with external APIs involves handling HTTP requests and responses, managing rate limits, and implementing caching strategies. By using `httpx` or similar libraries for making HTTP requests, you can interact with external APIs asynchronously and efficiently. Proper handling of API responses, including validation and error management, ensures that your application remains robust. Implementing rate limiting and caching mechanisms further enhances performance and reliability, providing a solid foundation for building scalable and interactive applications.

CHAPTER 22: IMPLEMENTING RATE LIMITING

In modern API development, protecting your service from abuse and ensuring fair usage is paramount. Implementing rate limiting is a fundamental technique to manage the number of requests clients can make within a given timeframe, thereby preventing overload and ensuring equitable access. This section delves into the principles of rate limiting, explores various techniques such as token bucket algorithms and fixed window counters, and provides practical examples of how to configure rate limiting in FastAPI.

Rate limiting involves setting rules that control the rate at which clients can make requests to an API. By enforcing these rules, you can prevent any single client from consuming disproportionate amounts of resources, thereby safeguarding the API's performance and availability. FastAPI, being a highly performant and flexible framework, supports various rate limiting strategies that can be tailored to your application's needs.

One of the foundational algorithms used for rate limiting is the token bucket algorithm. This algorithm allows clients a certain number of tokens that are refilled at a fixed rate. Each request consumes a token, and if tokens are unavailable, the request is either delayed or rejected. The token bucket algorithm is advantageous because it provides a smooth and flexible way to handle bursts of requests while maintaining a steady rate over time.

To implement token bucket rate limiting in FastAPI, you might use a middleware approach combined with a caching or storage solution to track tokens. Here is a simplified example using an in-memory approach:

```python
from fastapi import FastAPI, Request, HTTPException
from starlette.middleware.base import BaseHTTPMiddleware
import time

app FastAPI()
bucket_capacity 10 Maximum tokens
token_rate 1 Tokens added per second
buckets {} Dictionary to store token buckets for each client

class RateLimitMiddleware(BaseHTTPMiddleware):
  async def dispatch(self, request: Request, call_next):
    client_ip request.client.host
    current_time time.time()
    bucket buckets.setdefault(client_ip, {"tokens": bucket_capacity, "last_checked": current_time})

    Refill tokens
    elapsed_time current_time - bucket["last_checked"]
    bucket["tokens"] min(bucket_capacity, bucket["tokens"] + elapsed_time token_rate)
    bucket["last_checked"] current_time

    if bucket["tokens"] > 1:
      bucket["tokens"] - 1
      response await call_next(request)
    else:
      response HTTPException(status_code429, detail"Rate limit exceeded")
```

```
        return response

app.add_middleware(RateLimitMiddleware)
```

In this example, a middleware class `RateLimitMiddleware` manages the rate limiting. It keeps track of tokens for each client based on their IP address. Tokens are refilled at a rate defined by `token_rate`, and the bucket's capacity is set by `bucket_capacity`. If a client exceeds their token quota, the middleware responds with a 429 status code indicating that the rate limit has been exceeded.

Another popular rate limiting strategy is the fixed window counter. This approach divides time into fixed-size windows (e.g., one minute) and counts the number of requests within each window. If a client exceeds the allowed number of requests within a window, additional requests are denied until the next window. Fixed window counters are simpler to implement but may suffer from the "boundary effect," where clients may get an unfair advantage by making requests right before the window resets.

To illustrate a fixed window counter, consider the following implementation:

```python
from fastapi import FastAPI, Request, HTTPException
from starlette.middleware.base import BaseHTTPMiddleware
import time

app FastAPI()
window_size 60  Window size in seconds
request_limit 100  Maximum number of requests per window
requests {}  Dictionary to store request counts and timestamps
```

```
class RateLimitMiddleware(BaseHTTPMiddleware):
  async def dispatch(self, request: Request, call_next):
    client_ip request.client.host
    current_time time.time()
    if client_ip not in requests:
          requests[client_ip] {"count": 0, "window_start":
current_time}

      window_start requests[client_ip]["window_start"]
    if current_time - window_start > window_size:
          requests[client_ip] {"count": 1, "window_start":
current_time}
    else:
      if requests[client_ip]["count"] > request_limit:
        response HTTPException(status_code429, detail"Rate
limit exceeded")
      else:
        requests[client_ip]["count"] + 1
        response await call_next(request)


      return response

app.add_middleware(RateLimitMiddleware)
```

In this implementation, `RateLimitMiddleware` manages request counts for each client IP within a fixed window. If the number of requests exceeds the allowed limit within the window, further requests are denied. The window is reset after the `window_size` duration.

Both the token bucket algorithm and fixed window counters have their advantages and trade-offs. Token bucket algorithms offer more flexibility in handling bursts of traffic, while fixed window counters provide a simpler implementation. Choosing the appropriate method depends on the specific requirements of your application and the nature of the traffic it handles.

To continue with the token bucket algorithm example, let's delve deeper into its implementation. After checking and refilling the tokens, the next step is to determine whether a request can be processed. If the bucket contains sufficient tokens, the request is allowed; otherwise, it should be rejected or rate-limited.

Here's how the implementation continues:

```python
    if bucket["tokens"] > 1:
      bucket["tokens"] - 1
      response  await call_next(request)
    else:
        raise HTTPException(status_code429, detail"Rate limit
exceeded")


        return response

app.add_middleware(RateLimitMiddleware)
```

In this implementation, if there are enough tokens (greater than or equal to 1), the request is processed and the tokens are decremented. If not, an HTTP 429 Too Many Requests error is raised, signaling that the rate limit has been exceeded. This approach ensures that clients are given a fair number of requests while allowing for occasional bursts of activity.

Another common rate limiting strategy is the fixed window counter algorithm. This method divides time into fixed intervals or windows, counting the number of requests within each window. When a client exceeds the allowed number of requests within a single window, further requests are blocked until the window resets.

To implement the fixed window counter in FastAPI, you can use a similar middleware approach. This strategy is simpler than the token bucket algorithm but does not handle burstiness as effectively. Here's an example:

```python
from fastapi import FastAPI, Request, HTTPException
from starlette.middleware.base import BaseHTTPMiddleware
from datetime import datetime, timedelta

app FastAPI()
window_size timedelta(minutes1) Window size
max_requests 100 Max requests per window
request_counts {} Dictionary to store request counts for each
client

class
FixedWindowRateLimitMiddleware(BaseHTTPMiddleware):
  async def dispatch(self, request: Request, call_next):
    client_ip request.client.host
    current_time datetime.now()
    window_start current_time - window_size

      if client_ip not in request_counts:
        request_counts[client_ip] {"count": 0, "window_start":
current_time}


      client_data request_counts[client_ip]

      if current_time - client_data["window_start"] >
window_size:
      Reset window
      client_data["count"] 0
      client_data["window_start"] current_time

      if client_data["count"] > max_requests:
        raise HTTPException(status_code429, detail"Rate limit
```

```
exceeded")
        client_data["count"] + 1
    response await call_next(request)
    return response

app.add_middleware(FixedWindowRateLimitMiddleware)
```

In this example, `window_size` defines the length of the time window, and `max_requests` specifies the maximum number of requests allowed per window. The `request_counts` dictionary keeps track of the number of requests and the start time of the current window for each client IP. When a request is made, the middleware checks if the current window has expired. If it has, the request count is reset. If the request count exceeds the maximum allowed within the window, an HTTP 429 error is returned. Otherwise, the request count is incremented, and the request is processed.

Both rate limiting techniques, the token bucket algorithm and the fixed window counter, serve different purposes and come with their trade-offs. The token bucket algorithm allows for smoother handling of bursts but requires more complex implementation and state management. The fixed window counter is simpler but can lead to more abrupt rate limiting at the boundaries of each time window.

Beyond these basic strategies, you may also consider advanced techniques such as sliding window logs or dynamic rate limiting, which adjust limits based on the current load or other criteria. Implementing rate limiting effectively ensures that your API remains responsive and fair, even under high load or when facing potential abuse.

It's essential to test and monitor your rate limiting implementation thoroughly. Evaluate how it performs under various load conditions and adjust parameters like window size and token rates based on your application's requirements and traffic patterns. Moreover, consider using external tools and services for more sophisticated rate limiting and monitoring if needed, especially for high-traffic APIs.

If the elapsed time since the start of the window exceeds the `window_size`, we need to reset the request count and window start time. This is crucial because the fixed window counter must accurately track the number of requests made within the current time window to enforce rate limits correctly.

Here's the continuation of the implementation:

```python
            if current_time - client_data["window_start"] >
window_size:
        client_data["count"] 0
        client_data["window_start"] current_time


        if client_data["count"] < max_requests:
        client_data["count"] + 1
        response await call_next(request)
    else:
          raise HTTPException(status_code429, detail"Rate limit
exceeded")

        return response

app.add_middleware(FixedWindowRateLimitMiddleware)
```

In this code snippet, if the current time exceeds the window size from the window start, the count is reset to zero, and the window start time is updated to the current time. If the request count is below the maximum allowed requests, the request is processed and the count is incremented. If the limit is exceeded, an HTTP 429 Too Many Requests error is raised.

This method ensures that requests are restricted within each fixed time window.

While both the token bucket and fixed window counter algorithms are effective for rate limiting, each has its trade-offs. The token bucket algorithm is generally better for handling bursts of traffic, as it allows a certain degree of flexibility in the rate of requests. In contrast, the fixed window counter can be simpler to implement but may result in more rigid rate limiting, potentially causing issues if traffic spikes occur at the boundaries of the fixed time windows.

For more sophisticated rate limiting requirements, such as those involving distributed systems or high traffic volumes, it may be necessary to use a distributed rate limiting solution. Distributed rate limiting involves sharing the rate limit data across multiple instances of your application, ensuring that the rate limit is enforced consistently regardless of which instance handles the request.

Redis is a popular choice for implementing distributed rate limiting due to its support for fast in-memory operations and atomic operations. By using Redis, you can maintain a global count of requests and manage rate limiting across all instances of your application. Below is a basic example of how to integrate Redis with FastAPI to handle distributed rate limiting:

```python
import redis
from fastapi import FastAPI, Request, HTTPException
from starlette.middleware.base import BaseHTTPMiddleware
from datetime import datetime, timedelta

app FastAPI()
redis_client redis.StrictRedis(host'localhost', port6379, db0)
window_size timedelta(minutes1)
max_requests 100
```

```
class
DistributedRateLimitMiddleware(BaseHTTPMiddleware):
  async def dispatch(self, request: Request, call_next):
    client_ip request.client.host
    current_time datetime.now()
    window_start current_time - window_size
                redis_key        f"rate_limit:{client_ip}:
{window_start.strftime('%Y%m%d%H%M')}"


      request_count redis_client.get(redis_key)
    if request_count is None:
                        redis_client.set(redis_key,    1,
exint(window_size.total_seconds()))
      response await call_next(request)
    elif int(request_count) < max_requests:
      redis_client.incr(redis_key)
      response await call_next(request)
    else:
        raise HTTPException(status_code429, detail"Rate limit
exceeded")


      return response

app.add_middleware(DistributedRateLimitMiddleware)
```

In this example, Redis is used to store and manage the request counts for each client IP address. Each key in Redis represents the request count for a specific client and time window. The key is set with an expiration time equal to the window size, ensuring that old data is automatically cleaned up. If the request count is below the maximum allowed, it is incremented, and the request is processed. If the limit is exceeded, an HTTP 429 error is returned.

By integrating Redis, you can achieve a scalable rate limiting solution that can handle high traffic volumes and ensure consistent enforcement of rate limits across distributed application instances.

Implementing rate limiting effectively requires selecting the appropriate strategy based on your application's needs and traffic patterns. By understanding and applying techniques such as the token bucket algorithm, fixed window counters, and distributed rate limiting with Redis, you can ensure that your API remains performant, fair, and resistant to abuse.

CHAPTER 23: MANAGING APPLICATION CONFIGURATION

Effective configuration management is a cornerstone of building robust and maintainable applications. As your application transitions through various environments—such as development, testing, and production—proper management of configuration settings becomes increasingly important. In FastAPI, configuration management involves using environment variables, configuration files, and dynamic configuration loading to handle settings appropriately for each environment. This section will delve into these methods, providing a comprehensive understanding of how to manage application settings effectively.

Environment variables are a fundamental aspect of configuration management. They offer a way to separate configuration from code, allowing you to adjust settings without modifying your application's source code. This separation is particularly beneficial when deploying applications to different environments where settings might vary. For example, you might use environment variables to store database credentials, API keys, or feature flags.

To access environment variables in FastAPI, Python's built-in `os` module can be used. Here is an example of how to read an environment variable:

```python
import os

DATABASE_URL os.getenv('DATABASE_URL', 'sqlite:///./test.db')
```

In this snippet, the `os.getenv` function retrieves the value of the `DATABASE_URL` environment variable. If the variable is not set, it defaults to `'sqlite:///./test.db'`. This approach ensures that your application can run with default settings if the environment variable is not specified.

For more structured configuration management, configuration files can be used. These files, often in formats such as JSON, YAML, or TOML, provide a centralized location for settings that can be easily edited and version-controlled. FastAPI does not include built-in support for configuration files, but Python's `configparser`, `json`, and `pyyaml` libraries can be employed to handle various formats.

Here's an example of using a JSON configuration file:

```json
{
    "database_url": "postgresql://user:password@localhost/dbname",
  "debug": true
}
```

To load and use this configuration in FastAPI, you could do the following:

```python
import json
```

```
with open('config.json', 'r') as config_file:
  config json.load(config_file)

DATABASE_URL config.get('database_url', 'sqlite:///./test.db')
DEBUG config.get('debug', False)
```

In this example, the `json` module is used to read the JSON configuration file, which is then parsed to extract the configuration values. This method allows you to maintain environment-specific settings in a separate file, simplifying the process of adjusting configurations as needed.

Dynamic configuration loading provides an additional layer of flexibility, particularly useful in applications that require real-time configuration changes. FastAPI itself does not directly support dynamic configuration, but integrating external libraries or services can enable this functionality. For instance, you might use a configuration service like Consul or etcd, which provides APIs to fetch and update configuration data dynamically.

To integrate a configuration service with FastAPI, you would typically write a client that interacts with the service, fetching the latest configuration data as needed. Here's a basic example using a hypothetical configuration service:

```python
import requests

def get_config():
   response requests.get('https://config-service.example.com/
api/config')
  response.raise_for_status()
  return response.json()

config get_config()
DATABASE_URL config.get('database_url', 'sqlite:///./test.db')
```

```
DEBUG config.get('debug', False)
```

In this code, the `requests` library is used to fetch the latest configuration from a remote service. This allows your application to stay updated with the most recent settings without needing to restart or redeploy.

In addition to these methods, it is essential to handle configuration secrets securely. For sensitive information such as API keys or database credentials, consider using secret management solutions like AWS Secrets Manager, Azure Key Vault, or HashiCorp Vault. These tools provide secure storage and access controls for sensitive data, ensuring that your application remains secure while managing configurations.

In conclusion, managing application configuration effectively in FastAPI involves using a combination of environment variables, configuration files, and dynamic configuration loading. By understanding and applying these techniques, you can ensure that your application is well-configured for various environments and can adapt to changing requirements. This approach not only enhances the maintainability and security of your application but also simplifies the process of deploying and managing applications across different stages of their lifecycle.

When managing application settings in FastAPI, dynamic configuration loading can offer an additional layer of flexibility and adaptability. Dynamic configuration loading allows an application to adjust its behavior at runtime based on changes to configuration sources without requiring a restart. This can be particularly useful in production environments where uptime and responsiveness are critical.

One approach to implementing dynamic configuration is to use a configuration management library that supports reloading. For instance, libraries like `pydantic` provide a robust mechanism for defining and managing configuration settings. Using `pydantic`, you can create a configuration class with fields that are automatically validated and loaded from environment variables or configuration files.

Here is a basic example of using `pydantic` to manage configuration:

```python
from pydantic import BaseSettings

class Settings(BaseSettings):
  database_url: str
  debug: bool

    class Config:
     env_file ".env"
     env_file_encoding "utf-8"

settings Settings()
```

In this example, the `Settings` class inherits from `BaseSettings`, which allows it to load configuration values from environment variables. The `Config` class nested within specifies that the configuration should also be read from a `.env` file. The `Settings` class automatically validates the values and provides default values if necessary. This setup makes it straightforward to manage configuration in a way that is both structured and dynamic.

For applications where configurations need to be updated without restarting the application, you may integrate more advanced solutions such as using a configuration management service or implementing a custom configuration watcher. Services like Consul or etcd provide centralized configuration management and allow applications to fetch updated settings from a remote source.

Implementing a custom configuration watcher involves setting up a mechanism that periodically checks for changes in configuration files or other sources and updates the application's configuration in response to these changes. This can be done using file watchers or scheduled tasks that read the updated configuration and apply changes accordingly.

Here's a simplified example of how you might set up a basic file watcher to reload configuration dynamically:

```python
import time
import threading
from pathlib import Path

class ConfigWatcher(threading.Thread):
  def __init__(self, config_file_path, reload_callback):
    super().__init__()
    self.config_file_path  Path(config_file_path)
    self.reload_callback  reload_callback
                                             self.last_modified_time
self.config_file_path.stat().st_mtime
    self.running  True

   def run(self):
    while self.running:
                                             current_modified_time
self.config_file_path.stat().st_mtime
      if current_modified_time ! self.last_modified_time:
        self.last_modified_time  current_modified_time
        self.reload_callback()
      time.sleep(5)  Check for changes every 5 seconds

   def stop(self):
    self.running  False
```

In this implementation, `ConfigWatcher` is a thread that

monitors a specified configuration file for changes. When a modification is detected, it triggers the `reload_callback` function to apply the new configuration. This approach ensures that the application adapts to configuration changes without requiring a restart, improving its responsiveness to dynamic environments.

Integrating these approaches into a FastAPI application involves setting up the appropriate configuration mechanisms during application startup and ensuring that the configuration is accessed consistently throughout the application. For instance, you might initialize your settings and start the configuration watcher in the application's startup event:

```python
from fastapi import FastAPI

app FastAPI()

@app.on_event("startup")
async def startup_event():
  global settings
  settings Settings()
  config_watcher ConfigWatcher(".env", reload_config)
  config_watcher.start()

def reload_config():
  global settings
  settings Settings()
```

By using this setup, the application initializes its configuration at startup and sets up a watcher to reload settings dynamically. The `reload_config` function is called whenever the configuration file is updated, ensuring that changes are applied without disrupting the application's operation.

In conclusion, managing application configuration in

FastAPI requires careful consideration of various strategies to accommodate different environments and requirements. Using environment variables provides a straightforward method for configuration management, while configuration files offer a more structured approach. Dynamic configuration loading and custom watchers further enhance flexibility, allowing applications to adapt to changes without downtime. By leveraging these techniques, you can build robust and adaptable applications that effectively handle environment-specific settings.

Continuing with the topic of managing application configuration, it's also important to consider how to handle and manage configurations specific to different environments —development, testing, and production. This approach ensures that your application behaves correctly and securely in each environment, addressing potential issues related to configuration drift or accidental exposure of sensitive data.

When dealing with different environments, it is common to use a combination of environment-specific configuration files and environment variables. For example, you might maintain separate configuration files for development and production environments, with each file containing settings tailored to the specific needs of that environment. This strategy helps to avoid the pitfalls of hardcoding configuration values, which can lead to errors and security vulnerabilities.

You can achieve this separation by organizing your configuration files in a structured directory layout. For instance, you could have a directory structure like this:

```
config/
├── development.json
├── production.json
└── testing.json
```

In your application, you can dynamically load the appropriate configuration file based on the current environment. This can be managed using environment variables to specify which configuration file to load. Here is an example of how to load a configuration file based on an environment variable:

```python
import json
import os

environment os.getenv('APP_ENV', 'development')
config_file f'config/{environment}.json'

with open(config_file, 'r') as f:
  config json.load(f)

DATABASE_URL config.get('database_url', 'sqlite:///./test.db')
DEBUG config.get('debug', False)
```

In this setup, the `APP_ENV` environment variable determines which configuration file is loaded. If `APP_ENV` is set to `'production'`, the application will load `production.json`. This approach makes it straightforward to manage different configurations for various environments.

When working with configuration files and environment variables, it's essential to handle sensitive information, such as API keys and database credentials, securely. This typically involves using environment variables for sensitive data instead of storing them in configuration files. Sensitive data should be kept out of source control and only be accessible in a controlled manner. Tools such as `dotenv` can help manage environment variables in a local development environment by loading them from a `.env` file, which should also be excluded from version control.

```python
```

```
from dotenv import load_dotenv
import os

load_dotenv()

DATABASE_URL os.getenv('DATABASE_URL')
SECRET_KEY os.getenv('SECRET_KEY')
```

In addition to managing configuration files and environment variables, consider implementing a robust approach for handling configuration updates. This could involve versioning your configuration files or using a centralized configuration management service that supports versioning and auditing. Services like HashiCorp Consul, AWS Systems Manager Parameter Store, or Azure App Configuration offer centralized management of configuration settings and provide features such as version control, secure storage, and dynamic reloading.

For applications requiring sophisticated configuration management, integrating with such services can enhance the maintainability and security of your application. These services often provide client libraries or APIs that your application can use to fetch and update configuration settings as needed.

Lastly, it's vital to implement comprehensive testing strategies to ensure that your configuration management approach works as expected. This includes testing configuration loading in different environments and validating that configuration changes do not introduce regressions or unexpected behavior. Automated tests can help ensure that your configuration setup is reliable and robust, covering scenarios such as missing configuration files, incorrect values, and environment-specific issues.

By thoughtfully managing application configuration through

environment variables, configuration files, dynamic loading, and centralized services, you can build applications that are adaptable, secure, and maintainable across different environments. This comprehensive approach to configuration management not only enhances the functionality of your application but also contributes to its overall reliability and ease of maintenance.

CHAPTER 24: BUILDING AND USING CUSTOM VALIDATORS

In FastAPI, while the built-in validation mechanisms provided by Pydantic cover a broad range of standard use cases, there are situations where more complex validation rules are required. Custom validators are essential for enforcing these non-standard validation requirements. In this section, I will guide you through the process of creating and using custom validators in FastAPI, demonstrating how to handle specific and advanced validation needs by integrating them into your request and response models.

To begin, it is important to understand the foundation of validation in FastAPI. FastAPI utilizes Pydantic for data validation and parsing. Pydantic allows you to define data models with field constraints and types, automatically validating incoming data against these constraints. However, for cases where the built-in validators do not suffice, custom validators offer a flexible solution.

Custom validators in Pydantic can be implemented in two primary ways: through the use of validator functions and custom types. Validator functions provide a straightforward method for adding custom logic to field validation, while custom types enable the creation of entirely new data types with built-in validation rules.

Validator Functions

To create a custom validator function in Pydantic, you can use the `@validator` decorator. This decorator allows you to define methods within your Pydantic model that will be used to perform additional validation. These methods can be applied to single fields or to the entire model.

Consider a scenario where you need to validate that a user's email address is in a specific domain. The standard email validation provided by Pydantic ensures that the email is properly formatted, but it does not check the domain. Here's how you might implement a custom validator to enforce this rule:

```python
from pydantic import BaseModel, EmailStr, validator

class User(BaseModel):
    email: EmailStr
    username: str

    @validator('email')
    def email_domain(cls, value):
        if not value.endswith('@example.com'):
            raise ValueError('Email domain must be @example.com')
        return value
```

In this example, the `email_domain` method checks whether the email address ends with '@example.com'. If not, it raises a `ValueError`, which Pydantic will handle by rejecting the input data.

The `@validator` decorator can also be applied to the entire model to perform cross-field validation. For instance, if you want to ensure that a password and its confirmation match, you can add a custom validator like this:

```python
from pydantic import BaseModel, validator

class UserRegistration(BaseModel):
  password: str
  confirm_password: str

   @validator('confirm_password')
  def passwords_match(cls, value, values):
    if 'password' in values and values['password'] ! value:
      raise ValueError('Passwords do not match')
    return value
```

In this case, the `passwords_match` method compares the `confirm_password` field against the `password` field, ensuring they are identical.

Custom Types

For more complex validation scenarios, you might define a custom type that includes built-in validation rules. This approach is useful when you need a reusable data type across multiple models. You can create a custom type by subclassing Pydantic's `BaseModel` and implementing the desired validation logic.

Here is an example of defining a custom type for validating phone numbers with a specific format:

```python
import re
from pydantic import BaseModel, constr

class PhoneNumber(constr):
  @classmethod
  def __get_validators__(cls):
```

```
    yield cls.validate

   @classmethod
  def validate(cls, value):
    pattern re.compile(r'^\+\d{1,3}\s\d{1,15}$')
    if not pattern.match(value):
      raise ValueError('Invalid phone number format')
    return value
```

In this example, `PhoneNumber` is a custom type that enforces a specific phone number format using a regular expression. The `__get_validators__` method returns the validation method, which will be used whenever the `PhoneNumber` type is instantiated.

You can then use this custom type within your Pydantic models:

```python
class Contact(BaseModel):
  name: str
  phone: PhoneNumber
```

This approach ensures that any `phone` value assigned to the `Contact` model will be validated against the specified format.

Integrating Custom Validators

To integrate custom validators into your FastAPI application, you simply define your models with the appropriate validators and use them in your endpoints. FastAPI will automatically apply the validators when processing incoming requests and generating responses.

For example, if you have an endpoint that accepts user registration data, you can use the `UserRegistration` model with custom validators:

```python
from fastapi import FastAPI, HTTPException

app FastAPI()

@app.post('/register')
def register(user: UserRegistration):
    Handle registration logic
   return {"message": "User registered successfully"}
```

In this endpoint, FastAPI will validate the `UserRegistration` data using the custom validators defined in the model. If the data fails validation, FastAPI will return a `422 Unprocessable Entity` response with detailed error messages.

By leveraging custom validators, you can address complex validation requirements and ensure that your FastAPI application handles data accurately and securely. This approach provides a powerful tool for enforcing specific rules and constraints, enhancing the reliability and robustness of your application.

In addition to the basic field-level validation, Pydantic also provides the ability to perform validation across multiple fields using the `@root_validator` decorator. This is particularly useful when the validation rules depend on the relationships between different fields in your model. The `@root_validator` is applied to a method that operates on the entire model instance, allowing you to enforce constraints that span multiple attributes.

For instance, consider a scenario where you need to validate that the `start_date` is always before the `end_date` in an event model. A `@root_validator` can be used to check this condition across the relevant fields:

```python
from pydantic import BaseModel, root_validator
from datetime import datetime

class Event(BaseModel):
    start_date: datetime
    end_date: datetime

     @root_validator(preTrue)
    def check_dates(cls, values):
        start_date  values.get('start_date')
        end_date  values.get('end_date')
        if start_date and end_date and start_date > end_date:
            raise ValueError('start_date must be before end_date')
        return values
```

In this example, the `check_dates` method ensures that `start_date` is earlier than `end_date`. The `preTrue` argument to `@root_validator` ensures that this validation is performed before any default values are assigned, allowing for a more accurate comparison of the fields.

Custom types in Pydantic offer another approach for implementing complex validation rules. By defining a custom type, you can encapsulate specific validation logic within a class that represents a new data type. This approach is beneficial when you need to reuse the validation logic across multiple models or when the validation rules are intricate enough to warrant their own class.

Creating a custom type involves defining a class that inherits from `Pydantic`'s `BaseModel` or from Python's standard data types, and implementing the desired validation logic within it. For example, if you need a custom type that validates a complex structure, such as a specific pattern in a string or a number within a particular range, you can define this type as follows:

```python
from pydantic import BaseModel, constr

class PositiveInteger(int):
    def __new__(cls, value):
        if value < 0:
            raise ValueError('Value must be positive')
        return int.__new__(cls, value)

class Order(BaseModel):
    order_id: PositiveInteger
    quantity: int
```

Here, the `PositiveInteger` class ensures that only positive integers are accepted, raising an error if a non-positive integer is provided. By using this custom type in the `Order` model, you ensure that the `order_id` must always be a positive integer, enforcing the validation rule automatically whenever an instance of `Order` is created.

When integrating custom validators into FastAPI, it is crucial to ensure that these validators are seamlessly incorporated into the request and response handling. This involves not only defining the validators but also ensuring that they are properly utilized in the context of FastAPI's request handling pipeline. FastAPI's dependency injection system and request parsing capabilities work harmoniously with Pydantic's validators, allowing you to validate incoming data effectively before it reaches your endpoint logic.

To test the effectiveness of your custom validators, it is essential to write comprehensive test cases. Unit tests should cover various scenarios, including valid and invalid inputs, to ensure that your validators behave as expected. Using frameworks such as pytest allows for the systematic testing of these validators, ensuring robustness and reliability in your API's data handling.

In summary, custom validators in FastAPI and Pydantic provide a powerful mechanism for enforcing complex validation rules. By using validator functions, root validators, and custom types, you can implement sophisticated validation logic that meets your application's specific needs. Integrating these validators into your request and response models ensures that your API handles data consistently and accurately, contributing to the overall reliability and quality of your FastAPI application.

To implement custom validators effectively, understanding how they integrate with FastAPI's request and response models is essential. In FastAPI, custom validation functions can be incorporated directly into Pydantic models, which are the cornerstone of request and response validation. This integration ensures that your custom validation logic is seamlessly applied when FastAPI processes incoming data or prepares outgoing responses.

A pivotal aspect of using custom validators in FastAPI is ensuring that they align with the structure of your models. The `@validator` decorator, which is a key tool in Pydantic, allows for field-specific validation. When used within a Pydantic model, this decorator provides a method to validate and potentially modify individual fields based on custom logic. For instance, you might need to ensure that a string field adheres to a specific format or range. The following example illustrates how you can use the `@validator` decorator to enforce such rules:

```python
from pydantic import BaseModel, validator, constr

class UserProfile(BaseModel):
  username: constr(min_length3, max_length20)
```

```
    age: int

    @validator('age')
    def check_age(cls, value):
        if value < 18:
            raise ValueError('Age must be at least 18')
        return value
```

In this example, the `UserProfile` model includes a custom validator for the `age` field. The `check_age` method ensures that the `age` value is not less than 18. If the condition is not met, a `ValueError` is raised, which will be handled by FastAPI to generate an appropriate error response for the client.

When designing custom validators, it's crucial to consider the user experience and ensure that the feedback provided is both clear and actionable. Custom error messages help in this regard, guiding users to correct any issues with their input. In the previous example, the custom error message 'Age must be at least 18' directly informs the user of the validation failure.

Moreover, FastAPI allows you to manage validation for more complex scenarios, such as handling nested models. When working with nested models, custom validators can be applied to ensure that both parent and child models adhere to the expected constraints. For example, if you have a model that includes a list of items, you can validate each item within the list using custom validators. Here's how you can handle such cases:

```python
from pydantic import BaseModel, validator, conlist

class Item(BaseModel):
    name: str
    price: float
```

```
    @validator('price')
  def check_price(cls, value):
    if value < 0:
      raise ValueError('Price must be greater than zero')
    return value

class Order(BaseModel):
  items: conlist(Item, min_items1)

    @validator('items', each_itemTrue)
  def validate_items(cls, item):
    if item.price > 1000:
      raise ValueError('Item price cannot exceed 1000')
    return item
```

In this case, the `Order` model uses a `conlist` to ensure that the list of items contains at least one item. Additionally, each item's price is validated to ensure it does not exceed 1000, demonstrating how custom validators can be used in conjunction with list constraints.

Dynamic configuration of validators adds another layer of flexibility. For more advanced use cases, where validation rules might change based on external conditions or configurations, you can dynamically adjust validators by using callable validators. This approach allows you to define validation logic that can adapt to different scenarios. Consider the following example where validation behavior is determined by an external configuration:

```python
from pydantic import BaseModel, validator
from typing import Callable

class ConfigurableValidator(BaseModel):
  value: int
  validate_func: Callable[[int], bool]
```

```
@validator('value')
    def apply_dynamic_validation(cls, value, values, config_func):
    if not config_func(value):
        raise ValueError('Value does not meet the dynamic validation criteria')
    return value
```

In this example, the `ConfigurableValidator` model allows the `validate_func` parameter to define custom validation logic. This function is applied during validation, enabling the model to use different validation criteria based on the provided callable.

In summary, building and using custom validators in FastAPI involves leveraging Pydantic's capabilities to enforce specific rules for individual fields, across multiple fields, and even within nested models. By incorporating custom validation functions, you ensure that your application can handle complex validation scenarios effectively. This approach not only enhances data integrity but also provides a robust mechanism for managing non-standard validation requirements in your FastAPI applications.

CHAPTER 25: SECURING YOUR API WITH HTTPS

Ensuring secure communication between clients and your API is crucial for maintaining data integrity and confidentiality. HTTPS (HyperText Transfer Protocol Secure) is the protocol used to secure data transmitted over the internet by encrypting it with SSL/TLS (Secure Sockets Layer/Transport Layer Security) certificates. In this section, I will guide you through the process of setting up HTTPS for your FastAPI application, including how to obtain and configure SSL/TLS certificates, and how to enforce secure connections to protect data in transit.

The first step in securing your FastAPI application with HTTPS is to acquire an SSL/TLS certificate. This certificate serves as a cryptographic key pair: a public key, which is shared with clients, and a private key, which is kept confidential on your server. The SSL/TLS certificate validates the identity of your server and encrypts data transmitted between the server and the client.

There are several ways to obtain an SSL/TLS certificate. For production environments, it's advisable to use a certificate issued by a trusted Certificate Authority (CA). Providers like Let's Encrypt offer free SSL/TLS certificates with automated renewal, which can be easily integrated into your deployment pipeline. For development or testing environments, you might use self-signed certificates, although these are not recommended for production due to their lack of trust from browsers and clients.

Once you have acquired an SSL/TLS certificate, the next step is to configure your FastAPI application to use it. FastAPI itself does not directly handle SSL/TLS certificates; instead, this configuration is typically managed by the web server or reverse proxy that sits in front of your FastAPI application. Common choices for web servers include Nginx and Apache, while reverse proxies like Gunicorn or Uvicorn can be used for serving your FastAPI app.

If you are using Uvicorn to serve your FastAPI application, you can configure HTTPS by specifying the path to your SSL/TLS certificate and key files using the `--ssl-keyfile` and `--ssl-certfile` options. Here's an example of how you might start your Uvicorn server with HTTPS enabled:

```bash
uvicorn myapp:app --host 0.0.0.0 --port 443 --ssl-keyfile /path/to/your/ssl/keyfile.pem --ssl-certfile /path/to/your/ssl/certfile.pem
```

In this example, replace `/path/to/your/ssl/keyfile.pem` and `/path/to/your/ssl/certfile.pem` with the actual paths to your private key and certificate files. Note that port 443 is the default port for HTTPS traffic.

For more advanced setups, particularly in production environments, it's common to use a reverse proxy like Nginx in front of your FastAPI application. Nginx can be configured to handle SSL/TLS termination, meaning it will manage the encryption and decryption of HTTPS traffic before passing requests to your FastAPI application over HTTP. Here's a basic example of an Nginx configuration file for handling HTTPS:

```nginx
server {
  listen 443 ssl;
  server_name yourdomain.com;

    ssl_certificate /etc/nginx/ssl/your_certificate.pem;
  ssl_certificate_key /etc/nginx/ssl/your_private_key.pem;

    location / {
     proxy_pass http://localhost:8000;
     proxy_set_header Host $host;
     proxy_set_header X-Real-IP $remote_addr;
                           proxy_set_header    X-Forwarded-For
$proxy_add_x_forwarded_for;
     proxy_set_header X-Forwarded-Proto $scheme;
  }
}
```

In this Nginx configuration, replace `yourdomain.com` with your domain name and update the paths to your SSL certificate and private key files accordingly. The `proxy_pass` directive specifies the backend FastAPI application running on port 8000.

Enforcing secure connections is an additional step to ensure that all communication with your API occurs over HTTPS. This can be achieved by configuring HTTP Strict Transport Security (HSTS), a security feature that instructs browsers to only use HTTPS for future requests to your domain. HSTS can be enabled in your Nginx configuration with the following directive:

```nginx
add_header   Strict-Transport-Security   "max-age31536000;
includeSubDomains" always;
```

This directive sets the HSTS policy to one year (31,536,000 seconds) and applies it to all subdomains as well.

In addition to HSTS, it's crucial to regularly test your SSL/TLS setup for vulnerabilities and ensure that you are using strong encryption algorithms. Tools like SSL Labs' SSL Test can be used to evaluate your server's SSL/TLS configuration and identify any potential weaknesses.

Finally, consider setting up automatic renewal for your SSL/TLS certificates, especially if you are using services like Let's Encrypt. This can typically be managed using tools like Certbot, which can handle certificate issuance and renewal with minimal manual intervention.

By following these practices, you will enhance the security of your FastAPI application, ensuring that data exchanged between clients and your API remains confidential and protected against potential threats.

To continue securing your FastAPI application with HTTPS, once you have set up the initial SSL/TLS configuration with Uvicorn, it's important to address additional aspects of HTTPS deployment to ensure robust security.

Firstly, managing and renewing SSL/TLS certificates is crucial for maintaining uninterrupted secure connections. Certificates issued by trusted Certificate Authorities typically have an expiration period, after which they must be renewed. Let's Encrypt, for example, provides certificates with a 90-day validity period, and it's advisable to automate the renewal process to avoid any lapse in security. Tools such as Certbot can automate the renewal of Let's Encrypt certificates, integrating seamlessly with your server environment. If you are using self-signed certificates, you will need to manually renew and update these certificates periodically.

Additionally, you need to configure your web server or reverse proxy to enforce HTTPS connections. While FastAPI itself does not handle HTTPS, web servers like Nginx or Apache can be configured to ensure that all traffic is encrypted. For Nginx, you would set up an SSL/TLS configuration block within your server block. An example configuration might look like this:

```nginx
server {
  listen 443 ssl;
  server_name example.com;

    ssl_certificate /etc/nginx/ssl/example.com.crt;
  ssl_certificate_key /etc/nginx/ssl/example.com.key;

    ssl_protocols TLSv1.2 TLSv1.3;
                                                    ssl_ciphers
'TLS_AES_128_GCM_SHA256:TLS_AES_256_GCM_SHA384:TL
S_ECDHE_RSA_WITH_AES_128_GCM_SHA256';
  ssl_prefer_server_ciphers off;

    location / {
     proxy_pass http://localhost:8000;
     proxy_set_header Host $host;
     proxy_set_header X-Real-IP $remote_addr;
                        proxy_set_header     X-Forwarded-For
$proxy_add_x_forwarded_for;
     proxy_set_header X-Forwarded-Proto $scheme;
  }
}
```

In this configuration, Nginx listens on port 443 for HTTPS connections and proxies the requests to the FastAPI application running on port 8000. The `ssl_certificate` and `ssl_certificate_key` directives point to your SSL/TLS certificate and key files, respectively. The `ssl_protocols` and `ssl_ciphers` directives ensure that only secure protocols and ciphers are used, enhancing the security of your HTTPS connections.

Furthermore, it is essential to implement HTTP Strict Transport Security (HSTS) to enforce secure connections. HSTS is a security feature that tells browsers to always use HTTPS when connecting to your site, even if the user initially tries to connect via HTTP. You can enable HSTS in Nginx with the following configuration directive:

```nginx
add_header Strict-Transport-Security "max-age31536000;
includeSubDomains" always;
```

This header instructs browsers to use HTTPS for the next year (31,536,000 seconds) and includes all subdomains in the policy. Enabling HSTS helps prevent man-in-the-middle attacks by ensuring that all connections to your site are secured.

Another aspect to consider is managing HTTP to HTTPS redirects. Redirects ensure that users who attempt to access your site over HTTP are automatically redirected to the secure HTTPS version. In Nginx, this can be done with a separate server block that listens on port 80:

```nginx
server {
  listen 80;
  server_name example.com;
  return 301 https://$host$request_uri;
}
```

This configuration will redirect all HTTP requests to HTTPS, preserving the original request URI.

Lastly, regularly monitoring and auditing your HTTPS configuration is vital for maintaining security. Use tools such as SSL Labs' SSL Test to assess your server's SSL/TLS configuration and identify any vulnerabilities or misconfigurations. Keeping your server software and dependencies up to date is equally important to protect against known vulnerabilities.

By addressing these additional aspects—automating certificate renewal, configuring web servers or reverse proxies, implementing HSTS, managing redirects, and monitoring your configuration—you can ensure that your FastAPI application remains secure and that data transmitted between clients and your server is encrypted and protected. This comprehensive approach to HTTPS implementation will safeguard your application against potential security threats and contribute to a more trustworthy and secure user experience.

Beyond configuring SSL/TLS certificates and setting up HTTPS with your web server, there are additional considerations to enhance the security of your FastAPI application. One of these considerations is the implementation of HTTP Strict Transport Security (HSTS). HSTS is a security feature that forces web browsers to interact with your server only over secure connections. By enabling HSTS, you reduce the risk of man-in-the-middle attacks and ensure that users' interactions with your API are always encrypted.

To enable HSTS in your FastAPI application through Nginx, you need to add a specific header to your server configuration. The `Strict-Transport-Security` header instructs browsers to use HTTPS for all future requests. Here's how you would configure it:

```nginx
server {
  listen 443 ssl;
  server_name example.com;
```

```
   ssl_certificate /etc/nginx/ssl/example.com.crt;
  ssl_certificate_key /etc/nginx/ssl/example.com.key;

   ssl_protocols TLSv1.2 TLSv1.3;
                                                   ssl_ciphers
'TLS_AES_128_GCM_SHA256:TLS_AES_256_GCM_SHA384:TL
S_ECDHE_RSA_WITH_AES_128_GCM_SHA256';
  ssl_prefer_server_ciphers off;

   add_header Strict-Transport-Security "max-age31536000;
includeSubDomains" always;

   location / {
    proxy_pass http://localhost:8000;
    proxy_set_header Host $host;
    proxy_set_header X-Real-IP $remote_addr;
                        proxy_set_header    X-Forwarded-For
$proxy_add_x_forwarded_for;
    proxy_set_header X-Forwarded-Proto $scheme;
  }
}
```

In this configuration, the `add_header` directive includes the `Strict-Transport-Security` header, specifying a `max-age` of one year (31,536,000 seconds) and the `includeSubDomains` option to apply HSTS to all subdomains. The `always` flag ensures that the header is set even in error responses.

Another crucial aspect of securing your API is ensuring that sensitive data is not inadvertently exposed or mismanaged. One method to achieve this is by using secure cookie attributes when dealing with session cookies. For FastAPI applications, you may manage cookies via dependencies or middleware. It is important to set cookies with the `Secure`, `HttpOnly`, and `SameSite` attributes to enhance their security.

The `Secure` attribute ensures that cookies are only sent over HTTPS connections, `HttpOnly` prevents JavaScript from accessing cookies, mitigating the risk of cross-site scripting attacks, and `SameSite` helps to prevent cross-site request forgery (CSRF) attacks by restricting how cookies are sent with cross-site requests. For example, you can set these attributes when creating a cookie in FastAPI as follows:

```python
from fastapi import FastAPI, Response
from starlette.middleware.sessions import SessionMiddleware
from starlette.requests import Request

app FastAPI()

app.add_middleware(SessionMiddleware, secret_key"your-secret-key")

@app.get("/set-cookie")
async def set_cookie(response: Response):
  response.set_cookie(
    key"session",
    value"your-session-value",
    secureTrue,
    httponlyTrue,
    samesite"Strict"
  )
  return {"message": "Cookie set with secure attributes"}
```

In this code snippet, the `set_cookie` function sets a cookie with the specified secure attributes. This practice ensures that cookies are transmitted securely and are protected from common vulnerabilities.

Furthermore, it is essential to regularly review and update your security practices as new threats emerge and best practices evolve. Keeping your dependencies up to date, applying security patches promptly, and performing regular security audits can help identify and mitigate vulnerabilities.

For comprehensive protection, consider integrating additional security mechanisms such as Web Application Firewalls (WAFs) and security monitoring tools. WAFs can help filter and monitor HTTP requests to prevent attacks like SQL injection and cross-site scripting. Security monitoring tools, on the other hand, can provide real-time alerts and insights into potential security incidents.

Finally, documenting your security practices and conducting regular training for your development team on security best practices can help foster a security-conscious culture. By combining proper configuration, secure coding practices, and proactive security measures, you can ensure that your FastAPI application remains secure and resilient against potential threats.

CHAPTER 26: IMPLEMENTING API VERSIONING

In the realm of API development, managing changes and updates to your API over time is crucial for maintaining backward compatibility and ensuring a smooth user experience. Implementing API versioning is a strategy that allows you to manage these changes effectively, providing a structured way to evolve your API without disrupting existing clients. This section will explore various approaches to API versioning in FastAPI, including URI versioning, query parameter versioning, and header-based versioning, and will demonstrate how to structure your API to support multiple versions gracefully.

The most common method of API versioning is URI versioning. This approach involves including the version number directly in the URL path. For instance, you might structure your endpoints like `/api/v1/resource` for version 1 and `/api/v2/resource` for version 2. This method is straightforward and makes it clear which version of the API a client is interacting with, both for developers and users.

To implement URI versioning in FastAPI, you can create separate routers for each version of your API. Each router will handle the routes specific to its version. Here's how you might set up versioning with FastAPI:

```python
from fastapi import FastAPI, APIRouter

app FastAPI()

Version 1 of the API
v1_router APIRouter()

@v1_router.get("/resource")
def get_resource_v1():
  return {"message": "This is version 1"}

app.include_router(v1_router, prefix"/api/v1")

Version 2 of the API
v2_router APIRouter()

@v2_router.get("/resource")
def get_resource_v2():
  return {"message": "This is version 2 with new features"}

app.include_router(v2_router, prefix"/api/v2")
```

In this setup, each version of the API has its own router and is prefixed accordingly. Clients can then request the specific version of the API they need by including the version number in the URL.

Another approach is query parameter versioning, where the version number is included as a query parameter in the URL. For example, a request might look like `/api/resource?v1` or `/api/resource?v2`. This method allows you to keep a single endpoint URL and differentiate versions through query parameters.

To implement query parameter versioning in FastAPI, you can use dependency injection to check the version parameter and route the request accordingly. Here's an example:

```python
from fastapi import FastAPI, Query, Depends

app  FastAPI()

def get_version(v: int  Query(..., alias"v")):
  if v  1:
    return "v1"
  elif v  2:
    return "v2"
  else:
    raise ValueError("Invalid version")

@app.get("/api/resource")
def get_resource(version: str  Depends(get_version)):
  if version  "v1":
    return {"message": "This is version 1"}
  elif version  "v2":
    return {"message": "This is version 2 with new features"}
```

In this example, the `get_version` function extracts the version from the query parameters and routes the request to the appropriate version handler based on the provided version.

Header-based versioning is another technique where the version number is included in the request headers rather than in the URL or query parameters. This method is less visible than URI or query parameter versioning but can be useful for clients that prefer to keep versioning information out of the URL.

To implement header-based versioning in FastAPI, you can create a dependency that reads the version information from the request headers. Here's how you might do this:

```python
from fastapi import FastAPI, Header, HTTPException
```

```
app FastAPI()

def get_version(x_api_version: str Header(...)):
  if x_api_version "1":
    return "v1"
  elif x_api_version "2":
    return "v2"
  else:
      raise HTTPException(status_code400, detail"Invalid API
version")

@app.get("/api/resource")
def get_resource(version: str Depends(get_version)):
  if version "v1":
    return {"message": "This is version 1"}
  elif version "v2":
    return {"message": "This is version 2 with new features"}
```

In this setup, the `get_version` function retrieves the version information from the `X-API-Version` header and directs the request to the appropriate version handler. Clients must include this header in their requests to specify which version of the API they wish to use.

Each of these versioning strategies has its own advantages and trade-offs. URI versioning is clear and explicit but can lead to URL bloat if many versions are supported. Query parameter versioning keeps URLs clean but requires clients to include versioning information in query parameters. Header-based versioning offers a cleaner URL structure but requires clients to handle custom headers.

Selecting the appropriate versioning strategy depends on your API's specific requirements and client preferences. Regardless of the method chosen, it is essential to provide clear documentation on how clients should specify the API version and how different versions of the API differ in terms of functionality and behavior.

Continuing from our discussion on API versioning strategies, let us delve into query parameter versioning and header-based versioning, exploring how these methods can be implemented in FastAPI and their respective advantages and considerations.

Query parameter versioning is a technique where the version information is included as a query parameter in the URL. This method allows for a more flexible and less intrusive approach compared to URI versioning. Instead of modifying the URL structure to include version numbers, you append a version identifier as a query string, such as `/api/resource?v1` or `/api/resource?v2`. This allows a single endpoint to handle multiple versions based on the query parameter.

To implement query parameter versioning in FastAPI, you can use a combination of request parameters and dependency injection to route requests to the appropriate version of your API. Here is an example illustrating this approach:

```python
from fastapi import FastAPI, Query, Depends

app FastAPI()

def get_version(version: int Query(default1, alias"v")):
  return version

@app.get("/api/resource")
def get_resource(version: int Depends(get_version)):
  if version 1:
    return {"message": "This is version 1"}
  elif version 2:
    return {"message": "This is version 2 with new features"}
  else:
    return {"message": "Version not supported"}, 400
```

In this example, the `get_version` function extracts the version number from the query parameter. The `get_resource` endpoint then uses this version number to determine which response to provide. This method is advantageous for maintaining a single endpoint and allows for flexibility in version management without altering the core URL structure.

Moving on to header-based versioning, this approach involves sending the version information in the HTTP headers rather than in the URL or query parameters. This method can be beneficial in scenarios where you want to keep the URL clean and versioning information separate from the resource path. Clients specify the API version using a custom header, such as `X-API-Version`.

Implementing header-based versioning in FastAPI requires creating a dependency that reads the version information from the headers. Here is a practical example:

```python
from fastapi import FastAPI, Header, HTTPException

app FastAPI()

def get_api_version(x_api_version: str Header(None)):
  if x_api_version is None:
      raise HTTPException(status_code400, detail"API version
header missing")
  return x_api_version

@app.get("/api/resource")
def get_resource(api_version: str Depends(get_api_version)):
  if api_version "1":
    return {"message": "This is version 1"}
  elif api_version "2":
    return {"message": "This is version 2 with enhancements"}
  else:
```

raise HTTPException(status_code400, detail"Version not supported")
```

In this implementation, the `get_api_version` function reads the `X-API-Version` header from incoming requests. The `get_resource` endpoint uses this header value to route requests to the appropriate version of the API. This approach maintains a clean URL structure and provides clear versioning information in the headers, which can be useful for clients that prefer to manage versioning separately from their URLs.

Each versioning method has its own set of trade-offs. URI versioning is clear and straightforward, making it easy for both developers and clients to understand which version they are interacting with. Query parameter versioning is flexible and keeps the URL clean but might require additional logic to handle versioning properly. Header-based versioning separates versioning information from the URL and can make it easier to manage versions, but requires clients to include custom headers and may complicate the API's integration with tools that do not easily support custom headers.

Choosing the right versioning strategy depends on various factors, including the needs of your API users, the complexity of your API, and how you plan to manage future changes. Each approach can be effective when used appropriately, and often, the choice is influenced by your specific use case and preferences for API design.

In addition to selecting a versioning strategy, it's also important to plan for deprecating old versions and providing clear communication to users about changes. Implementing proper deprecation strategies ensures that users have ample time to transition to new versions and that your API remains maintainable and user-friendly over time.

In the previous sections, we explored query parameter
```

and header-based versioning. To complete our examination, it's essential to address the practical considerations and best practices for implementing these versioning strategies in FastAPI. This involves understanding how to maintain backward compatibility, manage transitions between versions, and ensure that clients interact with your API in a way that minimizes disruption.

When managing multiple API versions, it is crucial to maintain backward compatibility to avoid breaking existing clients when new versions are introduced. This often involves providing support for older versions for a period, ensuring that clients can migrate to the new versions at their own pace. You should clearly document version changes and communicate with your users about deprecations and upgrades.

In FastAPI, backward compatibility can be managed through careful design of your routes and handlers. Each version of your API should ideally be able to co-exist with others, with clear distinctions made between the features and endpoints of each version. This allows clients to transition gradually without sudden interruptions in service. For instance, you might provide version 1 and version 2 endpoints concurrently until all users have migrated to the newer version.

Additionally, implementing a deprecation strategy is an important aspect of API versioning. This involves notifying users when a particular version is scheduled for deprecation, and providing ample time for them to migrate to newer versions. FastAPI does not natively support deprecation notices in routes, so you would need to manually include deprecation messages in your documentation and possibly implement custom logic in your endpoints to alert users when they are accessing a deprecated version.

To streamline the management of API versions, consider

leveraging automated tools and services that assist with version management and documentation. Tools such as Swagger UI, which FastAPI integrates with by default, can help in documenting different versions of your API. By configuring Swagger to include versioning information, you can provide clients with a clear view of available versions and their corresponding endpoints.

Moreover, establishing a clear versioning policy and documentation is essential for the long-term maintenance of your API. Your versioning strategy should be aligned with your development and release cycles, and all changes should be well-documented. This includes specifying which features are available in each version, the changes made from one version to another, and any known issues or limitations.

In terms of security and best practices, each version of your API should be subjected to the same security measures and testing processes. This ensures that newer versions do not introduce vulnerabilities that could be exploited. Regular security audits and adherence to best practices in API development will help in maintaining the integrity and security of your API across different versions.

Additionally, consider implementing automated testing for your API versions. Automated tests can help ensure that new versions do not break existing functionality and that all versions continue to operate correctly. FastAPI supports integration with testing frameworks such as pytest, which can be utilized to create comprehensive test suites for each version of your API.

When it comes to deploying multiple versions, it is important to have a robust deployment strategy that can handle version-specific configurations and environments. This may involve configuring different endpoints or load balancers to route traffic to the appropriate version of your API, ensuring that users receive the correct version based on their requests.

Lastly, continually monitoring and evaluating the performance and usage of different API versions can provide valuable insights into how your API is being utilized. This information can guide future versioning decisions and help in optimizing your API's performance and user experience. FastAPI's integration with monitoring and analytics tools can aid in gathering and analyzing this data effectively.

In summary, implementing API versioning in FastAPI involves choosing the right versioning strategy, ensuring backward compatibility, managing transitions, and maintaining clear documentation. Whether you use URI versioning, query parameters, or headers, each approach has its advantages and trade-offs. By adhering to best practices in API development and version management, you can build a robust and flexible API that meets the needs of your users while accommodating future changes and enhancements.

CHAPTER 27: WORKING WITH GRAPHQL

Integrating GraphQL with FastAPI offers a powerful alternative to traditional RESTful APIs, providing more flexibility and efficiency in querying data. In this section, we will delve into how to set up a GraphQL endpoint in FastAPI, define schemas, and handle both queries and mutations.

To begin, it is essential to understand the fundamentals of GraphQL. Unlike REST, where each endpoint corresponds to a specific resource, GraphQL provides a single endpoint where clients can request exactly the data they need. This is achieved through a flexible query language that allows clients to specify their data requirements in a precise manner. This flexibility can lead to more efficient data retrieval and reduced over-fetching or under-fetching of data.

The first step in integrating GraphQL with FastAPI is setting up a GraphQL endpoint. FastAPI itself does not provide built-in support for GraphQL, but you can use additional libraries such as `graphene` or `ariadne` to bridge this gap. For this example, we will use `graphene`, a popular library for building GraphQL APIs in Python.

Start by installing the required packages. You can do this using pip:

```bash
pip install graphene fastapi-graphql
```

Once you have installed these packages, you need to define your GraphQL schema. The schema is the core of your GraphQL API, defining the types of data that can be queried and the operations that can be performed. In GraphQL, schemas are defined using a combination of type definitions and resolvers.

Create a file named `schema.py` and define your types and queries. Here is a basic example to illustrate:

```python
import graphene

class Query(graphene.ObjectType):
    hello graphene.String(namegraphene.String(default_value"stranger"))

    def resolve_hello(self, info, name):
     return f"Hello, {name}!"

schema graphene.Schema(queryQuery)
```

In this example, we define a single query `hello` that takes an optional argument `name` and returns a greeting message.

With the schema defined, the next step is to integrate it with FastAPI. You will create a FastAPI application and add a GraphQL endpoint using the `FastAPI-GraphQL` integration. Create your main application file, `main.py`, with the following code:

```python
from fastapi import FastAPI
```

```
from fastapi_graphql import GraphQLApp
from schema import schema

app FastAPI()

app.add_route("/graphql", GraphQLApp(schemaschema))
```

In this setup, we import the `FastAPI` framework and the `GraphQLApp` from `fastapi-graphql`. We then add a new route `/graphql` to the FastAPI app that handles GraphQL queries using the defined schema.

To test your GraphQL endpoint, you can run the FastAPI application using Uvicorn:

```bash
uvicorn main:app --reload
```

Once the server is running, navigate to `http://localhost:8000/graphql` in your web browser or API client to access the GraphQL interface. You can use this interface to perform queries and see the responses directly.

Handling mutations in GraphQL involves defining operations that modify data. Just as with queries, you will need to define mutations in your schema and implement resolvers for them. Here's an example of how to add a mutation to the schema:

```python
class CreateGreeting(graphene.Mutation):
  class Arguments:
    name graphene.String(requiredTrue)


   success graphene.Boolean()
  message graphene.String()
```

```
    def mutate(self, info, name):
        return CreateGreeting(successTrue, messagef"Greeting created for {name}")

class Mutation(graphene.ObjectType):
  create_greeting CreateGreeting.Field()

schema graphene.Schema(queryQuery, mutationMutation)
```

In this example, we define a `CreateGreeting` mutation that takes a `name` argument and returns a success flag and a message. We then add this mutation to the `Mutation` type in our schema.

When implementing mutations, ensure that you handle any potential errors and edge cases, such as validation errors or conflicts. Proper error handling is crucial for maintaining a robust and user-friendly API.

In conclusion, integrating GraphQL with FastAPI involves defining a GraphQL schema, setting up a GraphQL endpoint, and handling queries and mutations. By following these steps, you can leverage the flexibility and efficiency of GraphQL in your FastAPI applications, allowing clients to interact with your data in a more dynamic and precise manner.

Once the schema is defined, integrating it into a FastAPI application involves setting up an appropriate GraphQL endpoint. This integration allows clients to interact with the GraphQL API, querying and mutating data as needed.

Create your main application file, where you will define your FastAPI app and set up the GraphQL endpoint. For this integration, you'll use the `FastAPI-GraphQL` package. This package provides a convenient way to expose a GraphQL endpoint in a FastAPI application. Here's a basic setup:

```python
```

from fastapi import FastAPI
from fastapi_graphql import GraphQLRouter
from schema import schema Import your GraphQL schema

app FastAPI()

Create a GraphQL router with the defined schema
graphql_app GraphQLRouter(schemaschema)

Add the GraphQL router to your FastAPI app
app.include_router(graphql_app, prefix"/graphql")
```

In this setup, you import your FastAPI application and the schema you defined earlier. The `GraphQLRouter` from the `fastapi-graphql` package is used to create a router that serves the GraphQL schema. You then include this router in your FastAPI application, specifying a prefix (e.g., `/graphql`) that will be used to access the GraphQL endpoint.

With this setup, your FastAPI application now has a `/graphql` endpoint that clients can use to send queries and mutations. You can test this endpoint using GraphQL client tools such as GraphiQL or Apollo Studio. These tools allow you to interactively explore your GraphQL API, run queries, and see the results.

Handling queries and mutations in GraphQL involves defining resolver functions. These resolvers are responsible for fetching and returning the data requested by the client. In the schema definition, you specify the types and fields available for querying and the functions that resolve these fields.

Consider extending the schema to include more complex queries and mutations. For example, you might want to add a mutation that allows clients to create or update data. Here's an example of how you might define a mutation:

```python

```
class Mutation(graphene.ObjectType):
                                                create_message
graphene.String(messagegraphene.String(requiredTrue))

    def resolve_create_message(self, info, message):
     Logic to create a new message
     return f"Message created: {message}"

schema  graphene.Schema(queryQuery, mutationMutation)
```

In this example, we define a `Mutation` class with a `create_message` field that takes a required `message` argument. The `resolve_create_message` function handles the creation of a new message and returns a confirmation string. The schema is updated to include both the `Query` and `Mutation` classes.

By integrating mutations into your GraphQL schema, you enable clients to modify data on the server. This is in addition to querying data, allowing for a more interactive and flexible API.

In summary, integrating GraphQL with FastAPI involves defining a GraphQL schema with types, queries, and mutations, and then exposing this schema via a GraphQL endpoint in your FastAPI application. This setup provides a powerful and flexible way to interact with your API, offering clients the ability to request exactly the data they need and perform complex data manipulations.

When working with GraphQL in FastAPI, another critical aspect is handling more complex queries and mutations that might involve interacting with databases or other external services. For such tasks, resolvers need to be carefully designed to ensure efficiency and accuracy.

In GraphQL, resolvers are the functions responsible for fetching the data for each field in a query. The design of resolvers should take into consideration the performance impact of database operations, especially when dealing with large datasets or complex relationships. For example, if a query requests a list of items with nested fields, each nested field might require additional database queries. This scenario is known as the "N+1 query problem," where an inefficient data fetching strategy results in many unnecessary queries. To mitigate this issue, use techniques such as query batching or join operations to reduce the number of queries made to the database.

Here's an example of how a resolver might interact with a database. Suppose you have a query that retrieves a list of users and their associated posts. You would want to ensure that your resolver efficiently fetches all the relevant data. In SQLAlchemy, this might involve using eager loading to fetch related data in a single query:

```python
from sqlalchemy.orm import joinedload

def resolve_users(self, info):
  Fetch users with their posts in one query
                                                return
db_session.query(User).options(joinedload(User.posts)).all()
```

In this resolver, `joinedload(User.posts)` ensures that posts related to each user are fetched in the same query, reducing the need for additional queries.

For mutations, which modify data, resolvers often need to handle input validation and error handling. Suppose you have a mutation to create a new user. Your resolver should validate the input, check for any existing users with the same email, and handle any errors gracefully:

```python
```

```
class Mutation(graphene.ObjectType):
    create_user graphene.Field(UserType,
namegraphene.String(requiredTrue),
emailgraphene.String(requiredTrue))

    def resolve_create_user(self, info, name, email):
     if db_session.query(User).filter(User.email email).first():
       raise Exception("Email already exists.")
     new_user User(namename, emailemail)
     db_session.add(new_user)
     db_session.commit()
     return new_user
```

In this mutation resolver, an exception is raised if a user with the same email already exists, preventing duplicate entries. Additionally, make sure to handle other potential errors such as database connection issues or validation errors.

For a more comprehensive approach, you might want to implement error handling in a way that integrates with your GraphQL schema. This can be done by defining custom error types and using them in your resolvers to provide meaningful error messages to clients. For instance:

```python
class UserError(graphene.ObjectType):
  message graphene.String()

class Mutation(graphene.ObjectType):
    create_user graphene.Field(UserType,
namegraphene.String(requiredTrue),
emailgraphene.String(requiredTrue))
  errors graphene.Field(UserError)

    def resolve_create_user(self, info, name, email):
     if db_session.query(User).filter(User.email email).first():
       return UserError(message"Email already exists.")
```

```
    new_user User(namename, emailemail)
    db_session.add(new_user)
    db_session.commit()
    return new_user
```

This design allows the mutation to return a user-friendly error message if something goes wrong, enhancing the client's ability to handle errors effectively.

When integrating GraphQL with FastAPI, another consideration is ensuring that your API is secure. GraphQL APIs can expose sensitive data if not properly secured. Implementing authentication and authorization at the GraphQL layer is essential. You can use FastAPI's dependency injection system to enforce security measures such as OAuth2 or JWT authentication.

Here's an example of how to secure a GraphQL endpoint using FastAPI's dependency injection:

```python
from fastapi import Depends, HTTPException
from fastapi.security import OAuth2PasswordBearer
from graphql.execution.base import ResolveInfo

oauth2_scheme OAuth2PasswordBearer(tokenUrl"token")

def get_current_user(token: str Depends(oauth2_scheme)):
  user authenticate_user(token)
  if not user:
        raise HTTPException(status_code401, detail"Invalid
token")
  return user

class Query(graphene.ObjectType):
  current_user graphene.Field(UserType)

   def resolve_current_user(self, info: ResolveInfo):
```

```
                                                        user
get_current_user(info.context["request"].headers.get("Authori
zation"))
    return user
```

In this example, `get_current_user` is a dependency that verifies the provided token and ensures that the user is authenticated before allowing access to the `current_user` query. This approach helps protect your GraphQL API from unauthorized access.

By carefully designing your schema, resolvers, and security measures, you can build a robust GraphQL API that provides a flexible and efficient interface for clients while maintaining high standards of performance and security.

CHAPTER 28: INTERNATIONALIZATION AND LOCALIZATION

Supporting multiple languages and regions is vital for applications aiming to cater to a global audience. Implementing internationalization (i18n) and localization (l10n) in FastAPI involves several key steps, including managing translations, handling locale-specific formatting, and accommodating user preferences for different languages. This approach ensures that your application can effectively communicate with users in their preferred languages and adhere to regional formatting conventions.

The first step in internationalizing an API with FastAPI is to establish a framework for managing translations. This involves creating and organizing translation files that map strings in your application to their equivalents in various languages. Python's `gettext` library is a commonly used tool for this purpose, providing mechanisms to extract, compile, and apply translations. Here's a step-by-step guide to integrating `gettext` with FastAPI:

1. Setting Up Translation Files: Start by creating a directory structure for your translations. Typically, this involves creating `.po` files for each language you wish to support.

These files contain the original strings and their translations.

For example, you might have `locales/en/LC_MESSAGES/messages.po` for English and `locales/es/LC_MESSAGES/messages.po` for Spanish. The `.po` files are generated using tools like `pygettext` or manually crafted. Each entry in these files looks like this:

```plaintext
msgid "Welcome"
msgstr "Bienvenido"
```

In this example, `"Welcome"` is the original English string, and `"Bienvenido"` is its Spanish translation.

2. Compiling Translation Files: Once the `.po` files are created and updated, they need to be compiled into binary `.mo` files that can be read by the application. This compilation is done using the `msgfmt` command:

```bash
msgfmt locales/es/LC_MESSAGES/messages.po -o locales/es/
LC_MESSAGES/messages.mo
```

3. Integrating with FastAPI: FastAPI does not directly support `gettext`, but you can integrate it using middleware or custom dependency injections. You'll need to load the appropriate translation files based on the user's locale and apply translations to API responses.

Here is a basic example of how to set up `gettext` with FastAPI:

```python
from fastapi import FastAPI, Request
from gettext import translation

app FastAPI()
```

```
def get_translator(locale):
        return translation('messages', localedir'locales',
languages[locale])

@app.get("/welcome")
async def welcome(request: Request):
  locale request.headers.get('Accept-Language', 'en')
  translator get_translator(locale)
  return {"message": translator.gettext("Welcome")}
```

In this code snippet, the `get_translator` function loads the appropriate `.mo` file based on the `Accept-Language` header from the request. The translation is then applied to the response message.

Handling locale-specific formatting is another crucial aspect of internationalization. Different regions have varying conventions for date formats, currency symbols, and number representations. To manage this, Python's `babel` library is highly useful. Babel provides tools for locale-aware formatting and parsing.

For example, if you need to format a date according to the user's locale, you can use Babel's `format_date` function:

```python
from babel.dates import format_date
from fastapi import FastAPI, Request

app FastAPI()

@app.get("/date")
async def get_date(request: Request):
  locale request.headers.get('Accept-Language', 'en')
  date_str format_date(datetime.now(), localelocale)
  return {"date": date_str}
```

In this snippet, `format_date` formats the current date based on the locale specified in the request header.

Managing user preferences for different languages involves storing and retrieving these preferences in user profiles or session data. This can be achieved by implementing a system to save user settings, which can then be used to automatically apply language preferences across different requests.

A typical approach might include saving user language preferences in a database or session storage. Upon each request, you would retrieve these preferences and apply the appropriate translations and formatting. Here's a conceptual example:

```python
@app.get("/user-settings")
async def get_user_settings(user_id: int):
  user db_session.query(User).filter(User.id user_id).first()
  return {"preferred_language": user.preferred_language}

@app.get("/localized-content")
async def get_localized_content(user_id: int):
  user db_session.query(User).filter(User.id user_id).first()
  locale user.preferred_language or 'en'
  translator get_translator(locale)
      return {"content": translator.gettext("Welcome to our application")}
```

In this example, the user's language preference is retrieved from the database and used to apply the correct translations.

In summary, integrating internationalization and localization into a FastAPI application involves setting up and managing translation files, handling locale-specific formatting, and accommodating user preferences. By leveraging libraries such as `gettext` and `babel`, and incorporating these practices into your FastAPI application, you can build robust APIs that cater to a diverse global audience, ensuring that users receive content in their preferred languages and in formats familiar to their regions.

To effectively manage translations in FastAPI, it's essential to handle locale-specific formatting and user preferences with precision. The integration of these aspects ensures that your API is not only multilingual but also tailored to regional standards and individual user requirements.

Locale-specific formatting encompasses various aspects such as date and time formats, number formatting, and currency representation. These elements differ significantly between regions, making it crucial to address them appropriately. FastAPI itself does not provide built-in support for locale-based formatting, but you can leverage Python's `babel` library to handle these requirements.

To use `babel`, you first need to install it using pip:

```bash
pip install babel
```

After installation, you can configure `babel` to support different locales. Start by creating a configuration file, typically named `babel.cfg`, which specifies the file paths and formats for extraction:

```ini
[python: .py]
[jinja2: templates/.html]
```

You will use this configuration to extract translatable strings from your codebase and templates. Next, initialize and generate message catalogs using the `pybabel` command-line tool:

```bash
pybabel extract -F babel.cfg -o messages.pot .
pybabel init -i messages.pot -d translations -l en
```

In this process, `messages.pot` contains all the strings extracted from your code, and `translations` is the directory where the locale-specific translations will be stored.

After initializing the translations, you'll need to update the catalogs as new strings are added or modified:

```bash
pybabel update -i messages.pot -d translations
```

For locale-specific formatting, `babel` provides a suite of functions for formatting dates, times, numbers, and currencies according to locale-specific conventions. For instance, to format a date in a locale-aware manner, you would use:

```python
from babel.dates import format_date
from datetime import date

formatted_date format_date(date.today(), locale'es')
print(formatted_date) Output in Spanish locale
```

Integrating these formatting capabilities into your FastAPI application involves creating utility functions that apply the appropriate formatting based on the user's locale. You can then use these functions within your route handlers to ensure that all data presented to users conforms to their regional standards.

Another critical aspect of internationalization and localization is handling user preferences for different languages. In FastAPI, you can manage this by including locale information in user requests. Typically, this is done through HTTP headers, query parameters, or user settings stored in databases.

For example, if you are using HTTP headers to specify the desired language, you can implement a middleware that extracts the locale information and applies it throughout the request lifecycle. Here's how you might implement such middleware:

```python
from fastapi import FastAPI, Request
from starlette.middleware.base import BaseHTTPMiddleware

class LocaleMiddleware(BaseHTTPMiddleware):
  async def dispatch(self, request: Request, call_next):
    locale request.headers.get('Accept-Language', 'en')
    request.state.locale locale
    response await call_next(request)
    return response

app FastAPI()
app.add_middleware(LocaleMiddleware)
```

In this middleware, the `Accept-Language` header is used to determine the user's preferred locale, which is then stored in the request state for later use.

Additionally, you can create a dependency to extract the locale from the request state and apply it to various parts of your application:

```python
from fastapi import Depends

def get_locale(request: Request):
  return request.state.locale
```

```
@app.get("/some-endpoint")
async def some_endpoint(locale: str Depends(get_locale)):
    Use the locale to format responses
   return {"message": translate("Hello World", locale)}
```

In this endpoint, the `get_locale` dependency retrieves the locale from the request state, allowing you to tailor the response accordingly.

To sum up, integrating internationalization and localization in FastAPI involves several key practices: managing translations with `gettext` and `babel`, handling locale-specific formatting, and accommodating user preferences through headers or other mechanisms. By implementing these strategies, you can build APIs that provide a seamless experience for users across different languages and regions, ultimately enhancing the accessibility and usability of your application on a global scale.

To effectively handle user preferences for different languages in FastAPI, it is important to incorporate mechanisms for detecting and managing these preferences. This ensures that the application serves content in the language and format most suitable for each user.

First, consider how to detect and manage user preferences. Often, these preferences are communicated via HTTP headers, such as the `Accept-Language` header, which specifies the preferred languages of the user. In FastAPI, you can access this header through dependency injection. Here's how you might define a dependency to extract the user's preferred language:

```python
from fastapi import Request, Depends

def get_user_locale(request: Request):
   accept_language request.headers.get('accept-language', 'en')
```

```
    return accept_language.split(',')[0]  Return the first language preference
```

With this dependency, you can now use `get_user_locale` in your route handlers to determine the appropriate locale for each request. For example:

```python
from fastapi import FastAPI

app FastAPI()

@app.get("/greet")
def greet_user(locale: str  Depends(get_user_locale)):
    Assuming you have a function to get localized strings
    greeting  get_localized_greeting(locale)
    return {"message": greeting}
```

In this example, `get_localized_greeting` would be a function that returns a greeting string based on the provided locale. This function would use the translation files you've created with `babel` or any other localization library you are using.

Additionally, user preferences can be managed through session data or user profiles. If your application supports user accounts, you might store language preferences in user profiles. This method provides a more personalized experience, as users can set their preferred language manually, and it will be remembered across sessions.

Consider a scenario where users set their language preferences in their profile settings. When a user logs in, you retrieve their preference from the database and use it throughout their session. This can be implemented as follows:

```python
from fastapi import FastAPI, Depends
```

```
from pydantic import BaseModel

app FastAPI()

class UserProfile(BaseModel):
  user_id: int
  preferred_language: str

Dummy database simulation
user_profiles {
  1: UserProfile(user_id1, preferred_language"fr"),
  2: UserProfile(user_id2, preferred_language"en"),
}

def get_user_profile(user_id: int):
  return user_profiles.get(user_id, UserProfile(user_iduser_id,
preferred_language"en"))

@app.get("/greet")
def greet_user(user_id: int, profile: UserProfile
Depends(lambda: get_user_profile(user_id))):
  greeting get_localized_greeting(profile.preferred_language)
  return {"message": greeting}
```

In this setup, `get_user_profile` simulates fetching user profile data, including their language preference, which is then used to provide localized content.

Furthermore, managing translations and user preferences can be enhanced by implementing fallback mechanisms. These mechanisms ensure that if a user's preferred language is not available, the application defaults to a secondary language or a universal language like English. This approach ensures a consistent user experience even when certain translations are missing.

You can implement such fallback logic within your localization functions. For instance, if a translation is not found for a given locale, the function might default to English:

```python
from babel.support import Translations

def get_localized_greeting(locale: str) -> str:
  try:
        translations   Translations.load('translations', locales[locale])
    return translations.ugettext('greeting')
  except FileNotFoundError:
    Fallback to English if the locale-specific translations are not found
    translations  Translations.load('translations', locales['en'])
    return translations.ugettext('greeting')
```

In conclusion, effective internationalization and localization in FastAPI involve multiple aspects: managing translations, formatting locale-specific data, and handling user preferences. By integrating libraries like `babel`, leveraging FastAPI's dependency injection to handle locale detection, and implementing fallback mechanisms, you can build a robust system that caters to a diverse global audience. This holistic approach not only ensures that your API supports multiple languages but also adheres to regional formatting standards, thus enhancing the user experience for a worldwide audience.

CHAPTER 29: BUILDING COMMAND-LINE INTERFACES (CLI)

Building a command-line interface (CLI) for a FastAPI application involves understanding how to effectively leverage both Python's standard libraries and external tools to create commands that can automate tasks, manage configurations, and facilitate interactions with your API. This segment focuses on laying a solid foundation for integrating CLI functionality into your FastAPI application, beginning with the essentials of creating a CLI using Python's `argparse` library and then exploring how to integrate this with FastAPI.

The `argparse` module in Python's standard library serves as a fundamental tool for handling command-line arguments. This module provides a structured way to specify what arguments your CLI accepts and how these arguments should be processed. The first step in building a CLI is to create a command-line parser using `argparse`. This parser will be responsible for parsing the arguments provided by the user when they run the CLI command.

Let us start by examining a simple example. Importing the `argparse` module is the initial step. Once imported, you can create an `ArgumentParser` object. This object will hold all the information necessary to parse the command-line arguments. For instance, if you want to create a CLI tool that can start or stop a service, you might set up the parser as follows:

```python
import argparse

def main():
  parser argparse.ArgumentParser(description'CLI for FastAPI application.')
  parser.add_argument('command', typestr, help'Command to execute')
    parser.add_argument('--option', typestr, help'An optional argument')


    args parser.parse_args()


    if args.command 'start':
     print("Starting the application...")
  elif args.command 'stop':
     print("Stopping the application...")
  else:
     print("Unknown command.")

if __name__ '__main__':
  main()
```

In this code snippet, the `ArgumentParser` is instantiated with a description of what the CLI tool does. The `add_argument` method is used to define the command-line arguments the tool will accept. Here, `'command'` is a positional argument, meaning it is required and specifies the main action to be performed (e.g., `start` or `stop`). The `--option` is an optional argument that provides additional flexibility to the command.

Once the arguments are parsed with `parse_args()`, you can use conditional statements to execute different code based on the arguments provided. This is a straightforward example, but as we will see, `argparse` can handle much more complex scenarios, including subcommands and argument validation.

Next, integrating this CLI with a FastAPI application requires some additional considerations. FastAPI itself does not directly interact with command-line arguments; however, the CLI can be used to manage aspects of the FastAPI application such as starting or stopping the server, interacting with the application's database, or performing routine maintenance tasks.

To effectively integrate CLI commands with FastAPI, you should consider using third-party libraries designed to simplify this process. One such library is `Click`, which provides a more advanced and flexible way to build CLI applications compared to `argparse`. `Click` offers features like nested commands and automatic help generation, making it a popular choice for more complex CLI requirements.

Here's how you might set up a basic CLI using `Click`:

```python
import click

@click.group()
def cli():
    """CLI for managing FastAPI application."""
    pass

@cli.command()
def start():
    """Start the FastAPI application."""
    click.echo("Starting the FastAPI application...")
```

```
@cli.command()
def stop():
    """Stop the FastAPI application."""
    click.echo("Stopping the FastAPI application...")

if __name__ '__main__':
    cli()
```

In this example, the `@click.group()` decorator defines a CLI group, which acts as the entry point for the CLI commands. The `@cli.command()` decorators define individual commands within this group. Each command corresponds to a specific action that can be performed. `click.echo()` is used to print output to the console, similar to `print()` but more suited for CLI applications.

By using `Click`, you gain access to a range of advanced features such as argument validation, dynamic help messages, and command chaining. This can significantly streamline the development of complex CLI tools and make your FastAPI application more manageable.

In conclusion, building a CLI for a FastAPI application involves creating a parser for command-line arguments using libraries such as `argparse` or `Click`. These tools allow you to define commands and options that can automate tasks, interact with your FastAPI application, and improve the overall development workflow. The integration of CLI commands with FastAPI can enhance the application's usability and streamline various operational tasks. As you continue to develop and refine your CLI tools, consider the specific needs of your application and how these tools can best support your development and operational goals.

Having established the basic framework for a command-line interface (CLI) using Python's `argparse`, we can now turn our attention to integrating this functionality with a FastAPI application. The goal is to enhance the capabilities of your FastAPI app by enabling various command-line operations that can interact with your API, automate common tasks, and improve development workflows.

To integrate CLI commands with FastAPI, we need to consider how these commands will interact with the FastAPI application's code. This typically involves using the FastAPI application's internal functions or accessing its database directly from the CLI. For a more seamless integration, you may choose to use additional libraries like `click` or `Typer`. These libraries provide a more feature-rich interface compared to `argparse` and are often preferred for complex CLI applications due to their advanced features and ease of use.

Let's explore how to use `click` to enhance our CLI. `click` is a Python package that provides a straightforward way to build command-line interfaces. It offers features such as parameter typing, command chaining, and more flexible argument handling, which can be advantageous when developing a CLI for a FastAPI application.

First, you need to install the `click` library if it's not already included in your environment. You can install it using pip:

```bash
pip install click
```

Once installed, you can start using `click` to define your CLI commands. Unlike `argparse`, which relies on procedural programming, `click` uses decorators to define commands, making the code more modular and readable. Below is an example of how to use `click` to create a simple CLI that interacts with a FastAPI application:

```python
```

```
import click
from fastapi import FastAPI
from pydantic import BaseModel

app FastAPI()

class Item(BaseModel):
  name: str
  description: str

@app.post("/items/")
def create_item(item: Item):
  return {"name": item.name, "description": item.description}

@click.group()
def cli():
  """Command-line interface for FastAPI application."""
  pass

@cli.command()
@click.argument('name')
@click.argument('description')
def create(name, description):
  """Create a new item."""
   Simulating an API call or database operation
    print(f"Creating item with name '{name}' and description
'{description}'")

@cli.command()
def list_items():
  """List all items."""
   Simulating retrieval of items
  print("Listing all items...")

if __name__ '__main__':
  cli()
```

In this example, `click.group` defines a group of commands.

Each command is decorated with `@cli.command()` and is given a specific function that will be executed when the command is invoked. The `create` command takes two arguments, `name` and `description`, and simulates the creation of an item, while the `list_items` command simulates listing items.

To connect these commands to your FastAPI application, you would typically make actual API calls or interact with a database in the command functions. For instance, you might use the `httpx` library to make HTTP requests to your FastAPI endpoints from within the CLI commands.

Here's an example of how to use `httpx` to make an HTTP POST request from a CLI command:

```python
import click
import httpx

@click.command()
@click.argument('name')
@click.argument('description')
def create(name, description):
    """Create a new item using FastAPI."""
    url 'http://localhost:8000/items/'
    payload {'name': name, 'description': description}
    response httpx.post(url, jsonpayload)
    if response.status_code 200:
        print(f"Item created: {response.json()}")
    else:
        print(f"Failed to create item: {response.status_code}")
```

In this updated `create` command, `httpx.post` sends a POST request to the FastAPI endpoint for creating an item. The response from the server is then printed, providing feedback to the user.

The integration of a CLI with FastAPI can significantly streamline various tasks and interactions with your application. By leveraging `click` and `httpx`, you can build a robust CLI that allows for efficient management of your FastAPI application's data and functionality directly from the command line. This approach is not only useful for development and testing but can also be employed in production environments for administrative tasks and automated workflows.

In summary, building and integrating a CLI with a FastAPI application involves understanding both the basics of command-line argument parsing and the specific needs of your application. Using libraries such as `argparse` for simpler tasks or `click` for more complex CLI functionality allows you to enhance your FastAPI application's capabilities, automate repetitive tasks, and facilitate easier interaction with your API.

The integration of a command-line interface (CLI) with a FastAPI application involves not only creating commands that interact with the application but also ensuring these commands are effectively integrated into the development workflow. Beyond using `click` or `argparse`, which we have already discussed, it's crucial to understand how these CLI tools can be used to automate various tasks such as database migrations, testing, and deployment.

One important aspect of integrating CLI commands is managing the application's configuration. Often, a FastAPI application will have configuration settings that need to be adjusted or read during development and deployment. Using CLI commands to handle these configurations can greatly simplify the process of managing different environments (e.g., development, testing, production). For instance, you might create a CLI command to load configuration settings from a file or environment variables.

Consider a scenario where you need a CLI command to apply database migrations. If you're using an ORM like SQLAlchemy with FastAPI, you can integrate a migration tool like Alembic to manage your database schema changes. By defining a CLI command that invokes Alembic's migration commands, you can streamline the process of applying or rolling back migrations directly from the command line.

Here's an example of how you might set up such a command using `click` and Alembic:

```python
import click
from alembic import command
from alembic.config import Config

@click.group()
def cli():
    """Command-line interface for managing database migrations."""
    pass

@cli.command()
def upgrade():
    """Apply database migrations."""
    alembic_cfg Config("alembic.ini")
    command.upgrade(alembic_cfg, "head")
    print("Database migrations applied.")

@cli.command()
def downgrade():
    """Revert database migrations."""
    alembic_cfg Config("alembic.ini")
    command.downgrade(alembic_cfg, "-1")
    print("Database migrations reverted.")

if __name__ '__main__':
    cli()
```

In this example, the `upgrade` command applies the latest migrations, while the `downgrade` command reverts the most recent migration. The `alembic.ini` configuration file is used to specify the database connection and migration settings. This setup allows you to manage database schema changes efficiently from the command line.

Another common use case for CLI tools in a FastAPI application is testing. Automating testing via CLI commands can ensure that your codebase remains reliable and functional. You might use `pytest` for testing, and by creating a CLI command to run tests, you can easily incorporate this step into your development process.

Here's an example of how you might set up a CLI command to run tests using `click`:

```python
import click
import pytest

@click.group()
def cli():
    """Command-line interface for testing and other utilities."""
    pass

@cli.command()
def test():
    """Run tests using pytest."""
    result pytest.main()
    if result 0:
        print("All tests passed.")
    else:
        print("Some tests failed.")
    return result

if __name__ '__main__':
```

```
    cli()
```

In this code, the `test` command executes `pytest.main()`, which runs all tests in the codebase. Depending on the test results, it prints a message indicating whether all tests passed or if some failed. This command can be integrated into your continuous integration (CI) pipeline to automatically run tests on each commit.

Beyond testing and migration, you might also use CLI commands for deployment tasks. For example, you might create a command to package your FastAPI application and deploy it to a server or cloud service. Automating deployment tasks through CLI commands can reduce manual errors and streamline the deployment process.

Consider a CLI command for deploying your application to a cloud service. This command might involve packaging your application, uploading it to a cloud service, and starting the application. Here's a simplified example:

```python
import click
import subprocess

@click.group()
def cli():
    """Command-line interface for deployment tasks."""
    pass

@cli.command()
def deploy():
    """Package and deploy the FastAPI application."""
    print("Packaging the application...")
    subprocess.run(["tar", "-czf", "app.tar.gz", "app/"], checkTrue)


     print("Uploading to cloud service...")
```

```
Placeholder for upload command
        subprocess.run(["cloud-cli", "upload", "app.tar.gz"],
checkTrue)


 print("Starting application...")
Placeholder for start command
subprocess.run(["cloud-cli", "start", "app"], checkTrue)


 print("Deployment completed.")

if __name__ '__main__':
  cli()
```

In this example, the `deploy` command packages the application into a tarball and simulates uploading and starting the application on a cloud service. You would replace the placeholders with actual commands for your deployment process.

By leveraging CLI commands effectively, you can streamline various aspects of managing and deploying your FastAPI application. Whether it's running tests, applying database migrations, or handling deployment tasks, a well-designed CLI can greatly enhance your development workflow and improve productivity.

CHAPTER 30: INTEGRATING WITH FRONTEND FRAMEWORKS

FastAPI, a modern, high-performance web framework for building APIs with Python 3.7+, offers not only a robust backend solution but also seamless integration capabilities with various frontend frameworks. This integration process involves ensuring smooth communication between the backend API and the frontend application, handling Cross-Origin Resource Sharing (CORS) issues, setting up API endpoints, and managing the interactions between frontend and backend systems. In this section, we will explore how to connect FastAPI with popular frontend frameworks, including React, Vue.js, and Angular.

To start, it is essential to understand the principles behind integrating FastAPI with frontend frameworks. The primary goal is to enable the frontend application to communicate efficiently with the FastAPI backend. This involves setting up the backend API to handle requests and responses, configuring CORS to allow cross-origin requests, and ensuring that the frontend framework can make API calls to retrieve or send data.

Handling CORS

CORS is a security feature implemented by browsers to prevent unauthorized requests between different origins. When a frontend application hosted on one domain attempts to make a request to an API hosted on a different domain, the browser enforces CORS policies to ensure that the request is allowed. In the context of integrating FastAPI with frontend frameworks, configuring CORS correctly is crucial to ensure that the frontend application can communicate with the backend without encountering security errors.

FastAPI provides built-in support for configuring CORS via the `fastapi.middleware.cors.CORSMiddleware`. This middleware allows you to specify which origins are permitted to make requests to your API. To set up CORS, you need to include the `CORSMiddleware` in your FastAPI application and configure it with the appropriate parameters. Here is an example of how to configure CORS in a FastAPI application:

```python
from fastapi import FastAPI
from fastapi.middleware.cors import CORSMiddleware

app FastAPI()

orig_redirect_urls [
  "http://localhost:3000",  URL for React development server
  "http://localhost:8080",  URL for Vue.js development server
    "http://localhost:4200",   URL for Angular development server
]

app.add_middleware(
  CORSMiddleware,
  allow_originsorig_redirect_urls,
  allow_credentialsTrue,
  allow_methods[""],  Allows all HTTP methods
  allow_headers[""],  Allows all headers
```

)
```

In this configuration, `allow_origins` specifies the list of domains that are permitted to access the FastAPI application. The `allow_credentials` parameter enables the inclusion of credentials in requests, such as cookies or authentication tokens. The `allow_methods` and `allow_headers` parameters are set to `[""]` to permit all HTTP methods and headers, respectively. Adjust these settings according to your application's requirements for security and functionality.

Setting Up API Endpoints

Once CORS is properly configured, the next step is to set up the API endpoints in FastAPI. These endpoints define the routes that the frontend application can use to interact with the backend. FastAPI utilizes Python's type hints to provide automatic validation, serialization, and documentation of API endpoints. Defining endpoints is straightforward and follows a pattern of associating URL paths with functions that handle incoming requests.

Here is an example of defining a simple API endpoint in FastAPI:

```python
from fastapi import FastAPI

app FastAPI()

@app.get("/api/items/")
async def read_items():
    return {"items": ["item1", "item2", "item3"]}

@app.post("/api/items/")
async def create_item(item: dict):
    Simulate item creation
    return {"item": item, "status": "created"}
```
```

In this example, the `read_items` function handles GET requests to the `/api/items/` endpoint and returns a list of items. The `create_item` function handles POST requests to the same endpoint and simulates the creation of a new item based on the data provided in the request body.

The frontend application can use these endpoints to retrieve and send data. For instance, in a React application, you might use the `fetch` API or libraries like `axios` to make HTTP requests to these endpoints. Similarly, Vue.js and Angular have their respective methods and libraries for making API calls.

Managing Frontend-Backend Interactions

With CORS configured and API endpoints established, managing the interactions between the frontend and backend is the next critical step. This involves ensuring that the frontend application can make API requests and handle responses appropriately. Each frontend framework has its methods for making HTTP requests and managing asynchronous operations.

In React, for example, you might use the `fetch` API to make requests to the FastAPI backend:

```javascript
import React, { useState, useEffect } from 'react';

function App() {
  const [items, setItems] useState([]);

    useEffect(() > {
     fetch('http://localhost:8000/api/items/')
       .then(response > response.json())
       .then(data > setItems(data.items));
  }, []);

    return (
```

```
    <div>
      <h1>Items</h1>
      <ul>
        {items.map(item > (
          <li key{item}>{item}</li>
        ))}
      </ul>
    </div>
  );
}

export default App;
```

This example demonstrates how to use the `fetch` API to retrieve data from the FastAPI endpoint and update the React component's state with the received data. Vue.js and Angular follow similar patterns for making API calls and handling responses.

By effectively integrating FastAPI with frontend frameworks, you can create a cohesive and functional web application where the frontend and backend communicate seamlessly. Ensuring proper CORS configuration, setting up well-defined API endpoints, and managing frontend-backend interactions are crucial steps in achieving a successful integration.

Integrating FastAPI with frontend frameworks requires a thorough understanding of both backend and frontend development principles. To achieve a seamless interaction between these two layers, one must address several key aspects: handling Cross-Origin Resource Sharing (CORS), setting up API endpoints, and managing the interactions between the frontend and backend components.

Cross-Origin Resource Sharing (CORS) is a crucial aspect of integrating FastAPI with a frontend framework. When a frontend application makes requests to a backend server hosted on a different domain, CORS policies must be correctly configured to ensure that these requests are allowed. FastAPI simplifies this process through its support for CORS middleware. To enable CORS in a FastAPI application, one must first install the `fastapi` and `starlette` packages, as the latter provides the necessary middleware.

In your FastAPI application, you would configure CORS by importing the `CORSMiddleware` from `starlette.middleware.cors`. Here is a step-by-step guide on setting up CORS:

1. Installation: Ensure you have `fastapi` and `uvicorn` installed, and then install `starlette` if it is not already included.
```bash
pip install fastapi uvicorn starlette
```

2. Configuration: Import `CORSMiddleware` in your FastAPI application file.
```python
from fastapi import FastAPI
from starlette.middleware.cors import CORSMiddleware
```

3. Applying Middleware: Instantiate the FastAPI app and add `CORSMiddleware` to it.
```python
app FastAPI()

 app.add_middleware(
  CORSMiddleware,
   allow_origins[""],  Adjust this to specific domains for more
security
  allow_credentialsTrue,
  allow_methods[""],  Specify allowed HTTP methods
  allow_headers[""],  Specify allowed headers
```

```
)
```

The `allow_origins` parameter should be tailored to your deployment environment. For development, allowing all origins (`""`), as shown above, is acceptable. In a production setting, it is advisable to restrict this to specific domains to enhance security.

Once CORS is correctly set up, you can proceed to create and configure API endpoints that the frontend will interact with. FastAPI provides a straightforward way to define routes using Python's async functions, allowing for efficient and asynchronous processing of requests.

Here's an example of setting up a basic API endpoint:

1. Defining Routes: Use FastAPI's `@app.get` or `@app.post` decorators to define your endpoints.

```python
@app.get("/items/{item_id}")
async def read_item(item_id: int):
    return {"item_id": item_id}
```

This route handles GET requests and returns a JSON response with the item ID provided in the URL path.

2. Handling POST Requests: Similarly, you can handle POST requests by defining a route that processes request data.

```python
from pydantic import BaseModel

 class Item(BaseModel):
    name: str
    description: str  None
    price: float
    tax: float  None
```

```
 @app.post("/items/")
async def create_item(item: Item):
  return {"item": item}
```

This endpoint accepts a JSON payload that conforms to the `Item` model and returns the received data.

For frontend integration, you will typically use JavaScript or TypeScript code to interact with these API endpoints. Here's how you might handle API calls in popular frontend frameworks like React, Vue.js, and Angular:

1. React: Use the `fetch` API or a library like `axios` to make HTTP requests.

```javascript
import React, { useState, useEffect } from 'react';
import axios from 'axios';

 function App() {
  const [items, setItems]  useState([]);

    useEffect(() > {
    axios.get('http://localhost:8000/items/1')
      .then(response > setItems(response.data))
     .catch(error > console.error('Error fetching data:', error));
  }, []);

    return (
    <div>
      <h1>Items</h1>
      <pre>{JSON.stringify(items, null, 2)}</pre>
    </div>
  );
}

 export default App;
```

2. Vue.js: Similarly, use `axios` or Vue's `fetch` API to interact with the backend.

```javascript
<template>
  <div>
    <h1>Items</h1>
    <pre>{{ items }}</pre>
  </div>
</template>

<script>
import axios from 'axios';

export default {
  data() {
    return {
      items: null
    };
  },
  mounted() {
    axios.get('http://localhost:8000/items/1')
      .then(response > {
        this.items  response.data;
      })
      .catch(error > console.error('Error fetching data:', error));
  }
}
</script>
```

3. Angular: Use Angular's `HttpClient` to perform HTTP operations.

```typescript
import { Component, OnInit } from '@angular/core';
import { HttpClient } from '@angular/common/http';

@Component({
```

```
  selector: 'app-root',
  templateUrl: './app.component.html',
  styleUrls: ['./app.component.css']
})
export class AppComponent implements OnInit {
  items: any;

    constructor(private http: HttpClient) {}

    ngOnInit() {
    this.http.get('http://localhost:8000/items/1')
      .subscribe(
        data > this.items  data,
        error > console.error('Error fetching data:', error)
      );
  }
}
```

Each framework requires a slightly different approach for making HTTP requests and handling responses, but the fundamental concept remains the same: the frontend sends requests to the backend, which processes them and returns data for the frontend to display.

By combining FastAPI's efficient backend capabilities with the dynamic interfaces of modern frontend frameworks, you can build robust and interactive web applications. Ensuring proper CORS configuration, creating well-defined API endpoints, and using the appropriate methods for frontend-backend communication are essential steps in this integration process.

Setting up API endpoints is a fundamental aspect of integrating FastAPI with frontend frameworks. In FastAPI, defining endpoints involves creating path operations that correspond to HTTP methods. These endpoints can then be consumed by frontend applications through AJAX calls or other HTTP request methods.

To define an endpoint in FastAPI, you need to use decorators provided by the FastAPI framework, such as `@app.get()`, `@app.post()`, `@app.put()`, and `@app.delete()`. Each decorator specifies the HTTP method and the path of the endpoint. For instance, to create a simple API endpoint that returns a list of items, you would do the following:

```python
from fastapi import FastAPI
from typing import List

app FastAPI()

@app.get("/items/", response_modelList[str])
async def read_items():
  return ["Item 1", "Item 2", "Item 3"]
```

In this example, the `@app.get("/items/")` decorator defines a GET request endpoint at the path `/items/`, and the `response_model` parameter specifies that the endpoint will return a list of strings. FastAPI automatically generates the required JSON response format.

For POST requests, you can accept data from the client using request bodies. FastAPI supports various data types for request bodies, including Pydantic models, which allow for complex data validation. Here is an example of a POST endpoint that accepts a JSON object with specific fields:

```python
from pydantic import BaseModel

class Item(BaseModel):
  name: str
  description: str
  price: float

@app.post("/items/", response_modelItem)
```

```
async def create_item(item: Item):
    return item
```

In this case, the `Item` class, derived from `BaseModel`, defines the expected structure of the incoming request. The endpoint `/items/` accepts POST requests with a JSON body that conforms to this structure and returns the received item.

With your API endpoints defined, the next step is to manage the interactions between the frontend and backend. Frontend frameworks like React, Vue.js, and Angular each have their methods for making HTTP requests to these endpoints.

In React, you can use the `fetch` API or libraries such as Axios to perform HTTP requests. For example, to fetch a list of items from the `/items/` endpoint, you could use the following React code:

```javascript
import React, { useEffect, useState } from 'react';

function ItemList() {
  const [items, setItems]  useState([]);

    useEffect(() > {
     fetch('http://localhost:8000/items/')
        .then(response > response.json())
        .then(data > setItems(data));
  }, []);

    return (
     <ul>
        {items.map(item > (
           <li key{item}>{item}</li>
        ))}
     </ul>
  );
}
```

```
export default ItemList;
```

This component uses the `fetch` function to send a GET request to the FastAPI backend. The response is then processed and used to update the component's state.

In Vue.js, the `axios` library is commonly used for HTTP requests. Here is an example of how you might fetch data in a Vue component:

```javascript
<template>
  <ul>
    <li v-for"item in items" :key"item">{{ item }}</li>
  </ul>
</template>

<script>
import axios from 'axios';

export default {
  data() {
    return {
      items: []
    };
  },
  created() {
    axios.get('http://localhost:8000/items/')
      .then(response > {
        this.items  response.data;
      });
  }
};
</script>
```

In this Vue component, the `axios.get()` method sends a GET

request to the FastAPI server. Upon receiving the response, the data is stored in the `items` array, which is then rendered in the template.

Angular, on the other hand, uses its built-in `HttpClient` service for making HTTP requests. Here is how you can make a GET request in an Angular service:

```typescript
import { Injectable } from '@angular/core';
import { HttpClient } from '@angular/common/http';
import { Observable } from 'rxjs';

@Injectable({
  providedIn: 'root'
})
export class ItemService {
  private apiUrl  'http://localhost:8000/items/';

    constructor(private http: HttpClient) { }

    getItems(): Observable<string[]> {
     return this.http.get<string[]>(this.apiUrl);
  }
}
```

The `ItemService` class uses the `HttpClient` service to send a GET request to the FastAPI backend. This service can be injected into Angular components where the data can be consumed and displayed.

Each of these frontend frameworks offers unique tools and methods for integrating with FastAPI, but the principles of HTTP requests and responses remain consistent across them. Proper handling of CORS, correct setup of API endpoints, and effective management of frontend-backend interactions are essential for creating a functional and efficient full-stack application.

By understanding how to set up and interact with these APIs across different frontend frameworks, developers can ensure that their applications are well-integrated and responsive to user interactions.

CHAPTER 31: HANDLING AUTHENTICATION AND AUTHORIZATION

In the realm of API security, handling authentication and authorization is fundamental to safeguarding sensitive information and ensuring that users interact with the system according to their designated permissions. This section will elucidate the mechanisms and strategies for implementing robust authentication and authorization practices within an application. We will explore a range of methods including OAuth2, JWT tokens, and session-based authentication, and discuss the intricacies of role-based access control (RBAC) to manage user roles and permissions effectively.

Authentication is the process of verifying the identity of a user or system. It involves confirming that the entity attempting to access the system is who it claims to be. Authorization, on the other hand, determines what an authenticated entity is permitted to do within the system. Together, these processes form a comprehensive approach to protecting an API.

One of the most widely adopted authentication strategies is OAuth2, an authorization framework that allows applications to obtain limited access to user accounts on an HTTP service. OAuth2 operates through tokens, which serve as proof of authentication. In the OAuth2 flow, a user grants a third-party application access to their resources without sharing their credentials with the application. Instead, the application receives an access token, which it uses to access resources on behalf of the user.

OAuth2 supports several grant types, each suited to different use cases. The authorization code grant type is commonly used in web applications where users are redirected to an authorization server to log in. After successful authentication, the server redirects the user back to the application with an authorization code, which the application exchanges for an access token. This method is considered secure as it involves server-to-server communication for token exchange, reducing exposure to client-side vulnerabilities.

The implicit grant type is designed for client-side applications that run in the user's browser, such as single-page applications. In this flow, the access token is returned directly in the URL fragment after the user logs in, making it suitable for environments where the application cannot securely store secrets. However, this method is less secure compared to the authorization code grant because tokens are exposed in the URL.

The resource owner password credentials grant is used when the user trusts the application with their credentials directly. This approach is generally less secure and should only be used when there is a high level of trust between the user and the application. It involves sending the user's username and password to the authorization server to obtain an access token.

The client credentials grant is used for applications that need to access resources on their own behalf rather than on behalf of a user. This method is applicable for machine-to-machine communication where the application authenticates using its own credentials.

JSON Web Tokens (JWT) are another popular method for authentication and authorization. A JWT is a compact, URL-safe token format that encodes claims about an entity and optionally includes a signature. JWTs are self-contained, meaning they carry all the necessary information for authentication and authorization within the token itself, thereby reducing the need for server-side session storage.

A JWT consists of three parts: the header, payload, and signature. The header typically specifies the token type and signing algorithm. The payload contains claims, which are statements about an entity (e.g., user ID, roles) and other data. The signature is generated by signing the header and payload with a secret key or public/private key pair. This signature ensures the integrity of the token and verifies that it has not been tampered with.

JWTs are widely used for stateless authentication, where the server does not need to maintain session state between requests. This approach is particularly useful for distributed systems and microservices, where maintaining session state across different components can be challenging.

Session-based authentication, by contrast, involves creating and maintaining a session on the server side. When a user logs in, the server generates a unique session identifier, which is stored on the client side, typically in a cookie. The server then associates this identifier with the user's session data. Each subsequent request includes the session identifier, allowing the server to retrieve the associated session data and authenticate the user.

Session-based authentication is well-suited for traditional web applications where the server can maintain session state. It allows for centralized session management and can provide additional security features, such as session expiration and revocation. However, managing sessions across distributed systems can be complex and may require additional mechanisms like distributed session stores or session replication.

In addition to these authentication mechanisms, implementing role-based access control (RBAC) is essential for managing permissions and access to resources based on user roles. RBAC involves defining roles and assigning permissions to those roles. Users are then assigned to roles, which determines their access rights within the application.

In an RBAC system, roles represent a collection of permissions that can be assigned to users. Permissions define what actions users can perform and what resources they can access. For example, an application might have roles such as "Admin," "Editor," and "Viewer," each with different levels of access to various parts of the application.

RBAC simplifies the management of user permissions by grouping permissions into roles. When a user's role changes, only the role assignment needs to be updated, rather than modifying individual permissions. This approach enhances scalability and reduces the complexity of managing permissions across a large number of users.

Implementing RBAC effectively involves designing a role hierarchy and ensuring that roles are assigned appropriately based on users' responsibilities and needs. Additionally, it is crucial to review and update roles and permissions regularly to adapt to changes in the application and organizational requirements.

In summary, the choice of authentication and authorization strategies significantly impacts the security and usability of an API. By understanding and applying OAuth2, JWTs, and session-based authentication, along with implementing RBAC, developers can create secure and efficient systems that protect sensitive information and manage user access effectively.

The client credentials grant type is tailored for server-to-server communication where no user interaction is involved. In this scenario, the client itself is the resource owner. The client application exchanges its own credentials for an access token, which it uses to authenticate itself when accessing resources on a resource server. This grant type is particularly useful for automated processes and microservices that need to authenticate with an API without user intervention.

The final OAuth2 grant type, the device code grant, is used for devices with limited input capabilities, such as smart TVs or gaming consoles. In this flow, the user is provided with a code to enter on a separate device with a more robust interface. The device then polls the authorization server to exchange the code for an access token once the user has authenticated.

JSON Web Tokens (JWTs) are another popular mechanism for managing authentication. A JWT is a compact, URL-safe token that represents claims about an entity and is typically used in scenarios where tokens need to be transmitted over a network. JWTs contain three parts: a header, a payload, and a signature. The header typically indicates the algorithm used for signing the token, while the payload contains the claims or the actual data, such as user information or permissions. The signature is generated by encoding the header and payload with a secret key or public/private key pair.

One of the key advantages of using JWTs is that they are self-contained, meaning they carry the necessary information to authenticate the user and verify their identity without requiring additional queries to a database. This stateless nature of JWTs makes them highly scalable, as the server does not need to maintain session state between requests. However, because JWTs include claims within the token itself, they can become large if excessive data is included in the payload. Therefore, it's crucial to limit the size of the claims to avoid performance issues.

While JWTs are advantageous for their self-contained and stateless nature, session-based authentication remains a traditional and widely used approach. In session-based authentication, a server maintains session state for each user. After a user successfully authenticates, the server creates a session and returns a session ID to the client, which is typically stored in a cookie. This session ID is then sent with each subsequent request to authenticate the user.

The server retrieves the session data from a session store, which can be an in-memory store, a database, or a distributed cache. This approach provides a centralized way to manage user sessions and allows for easy revocation of access by deleting the session from the store. However, maintaining session state on the server introduces scalability challenges, as the server must handle and store session data for all users.

Session-based authentication also requires secure management of session identifiers to prevent session fixation and hijacking attacks. Implementing secure cookie attributes such as the `HttpOnly` and `Secure` flags can mitigate some of these risks. The `HttpOnly` flag ensures that cookies cannot be accessed through client-side scripts, while the `Secure` flag ensures that cookies are only sent over HTTPS.

Role-based access control (RBAC) is an essential strategy for managing user permissions and securing different parts of an application based on user roles. RBAC assigns users to roles, and roles are granted specific permissions or access rights. This approach simplifies permission management by grouping users with similar access needs into roles, which can then be easily managed and adjusted.

Implementing RBAC involves defining roles within the system

and associating them with specific permissions. For instance, an application might have roles such as "Admin," "Editor," and "Viewer," each with distinct levels of access to various resources. The Admin role might have full access to all resources, while the Editor role might have limited access to certain resources with the ability to create or modify content, and the Viewer role might only have read-only access.

Access control decisions are made based on the roles assigned to users and the permissions associated with those roles. This mechanism ensures that users can only access resources and perform actions that align with their role. For example, an Admin might be allowed to delete records, while an Editor might only be able to update or create records without deletion rights.

To implement RBAC effectively, it is important to establish a clear and consistent role hierarchy and ensure that permissions are accurately assigned and enforced. This requires careful planning and consideration of the various access needs of different user groups. Additionally, periodic reviews and audits of roles and permissions can help maintain the integrity of the access control system and address any potential security issues.

In summary, managing authentication and authorization is a multifaceted process that involves choosing the appropriate strategies and mechanisms to protect your API and manage user access. Whether using OAuth2 for delegated access, JWTs for stateless authentication, or session-based authentication for stateful management, each approach has its own strengths and considerations. Implementing role-based access control further enhances security by defining and enforcing access permissions based on user roles, ensuring that users only interact with resources according to their designated access levels.

or distributed cache, a database, or other persistent

storage mechanisms. This session data often includes user-specific information such as roles and permissions, which can be quickly accessed to authorize requests. Session-based authentication provides a straightforward method of managing user state but comes with its own set of challenges, particularly in scaling. As the number of users increases, the server must handle a larger volume of session data, potentially leading to performance bottlenecks.

To address these scaling concerns, session data can be stored in distributed caches such as Redis or Memcached, which provide fast access and are designed to handle large volumes of data. These systems help maintain session state across multiple server instances, making them suitable for high-traffic applications. Furthermore, load balancers can be employed to distribute requests across different servers, ensuring that no single server becomes a performance bottleneck.

Role-Based Access Control (RBAC) is a crucial concept in managing authorization. RBAC involves assigning users to roles and defining permissions associated with these roles. The fundamental principle is that access to resources is granted based on the roles assigned to users rather than individual user identities. This approach simplifies management by grouping permissions into roles, which can be assigned to users or user groups, and ensures that users have only the permissions necessary for their roles.

In implementing RBAC, it is essential to first identify the various roles within the application and the corresponding permissions each role should have. Roles are typically defined based on job functions, responsibilities, or access needs. For instance, a typical application might have roles such as Admin, Manager, and User, each with different levels of access to resources and functionalities.

Once roles are defined, the next step is to map these roles

to permissions. Permissions define what actions a role can perform on resources, such as read, write, or delete operations. For example, an Admin role might have permissions to create, read, update, and delete resources, while a User role might only have permission to read resources.

The implementation of RBAC can be achieved through various methods, depending on the technology stack and application requirements. In a database-driven application, roles and permissions are often stored in relational databases, with tables representing roles, users, and permissions. This data is then queried to enforce access control decisions. In web applications, RBAC is typically integrated into the authorization layer of the application's security architecture.

To enhance the security of RBAC, it is prudent to adopt the principle of least privilege, ensuring that users are granted only the permissions necessary for their specific roles. This minimizes the risk of unauthorized access and potential misuse of permissions. Additionally, regular audits and reviews of roles and permissions are essential to ensure that they remain aligned with the organization's security policies and user responsibilities.

Another aspect of access control is the concept of attribute-based access control (ABAC), which offers a more dynamic and granular approach compared to RBAC. In ABAC, access decisions are based on attributes such as user attributes, resource attributes, and environmental conditions. For example, access to a resource might be granted based on a combination of user department, resource sensitivity, and time of day. ABAC provides greater flexibility and can accommodate more complex access control scenarios.

Integrating authentication and authorization mechanisms effectively requires a comprehensive approach to security, ensuring that all potential vulnerabilities are addressed. This includes implementing secure communication channels, such as HTTPS, to protect tokens and credentials from being intercepted during transmission. Additionally, it is crucial to validate and sanitize all user inputs to prevent common security threats such as SQL injection and cross-site scripting (XSS).

Token management is another critical consideration. For both JWTs and OAuth2 tokens, it is important to implement mechanisms for token expiration and revocation. Tokens should have a limited lifespan to reduce the risk of misuse if they are compromised. Additionally, the application should provide functionality for revoking tokens when necessary, such as in cases of user account compromise or when a user's role or permissions change.

Overall, handling authentication and authorization effectively involves selecting appropriate strategies and implementing them in a secure manner. Whether using OAuth2, JWT tokens, session-based authentication, or RBAC, it is essential to ensure that the chosen methods align with the application's security requirements and provide a robust framework for protecting sensitive resources and managing user access. By combining these approaches with best practices in security management, you can create a secure and efficient system for managing user authentication and authorization.

CHAPTER 32: MANAGING DATABASE TRANSACTIONS

Effective management of database transactions is a cornerstone of ensuring data integrity and consistency within an application. This discussion delves into transaction management in FastAPI, focusing on handling commit and rollback operations, managing transaction scopes, and integrating with both SQL and NoSQL databases. The principles outlined here will equip you to handle transactions reliably, ensuring consistent and reliable database operations across different scenarios.

Transactions are fundamental to maintaining data integrity in a database system. A transaction represents a sequence of operations performed as a single logical unit of work. The key properties of transactions are encapsulated in the ACID model, which stands for Atomicity, Consistency, Isolation, and Durability. Atomicity ensures that a transaction is either fully completed or not executed at all, meaning that if any part of the transaction fails, the entire transaction is rolled back to its initial state. Consistency guarantees that a transaction transforms the database from one valid state to another, maintaining database constraints and rules. Isolation ensures that the operations of one transaction are not visible to other transactions until they are completed, thus preventing concurrent transactions from interfering with each other. Durability assures that once a transaction is committed, its effects are permanently recorded in the database, even in the event of a system crash.

In FastAPI, transaction management is typically handled through the use of database session objects, which are responsible for coordinating the execution of transactional operations. When using SQL databases, such as PostgreSQL or MySQL, the database session is often managed through an Object-Relational Mapping (ORM) tool like SQLAlchemy. SQLAlchemy provides a session object that encapsulates transaction management. The session object allows you to perform commit and rollback operations, ensuring that transactions are handled according to the ACID principles.

To manage transactions in FastAPI with SQLAlchemy, you begin by creating a session object, usually within a context manager to ensure proper resource management. The session object is used to execute database operations, and you can explicitly commit or rollback transactions based on the outcome of these operations. For example, within a context manager, you can execute a series of database operations and then commit the transaction if all operations succeed. If an error occurs, you can rollback the transaction to maintain data integrity.

Consider the following example, where a transaction is managed within a FastAPI route handler using SQLAlchemy:

```python
from fastapi import FastAPI, HTTPException
from sqlalchemy.orm import Session
from . import models, schemas, database

app FastAPI()
```

```
@app.post("/items/")
async def create_item(item: schemas.ItemCreate, db: Session
Depends(database.get_db)):
  db_item models.Item(item.dict())
  try:
    db.add(db_item)
    db.commit()
    db.refresh(db_item)
  except Exception as e:
    db.rollback()
        raise HTTPException(status_code500, detail"An error
occurred")
  return db_item
```

In this example, the `db.commit()` operation finalizes the transaction, while `db.rollback()` ensures that any changes are reverted if an exception is raised.

When dealing with NoSQL databases, such as MongoDB or Couchbase, the approach to transaction management can differ significantly due to the varying support for transactions in NoSQL systems. For instance, MongoDB provides support for multi-document transactions starting with version 4.0. When working with MongoDB, transactions are managed at the session level, and you can start, commit, or abort transactions using the MongoDB driver's API.

Here's a basic example of managing transactions in MongoDB using the `pymongo` library:

```python
from pymongo import MongoClient
from pymongo.errors import PyMongoError

client MongoClient('mongodb://localhost:27017/')
db client.mydatabase
```

```
def create_item(item):
  with client.start_session() as session:
    with session.start_transaction():
      try:
        db.items.insert_one(item, sessionsession)
         Additional operations can be performed here
      except PyMongoError as e:
        session.abort_transaction()
          raise HTTPException(status_code500, detail"An error
occurred")
```

In this case, `start_session()` begins a new session, and `start_transaction()` initiates a transaction within that session. If an error occurs, `abort_transaction()` is used to revert any changes made during the transaction.

Effective transaction management also involves understanding and managing transaction scopes. A transaction scope defines the boundaries within which a transaction operates. In a web application, this often means managing transactions within the lifecycle of a request. Ensuring that transactions are properly scoped prevents issues such as long-running transactions that can hold locks on database resources, potentially affecting system performance and concurrency.

In summary, managing database transactions involves ensuring that operations adhere to the ACID principles, using appropriate tools and methods based on the type of database employed. By effectively handling commit and rollback operations, and managing transaction scopes, you can ensure that your application maintains data integrity and consistency, regardless of the underlying database system.

When working with SQLAlchemy in FastAPI, managing transactions typically involves creating and managing a

`Session` object. This object is central to handling database interactions and ensuring that transactions adhere to the ACID properties. For instance, in a FastAPI application, you might use dependency injection to provide a `Session` object to your route handlers. This allows you to perform operations within a transactional context, ensuring that all database operations are completed successfully before committing the transaction.

To begin with, you would generally create a session factory using `sessionmaker` from SQLAlchemy, which configures how sessions are instantiated. When a request is made to your FastAPI application, a new session is created from this factory. Using a context manager ensures that the session is properly managed. Within the context of a request, operations are performed and tracked by the session. If all operations succeed, the transaction is committed, making all changes permanent. If an error occurs, the session is rolled back, undoing any partial changes made during the transaction.

For example, consider a FastAPI route that handles creating a new user. Within this route, you would start by opening a session, perform the necessary operations to insert the user into the database, and then commit the transaction if no errors are encountered. Here's a simplified illustration of how this might look in code:

```python
from fastapi import FastAPI, HTTPException, Depends
from sqlalchemy.orm import Session
from sqlalchemy.exc import SQLAlchemyError

app FastAPI()

Dependency to get the database session
def get_db():
  db SessionLocal()  SessionLocal is a session factory
  try:
```

```
    yield db
  finally:
    db.close()

@app.post("/users/")
def create_user(user: UserCreate, db: Session
Depends(get_db)):
  new_user User(user.dict())
  try:
    db.add(new_user)
    db.commit()
    return new_user
  except SQLAlchemyError:
    db.rollback()
        raise HTTPException(status_code400, detail"Failed to
create user")
```

In this example, `SessionLocal` is a session factory created earlier in the application configuration. The `create_user` function receives the `Session` object through dependency injection. It attempts to add and commit a new user. If an exception occurs, the transaction is rolled back to ensure that no partial changes are saved, maintaining the integrity of the database.

When it comes to integrating with NoSQL databases, the transaction management approach varies depending on the specific database technology. Many NoSQL databases, such as MongoDB, provide their own mechanisms for handling transactions. For instance, MongoDB offers support for multi-document transactions, which are essential for ensuring consistency across multiple operations.

In MongoDB, transactions are handled through the use of session objects provided by the database driver. When a transaction is started, operations are performed within the context of this session. The session tracks changes and can be committed or aborted based on the success of the operations. Here's an example of managing transactions with MongoDB using the Python driver:

```python
from pymongo import MongoClient
from pymongo.errors import PyMongoError

client MongoClient('mongodb://localhost:27017/')
db client.mydatabase

def create_user(user):
  session client.start_session()
  try:
    with session.start_transaction():
      db.users.insert_one(user, sessionsession)
       db.logs.insert_one({"action": "create_user", "user": user},
sessionsession)
  except PyMongoError:
    session.abort_transaction()
    raise
  finally:
    session.end_session()
```

In this code snippet, a session is started and used to handle a transaction involving multiple operations: inserting a new user and logging the action. If any part of the transaction fails, the transaction is aborted, and no changes are applied to the database. This ensures that either all operations are successfully applied or none are.

When managing transactions in FastAPI, whether using SQL or NoSQL databases, it's crucial to handle exceptions and roll back transactions appropriately to maintain data integrity. Additionally, understanding the specific transaction management features of your chosen database is essential for implementing reliable and consistent operations.

Transaction scopes, which define the boundaries within which transactions are managed, are also important. A transaction scope typically starts with the beginning of a transaction and ends with either a commit or a rollback. Properly managing these scopes ensures that all operations within a scope are treated as a single unit of work, either all succeeding or all failing together. This is vital for applications that require strong consistency and reliability in their database interactions.

Managing database transactions in FastAPI also extends to integrating with NoSQL databases, where the concepts of transaction management differ from those used in relational databases. NoSQL databases like MongoDB, Couchbase, and Cassandra often handle transactions in a manner specific to their underlying architecture and use cases.

For instance, in MongoDB, transactions are supported in replica sets and sharded clusters, allowing multiple operations to be executed as a single atomic operation. MongoDB's transactions provide isolation and atomicity, similar to ACID properties in relational databases. To use transactions in MongoDB with FastAPI, you need to work with the MongoDB client and manage sessions explicitly. The `pymongo` library, which is commonly used with MongoDB, allows you to create a client session and perform operations within that session. Transactions are initiated by starting a session, and operations within the session are committed or aborted based on success or failure.

Here's an example of handling transactions with MongoDB in a FastAPI application:

```python
from fastapi import FastAPI, HTTPException
from pymongo import MongoClient
```

```
from pymongo.errors import PyMongoError

app FastAPI()
client MongoClient("mongodb://localhost:27017/")
db client.mydatabase

@app.post("/users/")
def create_user(user: dict):
  session client.start_session()
  try:
    with session.start_transaction():
      db.users.insert_one(user, sessionsession)
      return user
  except PyMongoError:
    session.abort_transaction()
        raise HTTPException(status_code400, detail"Failed to create user")
  finally:
    session.end_session()
```

In this example, a session is started with `client.start_session()`, and a transaction is initiated within the context of the session. If an exception is raised, the transaction is aborted. Upon successful completion, the transaction is committed. This approach ensures that the operations either succeed as a unit or fail, maintaining data integrity.

For databases like Couchbase and Cassandra, transaction management is handled differently due to their distributed nature and eventual consistency models. Couchbase provides support for multi-document ACID transactions, whereas Cassandra, designed for high availability and scalability, uses an eventual consistency model with limited support for traditional transactions. For Cassandra, developers typically handle consistency at the application level, using techniques such as compensating transactions or conflict resolution strategies.

When dealing with NoSQL databases, it's essential to understand the database's transaction capabilities and limitations. For databases that do not support traditional ACID transactions, designing application-level mechanisms to ensure data consistency and integrity is crucial. This might involve implementing custom logic to handle retries, conflict resolution, and consistency checks.

Effective transaction management also involves understanding transaction scopes. The scope of a transaction defines the boundaries within which the operations are executed. In a web application context, the scope is often limited to the duration of a request. This means that each request can initiate and manage its transaction independently. However, in cases where multiple requests or processes need to coordinate transactions, additional mechanisms, such as distributed transactions or two-phase commits, may be required.

Distributed transactions are more complex and involve coordinating transactions across multiple systems or databases. Implementing distributed transactions typically requires specialized protocols and tools to ensure that all participating systems commit or rollback changes in a coordinated manner. Technologies like the two-phase commit protocol can be used to manage distributed transactions, ensuring that all involved systems reach a consensus on whether to commit or abort the transaction.

In FastAPI, transaction management is not limited to SQL and NoSQL databases but also extends to interactions with external services and APIs. For instance, when integrating with external services that require transactional guarantees, you might need to manage transactions at a higher level, coordinating between internal database operations and external service calls.

To summarize, managing database transactions effectively involves understanding the principles of ACID transactions, leveraging the capabilities of the chosen database system, and implementing appropriate mechanisms to ensure data integrity and consistency. Whether working with SQL or NoSQL databases, FastAPI provides the tools and flexibility to manage transactions, ensuring that your application operates reliably and maintains data integrity.

CHAPTER 33: IMPLEMENTING PAGINATION AND SORTING

In the context of API development, managing large datasets efficiently is crucial to ensuring performance and usability. One effective way to handle this challenge is by implementing pagination and sorting in your FastAPI application. Pagination allows users to navigate through large sets of data by retrieving a subset of records at a time, while sorting enables users to view data in a specified order. Both techniques help in managing large responses and improving the overall performance of the API.

Pagination is a technique used to divide a dataset into discrete pages, each containing a subset of records. This approach helps in reducing the amount of data transmitted over the network and limits the processing required on both the server and client sides. There are various methods to implement pagination, including offset-based, cursor-based, and keyset-based pagination. Each method has its own advantages and use cases.

Offset-based pagination is one of the simplest and most commonly used techniques. It involves specifying a `limit` and an `offset` in the query parameters of the API request.

The `limit` defines the number of records to return, while the `offset` specifies the starting point for the subset of records. For example, if a user requests the second page of results with a limit of 10 records per page, the offset would be set to 10, and the API would return records 11 through 20.

Here is an example of how to implement offset-based pagination in a FastAPI application using SQLAlchemy:

```python
from fastapi import FastAPI, Query
from sqlalchemy.orm import Session
from typing import List

app FastAPI()

@app.get("/items/", response_modelList[Item])
def get_items(limit: int  Query(10, gt0), offset: int  Query(0, ge0), db: Session  Depends(get_db)):
  items  db.query(Item).offset(offset).limit(limit).all()
  return items
```

In this example, the `limit` and `offset` parameters are specified in the query string. The `db.query(Item).offset(offset).limit(limit).all()` method retrieves the subset of records based on these parameters. This approach is straightforward but can become inefficient for large datasets, as the database must scan through the offset records before reaching the desired subset.

Cursor-based pagination, also known as keyset pagination, improves upon offset-based pagination by using a unique identifier or cursor to mark the starting point of the next page. Instead of specifying an offset, the client provides a cursor, which is typically the value of a unique field in the last record of the current page. This method is more efficient than offset-based pagination for large datasets, as it avoids the need to scan through skipped records.

Here is an example of cursor-based pagination:

```python
@app.get("/items/")
def get_items(cursor: str  None, limit: int  Query(10, gt0), db: Session  Depends(get_db)):
  query  db.query(Item).order_by(Item.id)
  if cursor:
    query  query.filter(Item.id > cursor)
  items  query.limit(limit).all()
  return items
```

In this example, the `cursor` parameter is used to filter records with IDs greater than the provided cursor. This method ensures efficient retrieval of records by leveraging indexed fields and avoids scanning through unnecessary records.

Sorting is another essential feature that enhances data retrieval by allowing users to view data in a specified order. Sorting can be implemented by adding an `order_by` clause to the query. This clause specifies the columns by which the results should be sorted, along with the sorting direction (ascending or descending). Sorting improves the usability of the API by presenting data in a structured and organized manner.

Here's how sorting can be implemented in a FastAPI application:

```python
from fastapi import FastAPI, Query
from sqlalchemy.orm import Session
from sqlalchemy import desc
from typing import List
```

```
app FastAPI()

@app.get("/items/", response_modelList[Item])
def get_items(sort_by: str  Query("id", enum["id", "name"]),
descending: bool Query(False), db: Session Depends(get_db)):
  if descending:
    order desc(getattr(Item, sort_by))
  else:
    order getattr(Item, sort_by)
  items db.query(Item).order_by(order).all()
  return items
```

In this example, the `sort_by` parameter specifies the column to sort by, while the `descending` parameter indicates the sorting direction. The `desc` function is used to apply descending order if needed. This method allows for flexible and user-defined sorting of data.

By combining pagination and sorting, you can provide users with powerful tools to navigate and view large datasets efficiently. Pagination ensures that only a manageable subset of records is retrieved at any given time, while sorting allows users to view data in a desired order. Together, these techniques contribute to an optimized and user-friendly API experience.

Cursor-based pagination, also known as keyset-based pagination, offers a more efficient alternative to offset-based pagination, especially for large datasets. Instead of using an offset to skip over records, cursor-based pagination uses a unique identifier or a pointer to the last record of the current page. This approach can significantly reduce the performance overhead associated with large offsets and ensure consistent pagination even when records are added or removed between requests.

In cursor-based pagination, the API response includes a cursor (usually an identifier or a token) that represents the position of the last record on the current page. The client then uses this cursor to fetch the next page of records. This method is particularly effective for applications with high data turnover, as it avoids the inefficiencies of scanning through large offsets.

To implement cursor-based pagination in FastAPI using SQLAlchemy, you need to design a mechanism to generate and handle cursors. Typically, the cursor is derived from the primary key of the last record in the current page. Here is an example of how to handle cursor-based pagination:

```python
from fastapi import FastAPI, HTTPException
from sqlalchemy.orm import Session
from typing import List
from sqlalchemy import desc

app FastAPI()

@app.get("/items/", response_modelList[Item])
def get_items(cursor: int  None, limit: int  10, db: Session
Depends(get_db)):
  query db.query(Item).order_by(desc(Item.id))

   if cursor:
    query query.filter(Item.id < cursor)

   items query.limit(limit).all()

   if not items:
        raise HTTPException(status_code404, detail"No more
items")

   next_cursor items[-1].id if len(items) limit else None

   return {"items": items, "next_cursor": next_cursor}
```

In this example, the `cursor` parameter represents the ID of the last item from the previous page. The query filters items based on whether their IDs are less than the cursor value, effectively retrieving the next set of records. The `next_cursor` is calculated from the ID of the last item in the current response, allowing the client to request the subsequent page. This approach is efficient and scales well with large datasets, as it avoids the performance drawbacks of offset-based pagination.

Another method of pagination is keyset-based pagination, which is similar to cursor-based but can include more complex keys composed of multiple columns. This method is useful when you need to paginate based on a combination of fields, such as a timestamp and an ID. Keyset-based pagination ensures that the pagination is consistent and efficient even in scenarios where data is frequently updated.

Sorting is another critical aspect of managing large datasets. Providing users with the ability to sort data based on various fields enhances usability and allows them to view data in a meaningful order. Sorting can be implemented in conjunction with pagination to enable users to navigate through and explore data more effectively.

In FastAPI, sorting can be integrated into your queries by including sort parameters in the API request. These parameters specify the field by which to sort and the direction of sorting (ascending or descending). For example, if you want to sort items based on their creation date, you would include a `sort_by` parameter in the request, along with a `sort_order` parameter to specify the direction.

Here is an example of how to implement sorting in FastAPI:

```python
from fastapi import FastAPI, Query
```

```
from sqlalchemy.orm import Session
from typing import List
from sqlalchemy import asc, desc

app FastAPI()

@app.get("/items/", response_modelList[Item])
def get_items(sort_by: str Query("created_at", enum["created_at", "name"]), sort_order: str Query("desc", enum["asc", "desc"]), limit: int 10, cursor: int None, db: Session Depends(get_db)):
  sort_column getattr(Item, sort_by)
      order desc(sort_column) if sort_order "desc" else asc(sort_column)

    query db.query(Item).order_by(order)

    if cursor:
     query query.filter(Item.id < cursor)

    items query.limit(limit).all()

    if not items:
         raise HTTPException(status_code404, detail"No more items")

    next_cursor items[-1].id if len(items) limit else None

    return {"items": items, "next_cursor": next_cursor}
```

In this example, the `sort_by` and `sort_order` parameters allow users to specify the field and direction for sorting. The query dynamically adjusts the sorting based on these parameters. By integrating sorting with pagination, you provide users with a flexible way to navigate and view data according to their preferences. This approach enhances the user experience and ensures that large datasets are handled efficiently.

In addition to pagination, implementing sorting capabilities is crucial for providing users with the ability to view data in a meaningful order. Sorting enables users to arrange data based on one or more attributes, such as date, name, or relevance. Effective sorting ensures that users can easily find and analyze data according to their preferences.

To implement sorting in a FastAPI application, you need to handle sorting parameters in your API requests and apply these parameters to your database queries. Sorting can be based on one or more fields and can be either ascending or descending. For SQL databases, sorting is typically achieved through the `ORDER BY` clause in SQL queries. For NoSQL databases, sorting is handled through specific query operations provided by the database driver or query language.

In FastAPI, sorting can be integrated into the API request parameters. For example, you might allow clients to specify the sort field and direction (ascending or descending) through query parameters. The sorting parameters are then applied to the database query to return results in the desired order.

Here's an example of how to implement sorting in a FastAPI route that retrieves items from a SQLAlchemy database:

```python
from fastapi import FastAPI, Query
from sqlalchemy.orm import Session
from sqlalchemy import asc, desc
from typing import List

app FastAPI()

@app.get("/items/", response_modelList[Item])
def get_items(sort_by: str  Query("id", alias"sort_by"), sort_order: str  Query("asc", alias"sort_order"), limit: int Query(10, gt0), db: Session  Depends(get_db)):
  if sort_order not in ["asc", "desc"]:
```

```
        raise HTTPException(status_code400, detail"Invalid sort order")

    if sort_order "asc":
        order asc(getattr(Item, sort_by))
    else:
        order desc(getattr(Item, sort_by))

    items db.query(Item).order_by(order).limit(limit).all()
    return items
```

In this example, the `sort_by` parameter specifies the field by which to sort the results, and `sort_order` determines whether the sorting is ascending or descending. The `getattr(Item, sort_by)` function dynamically retrieves the attribute of the `Item` model based on the `sort_by` parameter, allowing flexible sorting. The `asc` and `desc` functions from SQLAlchemy are used to apply the appropriate sorting direction.

Sorting in NoSQL databases, such as MongoDB, often involves using built-in methods provided by the database driver. For MongoDB, the `.sort()` method can be used to specify the fields and directions for sorting.

Here's an example of sorting in a FastAPI route using MongoDB with the `pymongo` driver:

```python
from fastapi import FastAPI, HTTPException, Query
from pymongo import MongoClient
from typing import List

app FastAPI()
client MongoClient("mongodb://localhost:27017/")
db client.mydatabase

@app.get("/items/", response_modelList[dict])
```

```
def get_items(sort_by: str Query("id"), sort_order: str
Query("asc"), limit: int Query(10, gt0)):
  if sort_order not in ["asc", "desc"]:
     raise HTTPException(status_code400, detail"Invalid sort
order")

   sort_direction 1 if sort_order "asc" else -1
              items      list(db.items.find().sort(sort_by,
sort_direction).limit(limit))
  return items
```

In this MongoDB example, the `sort_by` parameter specifies the field to sort by, and `sort_order` determines the sorting direction. The `sort_direction` variable is set to `1` for ascending order and `-1` for descending order, which are the respective values used by MongoDB for sorting. The `find()` method retrieves documents, and the `sort()` method applies the sorting parameters.

Combining pagination and sorting allows for more powerful data retrieval capabilities in your API. By providing users with the ability to sort and paginate data, you enhance the user experience and ensure that your application remains responsive even with large datasets. Properly handling these features requires careful design and implementation to balance performance and usability. In summary, implementing effective pagination and sorting strategies ensures that your FastAPI application can handle large volumes of data efficiently while offering a user-friendly interface for navigating and analyzing that data.

CHAPTER 34: ADVANCED TESTING STRATEGIES

Testing is an integral component of the software development lifecycle, particularly for applications built using frameworks like FastAPI. Advanced testing strategies are crucial to ensuring that your FastAPI application is both robust and reliable. This chapter delves into sophisticated methodologies for testing FastAPI applications, covering comprehensive unit tests, integration tests, and end-to-end tests. We will also explore useful testing tools, the intricacies of mocking dependencies, and strategies for maintaining a resilient API.

When approaching testing for FastAPI applications, the initial focus should be on unit tests. Unit tests are designed to validate the smallest testable parts of an application, typically individual functions or methods, in isolation. In the context of FastAPI, this often means testing individual routes or service functions that do not rely on external systems or databases. A robust unit test suite ensures that each piece of your application works correctly on its own before it is integrated with other components.

To effectively write unit tests for FastAPI applications, we begin by leveraging the `pytest` framework, which is highly recommended for its simplicity and power. For unit testing, the use of dependency injection is a key feature of

FastAPI that can be exploited to isolate components. FastAPI's dependency injection system allows developers to replace real dependencies with mock ones, enabling precise control over the behavior of your unit tests. For instance, if you have a route handler that depends on a database connection, you can substitute a mock database during testing to ensure that tests do not interact with a real database.

An example of this approach might involve testing a route that retrieves user information from a database. You would define a mock database client that returns predetermined data instead of querying a real database. Using `pytest`, you would write a test function to assert that the route correctly processes the data provided by the mock client. This method ensures that your unit tests are not only fast but also independent of external systems, leading to more reliable and repeatable test results.

Next, integration tests come into play. Integration tests evaluate how different parts of the application work together, typically involving real or mocked external services and databases. These tests are broader than unit tests and are designed to catch issues that arise when different components interact. For FastAPI applications, integration tests often involve the complete stack of the application, including routes, middleware, and service layers.

Writing integration tests for FastAPI involves setting up a test client that interacts with the application's endpoints. FastAPI's `TestClient` from the `starlette.testclient` module is particularly useful for this purpose. The `TestClient` allows you to make HTTP requests to your application and inspect the responses. This is particularly valuable for testing endpoints to ensure that they function correctly when integrated with other parts of the application.

In integration testing, it is important to test various scenarios, including successful operations, error handling, and edge cases. For instance, if your application includes a route for creating a new user, integration tests should verify not only that the user is created successfully but also that appropriate error messages are returned when invalid data is submitted. To ensure comprehensive coverage, integration tests should also include tests for different HTTP methods, authentication and authorization mechanisms, and data validation rules.

Following integration testing, end-to-end (E2E) tests are employed to validate the application as a whole. E2E tests are designed to simulate real user scenarios and ensure that the application functions correctly from start to finish. These tests often involve interacting with the application through its user interface and can include testing how the application behaves under different conditions, such as varying network speeds or browser types.

For FastAPI applications, E2E testing typically requires a combination of automated browser testing tools and API testing. Tools like Selenium or Playwright can be used for automating interactions with the application's front-end, while API testing tools ensure that the back-end services are functioning as expected. These tests should cover a wide range of user interactions, from simple actions like form submissions to more complex workflows involving multiple steps and interactions with various parts of the application.

An effective E2E testing strategy involves creating test scenarios that accurately reflect real user behavior. This might include scenarios such as a user logging in, performing a series of actions, and logging out, or more complex workflows involving interactions with multiple endpoints. By simulating these scenarios, E2E tests help to identify issues that may not be apparent in unit or integration tests, such as user interface bugs or issues with data synchronization between the front-end and back-end.

In conclusion, advanced testing strategies for FastAPI applications involve a multi-layered approach that includes unit tests, integration tests, and end-to-end tests. Each type of test plays a crucial role in ensuring that the application is robust and reliable. By leveraging tools such as `pytest`, `TestClient`, and browser automation frameworks, developers can create a comprehensive testing suite that not only verifies the correctness of individual components but also ensures that the entire application functions seamlessly as a whole.

Integration tests are pivotal in ensuring that the various components of a FastAPI application interact correctly. These tests provide a bridge between unit tests, which examine isolated units of functionality, and end-to-end tests, which evaluate the application's behavior as a whole. Integration tests are essential for identifying issues that may not be evident when testing components in isolation.

When writing integration tests for FastAPI applications, it is important to replicate a production-like environment as closely as possible. This means testing against a real or a well-mocked version of the external services that your application interacts with, such as databases, message queues, or third-party APIs. FastAPI provides tools to facilitate this process, such as dependency overrides and test clients.

One effective strategy for integration testing involves setting up a separate test database or using an in-memory database. For instance, if your application interacts with a SQL database, you can configure your test environment to use SQLite in-memory mode. This approach allows you to run integration tests without affecting the production database. FastAPI's dependency injection system can be utilized to swap the real database connection with a test-specific one, ensuring that tests are isolated and reproducible.

Furthermore, when writing integration tests, it is beneficial to employ FastAPI's `TestClient` from the `starlette.testclient` module. This client provides a way to simulate HTTP requests to your application and examine the responses, mimicking real-world interactions with your API. By using `TestClient`, you can send requests to various endpoints of your application, validate the responses, and ensure that the entire system behaves as expected. This approach is particularly useful for testing routes that involve complex logic or multiple dependencies.

To illustrate, consider a scenario where your application includes a route for creating user accounts. An integration test for this route would involve sending a POST request with user data, then verifying that the user was successfully created in the database. The test would assert not only that the HTTP response is correct but also that the user data persists as expected, ensuring that both the route handler and the database interaction work seamlessly together.

In addition to traditional integration testing, end-to-end testing provides a comprehensive evaluation of the entire application from the user's perspective. This type of testing simulates real user scenarios and interactions with the application to validate that all components function together as intended. End-to-end tests are particularly valuable for detecting issues that may arise from the interplay between the front-end and back-end of your application.

End-to-end testing typically involves using tools that can automate user interactions and validate the application's behavior across different layers. Tools such as Selenium or Playwright can be employed to automate browser-based tests, interacting with the application's user interface and asserting that it behaves correctly. For FastAPI applications, these tools can be integrated with your test suite to provide a thorough examination of your application's functionality.

A crucial aspect of end-to-end testing is the design of test scenarios that reflect real user workflows. These scenarios should cover a range of use cases, including typical user actions and edge cases. For instance, if your application includes a feature for searching and filtering data, your end-to-end tests should verify that users can perform searches, apply filters, and view the results as expected. This approach ensures that the application delivers a consistent and reliable user experience.

Another important consideration in end-to-end testing is the management of test data. Test scenarios should be designed to create and clean up test data as needed to ensure that tests are repeatable and do not interfere with each other. Automated scripts can be employed to set up the necessary data before tests run and clean it up afterward, maintaining a consistent testing environment.

As you implement these advanced testing strategies, it is also crucial to consider the tools and frameworks that support testing in FastAPI applications. In addition to `pytest` and `TestClient`, tools such as `factory_boy` for generating test data and `pytest-mock` for creating mock objects can greatly enhance your testing process. These tools help streamline the creation of test scenarios, simplify the management of test dependencies, and improve the overall efficiency of your testing efforts.

Finally, maintaining a robust and reliable API involves more than just writing tests; it requires a commitment to continuous testing and integration. Automated testing pipelines that run tests on code changes can help catch issues early in the development process, reducing the risk of defects reaching production. Implementing such pipelines, along with regular code reviews and quality checks, ensures that your

FastAPI application remains resilient and dependable.

In summary, advanced testing strategies for FastAPI applications encompass a range of methodologies, including unit tests, integration tests, and end-to-end tests. By leveraging tools and techniques such as dependency injection, `TestClient`, and automated testing frameworks, you can build a comprehensive testing suite that ensures the reliability and robustness of your application. As you develop and refine your testing strategies, remember that the goal is to create an application that performs consistently and meets user expectations, while also maintaining a high standard of code quality.

End-to-end testing provides a comprehensive approach to validating the functionality of your FastAPI application by simulating real-world use cases and interactions. This type of testing assesses whether all components of the system—ranging from frontend interfaces to backend services—work together harmoniously to deliver a seamless user experience. Given its breadth, end-to-end testing requires careful planning and execution to ensure that it accurately reflects the user journey.

To perform effective end-to-end testing for a FastAPI application, you typically employ testing frameworks and tools designed for this purpose. Tools such as Selenium or Playwright are popular choices for interacting with web applications' user interfaces. These tools can automate browser interactions, allowing you to simulate user actions such as clicking buttons, filling out forms, and navigating through pages. By running these automated scripts, you can verify that your application's frontend and backend are integrated correctly and that the overall user experience aligns with expectations.

Consider an example where your FastAPI application includes a user registration form. An end-to-end test for this feature would involve automating a browser to navigate to the registration page, enter user details, submit the form, and verify that the user is redirected to the appropriate page and that the registration process is completed successfully. Additionally, you would check that the new user data is correctly stored in the database and that any confirmation messages or emails are sent as intended. This comprehensive approach ensures that every step of the user journey is tested in a realistic manner.

Another critical aspect of end-to-end testing is dealing with asynchronous operations and real-time interactions. Many modern applications rely on asynchronous tasks such as background processing, real-time updates, or notifications. Testing these features requires special considerations to ensure that your tests accurately capture the asynchronous behavior of the application. For example, you might need to implement waiting strategies in your end-to-end tests to account for delays caused by network requests or background tasks. Tools like Playwright provide built-in support for handling such scenarios, allowing you to write tests that are resilient to the variability of real-time interactions.

Additionally, managing test data and environment setup is crucial for effective end-to-end testing. It is essential to ensure that each test run starts with a consistent and predictable environment. This might involve setting up test databases, seeding them with initial data, and tearing down any modifications made during the tests. For FastAPI applications, employing containerization tools such as Docker can streamline this process by providing isolated environments for each test run. By using Docker Compose, you can define and manage the necessary services and dependencies, ensuring that your end-to-end tests are executed in a controlled and reproducible manner.

Testing tools and strategies aside, mocking dependencies

is another essential consideration when testing FastAPI applications. Mocking involves replacing real dependencies with simulated versions to control their behavior and isolate the parts of the application under test. This technique is particularly useful for unit and integration tests where interactions with external systems need to be controlled. FastAPI's dependency injection system facilitates easy substitution of real components with mocks, ensuring that tests remain focused and reliable.

For instance, if your FastAPI application integrates with an external API, you can mock this API during testing to avoid making actual network calls. By defining mock responses, you can simulate various scenarios and edge cases without relying on the external service's availability or behavior. This approach is beneficial for testing how your application handles different responses or failures from the external API. Tools like `unittest.mock` in Python or `pytest-mock` can help you create and manage these mocks efficiently.

In summary, the advanced testing strategies for FastAPI applications encompass a range of methodologies designed to ensure the reliability and robustness of your API. By incorporating comprehensive unit tests, integration tests, and end-to-end tests, you can cover different aspects of your application's functionality and interaction. Utilizing testing tools, managing dependencies through mocking, and maintaining a consistent testing environment are all crucial elements of a successful testing strategy. As you implement these techniques, you will enhance the quality of your FastAPI application and be better equipped to address potential issues before they impact users.

CHAPTER 35: HANDLING ASYNCHRONOUS OPERATIONS

Asynchronous operations play a pivotal role in developing high-performance APIs, particularly in modern web applications where efficiency and responsiveness are paramount. FastAPI, with its robust support for asynchronous programming, allows developers to build applications that can handle concurrent requests effectively and maintain high responsiveness. This chapter explores how to leverage FastAPI's asynchronous capabilities, including async functions, coroutines, and background tasks, to optimize the performance of your API.

Understanding asynchronous programming begins with the concept of async functions and coroutines. In Python, async functions are defined using the `async def` syntax, and they enable the execution of asynchronous code. When an async function is called, it returns a coroutine object rather than executing immediately. This coroutine object can then be awaited using the `await` keyword, allowing the function to yield control back to the event loop, which can then execute other tasks while waiting for the initial function to complete. This approach facilitates non-blocking operations, which is especially beneficial in scenarios involving I/O-bound tasks such as database queries or external API calls.

In FastAPI, the use of async functions is particularly relevant when handling HTTP requests. By defining route handlers as async functions, you can perform I/O-bound operations without blocking the server's main thread, thereby improving the efficiency of handling concurrent requests. For instance, if your application needs to retrieve data from an external service, defining the route handler as an async function allows other requests to be processed concurrently while waiting for the external service to respond.

Consider an example where you have an API endpoint that queries a remote weather service for data. By defining this endpoint as an async function, you enable the FastAPI server to handle multiple requests to this endpoint simultaneously. This asynchronous handling prevents the server from being stalled by long-running requests, ensuring that other clients can continue to interact with the API without unnecessary delays.

Coroutines are the building blocks of asynchronous programming in Python. They are special types of functions that can pause their execution and resume later, making them ideal for tasks that involve waiting for external resources. FastAPI's integration with Python's `asyncio` library allows you to utilize coroutines to manage complex asynchronous workflows. For example, you might use coroutines to manage multiple asynchronous database queries or orchestrate tasks that depend on each other. By carefully designing your coroutines and managing their execution flow, you can build highly responsive applications that efficiently handle a large volume of requests.

In addition to async functions and coroutines, FastAPI supports background tasks, which are crucial for handling operations that do not need to be completed within the request-response cycle. Background tasks are ideal for performing time-consuming operations, such as sending emails or processing large datasets, without delaying the response to the client. FastAPI provides a simple interface for defining background tasks using the `BackgroundTasks` class, which can be used to schedule tasks to be executed after the response has been sent.

To illustrate, consider an API endpoint that handles user registrations. After a user registers, you might need to send a welcome email. By using FastAPI's background tasks, you can immediately respond to the user with a success message while the email is sent asynchronously in the background. This approach improves user experience by ensuring that the registration process is not delayed by the email-sending operation.

Handling concurrent requests is another critical aspect of asynchronous operations. In a high-performance API, it is essential to manage multiple simultaneous requests efficiently. FastAPI's asynchronous capabilities facilitate this by allowing the server to process multiple requests concurrently without blocking. This concurrency is achieved through the use of asynchronous I/O operations, which enable the server to perform non-blocking tasks and handle a higher volume of requests.

However, managing concurrency also requires careful consideration of thread safety and data integrity. When multiple requests are processed concurrently, shared resources such as in-memory data structures or external databases must be managed to prevent race conditions or data corruption. FastAPI's async and await mechanisms, combined with proper synchronization techniques, help mitigate these issues. For example, when accessing shared resources, you might use locks or other synchronization primitives to ensure that concurrent operations do not interfere with each other.

In conclusion, leveraging FastAPI's asynchronous capabilities allows developers to build efficient and responsive APIs that can handle a high volume of concurrent requests. By using async functions, coroutines, and background tasks, you can optimize your application's performance and ensure that it remains responsive under varying loads. Understanding and implementing these asynchronous strategies will enable you to create high-performance APIs that meet the demands of modern web applications.

Background tasks are another critical aspect of asynchronous programming in FastAPI, providing a mechanism for performing operations in the background without blocking the main request-response cycle. This feature is particularly useful for handling tasks that are time-consuming or do not need to be completed immediately, such as sending emails, processing data, or executing long-running computations.

In FastAPI, background tasks can be managed using the `BackgroundTasks` class from the `fastapi` module. This class allows you to define functions that will run asynchronously after the response has been sent to the client. To use background tasks, you need to instantiate a `BackgroundTasks` object within your route handler, register the functions you want to run in the background, and then pass this object to the `background_tasks` parameter.

Consider a scenario where your FastAPI application includes a route for user registration that involves sending a confirmation email to the user. Instead of sending the email synchronously, which could delay the response and affect the user experience, you can offload the email-sending operation to a background task. By doing so, the registration endpoint can respond promptly to the user while the email is sent in the background.

Here's a concise example of how to implement background tasks in FastAPI:

```python
from fastapi import FastAPI, BackgroundTasks
from typing import Union
import time

app FastAPI()

def send_email(email: str, message: str):
    Simulate a time-consuming email sending operation
    time.sleep(5)
    print(f"Sent email to {email} with message: {message}")

@app.post("/send/")
async def send_email_endpoint(email: str, message: str,
background_tasks: BackgroundTasks):
    background_tasks.add_task(send_email, email, message)
    return {"message": "Email is being sent"}
```

In this example, the `send_email` function simulates a delay representing the time taken to send an email. By adding this function as a background task, the `/send/` endpoint can immediately return a response to the client, while the email is processed in the background.

Handling concurrent requests effectively is a vital aspect of asynchronous programming and contributes significantly to the overall performance of your FastAPI application. Asynchronous programming allows your application to manage multiple simultaneous operations without waiting for each one to complete before starting the next. This is particularly advantageous for web APIs, where handling multiple requests efficiently can lead to a better user experience and higher throughput.

To handle concurrent requests, FastAPI relies on Python's `asyncio` library, which provides the necessary infrastructure for managing asynchronous tasks. By leveraging `asyncio`, FastAPI can efficiently schedule and execute coroutines, enabling the server to process multiple requests concurrently. This approach contrasts with traditional synchronous programming, where each request is handled sequentially, potentially leading to bottlenecks and reduced performance.

A practical consideration when handling concurrent requests is ensuring that your application's code is designed to be thread-safe and free of race conditions. Since asynchronous programming involves managing multiple tasks that run simultaneously, it is crucial to avoid situations where shared resources or data might be accessed concurrently in an unsafe manner. FastAPI and `asyncio` provide mechanisms to handle these scenarios, but developers must be vigilant in designing their code to prevent issues related to concurrency.

For instance, when working with shared resources such as a database or in-memory cache, you should ensure that your code properly handles concurrent access. This might involve using synchronization primitives like locks or semaphores to manage access to critical sections of code. Additionally, database operations should be designed to handle concurrent transactions and avoid conflicts, often by using transactional mechanisms or isolation levels provided by the database system.

In summary, mastering asynchronous operations in FastAPI involves understanding and applying async functions, coroutines, background tasks, and concurrency handling strategies. By leveraging these features, you can build APIs that are not only high-performance but also scalable and responsive to user demands. Asynchronous programming allows for the efficient management of multiple simultaneous tasks, contributing to a more responsive application and an improved overall user experience. As you continue to develop and optimize your FastAPI applications, these principles will play a critical role in achieving both performance and reliability.

Handling concurrent requests is a fundamental advantage of asynchronous programming, enabling your FastAPI application to manage multiple operations simultaneously. This capability significantly enhances the responsiveness and scalability of your application, especially under high load conditions. When your application handles requests asynchronously, it can process multiple incoming requests without waiting for one request to complete before starting another. This non-blocking behavior is crucial for building efficient and high-performance APIs.

FastAPI's integration with Python's `asyncio` library is central to its handling of concurrent operations. The `asyncio` library provides an event loop that manages the execution of asynchronous tasks. When an async function is called, it schedules the coroutine for execution and allows other tasks to proceed while waiting for the initial task to complete. This approach ensures that your application can continue to serve other requests while performing time-consuming operations, such as I/O operations or network communication.

To effectively manage concurrent requests, you need to ensure that your asynchronous code is designed to minimize blocking operations. Blocking operations, such as synchronous I/O calls or long-running computations, can negate the benefits of asynchronous programming. Therefore, it is essential to use asynchronous libraries and functions that are compatible with FastAPI's async capabilities. For example, when interacting with databases, you should use asynchronous database clients, such as `databases` or `asyncpg`, which support non-blocking operations.

Consider a scenario where your FastAPI application includes an endpoint that performs multiple database queries. By using an asynchronous database client, you can execute these queries concurrently, allowing the application to handle other requests while waiting for the database responses. This approach reduces latency and improves the overall throughput of your application. For instance, if you need to fetch user profiles and their associated posts, you can initiate both queries concurrently and then process the results once both queries are complete.

Another key consideration in handling asynchronous operations is managing shared resources, such as in-memory caches or external services. Concurrent access to shared resources can lead to race conditions or data inconsistency if not properly managed. FastAPI's asynchronous capabilities can help mitigate these issues by allowing you to use asynchronous locks or semaphores to control access to shared resources. These synchronization primitives ensure that only one coroutine can access a resource at a time, preventing conflicts and maintaining data integrity.

For example, if your application maintains a global cache that needs to be updated by multiple concurrent requests, you can use an asynchronous lock to serialize access to the cache. This ensures that updates to the cache are performed atomically, avoiding potential inconsistencies caused by concurrent modifications. FastAPI's support for asynchronous context managers and locks can simplify the implementation of such synchronization mechanisms.

Optimizing your application's responsiveness also involves monitoring and profiling asynchronous code to identify potential bottlenecks. Tools such as `asyncio`'s built-in tracing and logging features can help you gain insights into the performance of your asynchronous tasks. By analyzing the event loop's behavior and task execution times, you can identify areas where performance can be improved and make necessary adjustments to your code.

In addition to monitoring tools, comprehensive testing of asynchronous code is crucial for ensuring that your application behaves as expected under various conditions. Asynchronous code can introduce complexities that are not present in synchronous code, such as handling exceptions, managing task cancellations, and ensuring proper cleanup of resources. It is important to write tests that cover these aspects and verify that your application handles asynchronous operations correctly.

FastAPI's support for testing asynchronous code is facilitated by the `pytest-asyncio` plugin, which provides utilities for writing and running asynchronous tests. By using this plugin, you can write test functions that use `async def` syntax and utilize the `await` keyword to interact with your asynchronous code. This ensures that your tests accurately reflect the behavior of your application's asynchronous operations and help identify any issues or regressions.

In conclusion, leveraging FastAPI's asynchronous capabilities allows you to build high-performance APIs that handle concurrent requests efficiently. By using async functions, coroutines, and background tasks, you can optimize your application's responsiveness and scalability. Proper management of concurrent requests, careful handling of shared resources, and effective monitoring and testing are essential for ensuring that your asynchronous code performs reliably and meets the demands of modern web applications. Asynchronous programming, when applied thoughtfully, can significantly enhance the performance and user experience of your FastAPI application.

CHAPTER 36: DEPLOYING FASTAPI APPLICATIONS

Deploying FastAPI applications to production involves a series of critical steps and considerations to ensure that your application operates efficiently and reliably. Whether deploying using containerization with Docker, leveraging cloud platforms like AWS and Azure, or deploying on traditional servers, understanding the deployment process and adhering to best practices are essential for a successful production rollout. This section provides a comprehensive guide to deploying FastAPI applications, covering different deployment methods and offering best practices to facilitate a smooth deployment process.

One of the most popular methods for deploying FastAPI applications is containerization using Docker. Docker simplifies the deployment process by encapsulating the application and its dependencies into a lightweight, portable container. This approach ensures that the application runs consistently across different environments, from development to production. To deploy a FastAPI application with Docker, you start by creating a Dockerfile, which defines the environment and instructions for building the Docker image.

A typical Dockerfile for a FastAPI application might look as follows:

```dockerfile
Use the official Python image from the Docker Hub
FROM python:3.9-slim

Set the working directory in the container
WORKDIR /app

Copy the requirements file into the container
COPY requirements.txt .

Install the required dependencies
RUN pip install --no-cache-dir -r requirements.txt

Copy the rest of the application code into the container
COPY . .

Expose the port on which the application will run
EXPOSE 8000

Define the command to run the FastAPI application using Uvicorn
CMD ["uvicorn", "main:app", "--host", "0.0.0.0", "--port", "8000"]
```

In this Dockerfile, the `python:3.9-slim` image serves as the base image, providing a minimal Python environment. The working directory is set to `/app`, where the application code and dependencies are copied. The `requirements.txt` file lists the Python packages required by the application, and `pip` is used to install these dependencies. Finally, the `CMD` instruction runs the FastAPI application using Uvicorn, specifying the host and port.

Once the Dockerfile is created, you can build the Docker image using the `docker build` command and then run a container based on that image with the `docker run` command. This process ensures that your FastAPI application is packaged in a consistent environment, making it easier to deploy across different systems.

In addition to Docker, cloud platforms such as AWS and Azure offer robust services for deploying FastAPI applications. Both platforms provide various options for deployment, ranging from managed container services to serverless functions. For example, AWS Elastic Beanstalk and Azure App Services offer streamlined deployment solutions that abstract away much of the infrastructure management. These platforms support containerized deployments, allowing you to deploy Docker images directly to managed services.

To deploy a FastAPI application using AWS Elastic Beanstalk, you would first create an Elastic Beanstalk environment and configure it to use Docker. Elastic Beanstalk simplifies the deployment process by handling the provisioning of the underlying infrastructure, including load balancers, auto-scaling groups, and monitoring services. You would then upload your Docker image or Dockerfile to Elastic Beanstalk, and the platform handles the deployment and scaling of your application.

Similarly, Azure App Services provides a platform for deploying web applications, including those built with FastAPI. Azure App Services supports Docker containers, so you can deploy your application by specifying a Docker image or Dockerfile. Azure also offers built-in scaling and monitoring capabilities, allowing you to manage your application's performance and resource utilization effectively.

For traditional server deployments, you might use a virtual private server (VPS) or a dedicated server. Deploying a FastAPI application on traditional servers involves configuring the server environment, installing necessary software, and setting up a web server and application server. Common web servers used in conjunction with FastAPI include Nginx and Apache, while application servers such as Uvicorn or Gunicorn handle the execution of your FastAPI application.

To deploy a FastAPI application on a traditional server, you would typically start by installing Python and any required dependencies on the server. Next, you would set up a virtual environment and install the application's dependencies. Once the environment is configured, you would run your FastAPI application using an application server like Uvicorn, ensuring that it listens on the appropriate port.

Nginx can be configured as a reverse proxy to forward incoming HTTP requests to the Uvicorn server, providing additional features such as load balancing, SSL termination, and request routing. The Nginx configuration would include a server block that specifies the proxy settings and forwards requests to the Uvicorn server.

Regardless of the deployment method, several best practices can help ensure a smooth deployment process. First, thoroughly test your application in a staging environment that closely mirrors the production setup. This step helps identify and address potential issues before deploying to production. Additionally, implement proper monitoring and logging to track the application's performance and detect any anomalies or errors. Using automated deployment tools and continuous integration/continuous deployment (CI/CD) pipelines can streamline the deployment process and minimize human error.

Securing your deployment environment is also crucial. Implementing best practices for security, such as configuring firewalls, using secure protocols (e.g., HTTPS), and regularly updating dependencies, helps protect your application from vulnerabilities and attacks. Lastly, ensure that you have a robust backup and recovery plan in place to safeguard against data loss or system failures.

Once the Docker image is built, you can deploy it in

various environments. One common approach is to use cloud platforms like AWS and Azure, which offer managed services for deploying and scaling containerized applications. Both platforms provide services that simplify the deployment process and offer features for monitoring, scaling, and managing your FastAPI application.

For AWS, the Elastic Container Service (ECS) and Elastic Kubernetes Service (EKS) are popular choices for deploying Docker containers. ECS is a fully managed container orchestration service that supports Docker containers and integrates seamlessly with other AWS services. To deploy a FastAPI application using ECS, you would first push your Docker image to Amazon Elastic Container Registry (ECR), a managed container image registry service. After pushing the image, you can create an ECS task definition, which specifies the container configuration, including the Docker image to use and the ports to expose.

Once the task definition is created, you can set up an ECS cluster and launch tasks based on your definition. ECS also supports auto-scaling, which allows your application to handle varying loads by automatically adjusting the number of running tasks based on predefined metrics.

Alternatively, AWS EKS provides a managed Kubernetes service for deploying and managing containerized applications. Kubernetes offers advanced features for container orchestration, such as automated deployment, scaling, and management of containerized applications. To deploy your FastAPI application on EKS, you would first push your Docker image to ECR, create a Kubernetes deployment configuration file, and apply this configuration to your EKS cluster. The deployment configuration specifies the Docker image, the number of replicas, and the service settings for exposing your application.

Azure offers similar services for containerized applications, including Azure Kubernetes Service (AKS) and Azure Container Instances (ACI). AKS is a managed Kubernetes service that simplifies deploying, managing, and scaling containerized applications. To deploy a FastAPI application on AKS, you would push your Docker image to Azure Container Registry (ACR), create Kubernetes deployment and service configuration files, and apply these files to your AKS cluster.

Azure Container Instances provide a simpler option for deploying containers without needing a full-fledged Kubernetes cluster. ACI allows you to run Docker containers in a serverless environment, making it a suitable choice for lightweight applications or testing. You can deploy your FastAPI application to ACI by specifying the Docker image and configuration in the Azure portal or using the Azure CLI.

In addition to cloud platforms, deploying FastAPI applications on traditional servers is another viable approach. This method typically involves provisioning virtual machines or physical servers and manually configuring the environment. When deploying on traditional servers, you have full control over the server configuration, which can be advantageous for optimizing performance or integrating with existing infrastructure.

For a traditional server deployment, you would start by setting up a virtual machine or physical server with the necessary operating system and dependencies. After configuring the server, you can build and run the Docker image locally, ensuring that the FastAPI application functions as expected. Once verified, you can push the Docker image to a container registry and pull it onto the server. From there, you can use Docker commands to run the container and expose the necessary ports.

Regardless of the deployment method chosen, it is

crucial to implement best practices to ensure a smooth deployment process. This includes configuring robust logging and monitoring to track application performance and diagnose issues. FastAPI integrates well with various logging frameworks, and you can use tools like Prometheus and Grafana for monitoring. These tools provide insights into the application's behavior, resource usage, and potential bottlenecks.

Additionally, security is a critical consideration for deployment. Ensure that your application is secured using HTTPS by configuring TLS/SSL certificates. Many cloud platforms offer managed certificate services or integration with certificate authorities. It is also important to regularly update your dependencies and apply security patches to mitigate vulnerabilities.

Automating the deployment process with CI/CD pipelines is another best practice. Continuous Integration (CI) and Continuous Deployment (CD) pipelines streamline the deployment process by automating build, test, and deployment stages. Tools like GitHub Actions, Jenkins, and GitLab CI/CD can be used to set up pipelines that automatically build Docker images, run tests, and deploy your FastAPI application to production.

By adhering to these practices and choosing the appropriate deployment method, you can ensure that your FastAPI application is deployed effectively, performs well, and remains secure.

When deploying FastAPI applications on traditional servers, the approach differs from containerized or cloud-based deployments, focusing instead on configuring the server environment directly. This involves setting up the server infrastructure, installing necessary dependencies, and ensuring the application operates smoothly in a non-containerized environment.

One common method for deploying FastAPI applications on traditional servers is to use a combination of a web server gateway interface (WSGI) server and a reverse proxy. For FastAPI applications, the Uvicorn ASGI server is typically used as the application server due to its support for asynchronous operations and performance. However, Uvicorn itself is not a production-grade server but rather a lightweight ASGI server. To handle high loads and ensure robust performance, it is recommended to run Uvicorn behind a reverse proxy such as Nginx or Apache.

To deploy FastAPI on a traditional server, start by setting up the server environment, which includes installing Python and any dependencies specified in your `requirements.txt` file. You can use a virtual environment to isolate the application's dependencies, ensuring that they do not conflict with system packages or other applications. After creating the virtual environment and installing the required packages, configure Uvicorn to serve your FastAPI application.

For instance, you might run Uvicorn with a command similar to:

```bash
uvicorn main:app --host 0.0.0.0 --port 8000
```

This command starts the Uvicorn server, binding it to all network interfaces on port 8000. While this setup works for local testing, in a production environment, it is advisable to use a process manager like `gunicorn` or `supervisord` to manage Uvicorn processes, ensuring that the application is automatically restarted in case of failures and can handle multiple worker processes to handle concurrent requests.

When using Nginx as a reverse proxy, you will need to configure it to forward requests to Uvicorn. This involves setting up an Nginx configuration file with a server block that specifies the upstream server (Uvicorn) and the location directives for handling requests. A sample Nginx configuration for a FastAPI application might look like:

```nginx
server {
  listen 80;
  server_name example.com;

    location / {
     proxy_pass http://127.0.0.1:8000;
     proxy_set_header Host $host;
     proxy_set_header X-Real-IP $remote_addr;
     proxy_set_header X-Forwarded-For
$proxy_add_x_forwarded_for;
     proxy_set_header X-Forwarded-Proto $scheme;
  }
}
```

In this configuration, Nginx listens on port 80 and forwards incoming requests to the Uvicorn server running on localhost port 8000. The `proxy_set_header` directives ensure that the original request headers are preserved when passing requests through the proxy.

Another important consideration when deploying on traditional servers is ensuring that the application is secure and performs well. This involves configuring SSL/TLS for secure connections, optimizing server performance, and setting up monitoring and logging. For SSL/TLS, you can use Let's Encrypt to obtain free SSL certificates and configure Nginx to handle HTTPS requests. Performance optimization may include tuning server parameters, caching static files, and optimizing database queries.

Monitoring and logging are crucial for maintaining the

health of your application in production. You can use tools like Prometheus and Grafana for monitoring application metrics, and centralized logging solutions such as ELK Stack (Elasticsearch, Logstash, Kibana) or Fluentd for aggregating and analyzing logs. These tools help you track application performance, detect issues, and ensure that your application operates smoothly.

Lastly, deploying FastAPI applications requires careful planning for updates and maintenance. Implementing a deployment pipeline using tools like Jenkins, GitLab CI, or GitHub Actions can streamline the deployment process and reduce the risk of errors. Automated testing and continuous integration (CI) ensure that changes are thoroughly tested before being deployed to production. Additionally, implementing a rollback strategy allows you to revert to a previous version of your application if issues arise during deployment.

By following these best practices and leveraging the appropriate deployment methods, you can ensure that your FastAPI application is deployed effectively, performs optimally, and remains reliable in a production environment. Whether using containerization, cloud platforms, or traditional servers, understanding the deployment process and addressing potential challenges will contribute to a successful and resilient application deployment.

CHAPTER 37: MONITORING AND LOGGING

Effective monitoring and logging are critical components for maintaining the health, performance, and reliability of your FastAPI application. They provide essential insights into how your application is functioning, enabling you to track errors, assess performance issues, and ensure overall system health. Properly configured logging and monitoring systems can significantly aid in troubleshooting, optimizing performance, and maintaining a seamless user experience.

To begin with, setting up logging in FastAPI involves configuring Python's built-in logging module to capture and manage log messages. Logging is a crucial aspect of understanding application behavior, as it allows you to record various events, errors, and informational messages generated by your application. FastAPI itself does not impose specific logging requirements, so you can leverage the standard Python logging framework, which provides a flexible and powerful approach to logging.

You start by configuring the logging settings in your FastAPI application. This involves setting up a logging configuration that defines log levels, handlers, formatters, and log destinations. For example, you can configure logging to write messages to a file, console, or external logging service. The configuration typically includes specifying the log level (e.g., DEBUG, INFO, WARNING, ERROR, CRITICAL) to control the verbosity of the log messages.

Here's a sample configuration to set up logging for a FastAPI application:

```python
import logging

Configure the logging settings
logging.basicConfig(
  levellogging.INFO,  Set the logging level to INFO
      format'%(asctime)s - %(name)s - %(levelname)s - %
(message)s',  Define the log message format
  handlers[
    logging.StreamHandler(),  Output logs to the console
    logging.FileHandler('app.log')  Output logs to a file
  ]
)

logger  logging.getLogger(__name__)

Example of logging an informational message
logger.info('Logging has been configured')
```

In this configuration, the `basicConfig` function sets up the logging with a level of INFO, meaning that messages with a severity level of INFO and above will be recorded. The log format includes the timestamp, logger name, log level, and message, providing a clear and detailed log output. Logs are sent to both the console and a file named `app.log`.

In a production environment, logging configuration may need to be more sophisticated. For example, you might use different log levels for different environments (e.g., DEBUG for development and INFO or WARNING for production). Additionally, integrating with external logging services or platforms, such as ELK Stack (Elasticsearch, Logstash, Kibana), Splunk, or cloud-based services like AWS CloudWatch or Azure Monitor, can provide enhanced capabilities for aggregating, searching, and analyzing log data.

Beyond logging, monitoring application metrics is crucial for maintaining operational visibility. Monitoring involves collecting and analyzing data related to application performance, resource usage, and other critical metrics. FastAPI applications can benefit from integration with monitoring tools that track various aspects such as response times, error rates, system resource utilization, and request throughput.

One common approach to monitoring is to use tools that support Prometheus, a powerful open-source monitoring and alerting toolkit. Prometheus collects metrics from configured endpoints and stores them in a time-series database, which can then be queried and visualized using Grafana, a popular open-source analytics and monitoring platform.

To integrate Prometheus with FastAPI, you can use libraries such as `prometheus_client` to expose metrics endpoints. For instance, you can define a Prometheus metrics endpoint in your FastAPI application to provide metrics data that Prometheus can scrape. Here's an example of how to set up Prometheus metrics in FastAPI:

```python
from fastapi import FastAPI
from prometheus_client import start_http_server, Counter

app FastAPI()

Create a Prometheus counter metric
REQUESTS Counter('http_requests_total', 'Total number of HTTP requests')

@app.middleware("http")
```

```
async def count_requests(request: Request, call_next):
  REQUESTS.inc()  Increment the counter on each request
  response  await call_next(request)
  return response

Start the Prometheus HTTP server to expose metrics
if __name__  "__main__":
  start_http_server(8001)  Expose metrics on port 8001
  import uvicorn
  uvicorn.run(app, host"0.0.0.0", port8000)
```

In this example, the `prometheus_client` library is used to create a counter metric that tracks the total number of HTTP requests. The `count_requests` middleware increments the counter for each incoming request. Additionally, the `start_http_server` function exposes the metrics on a separate port, allowing Prometheus to scrape the metrics data.

Integrating with monitoring tools and platforms involves configuring these tools to scrape and visualize the metrics data collected by your application. This integration provides valuable insights into application performance and health, enabling proactive management and timely response to potential issues.

By implementing effective logging and monitoring strategies, you gain visibility into your FastAPI application's behavior, allowing you to track errors, performance issues, and overall health. This comprehensive approach to monitoring and logging is essential for maintaining a reliable and high-performing API in a production environment.

Lucas's confession left a palpable silence in the air, an almost tangible pause that seemed to stretch indefinitely. His eyes, usually so full of casual banter and effortless charm, were now earnest, vulnerable. For a moment, I felt as though time itself had stopped, leaving just the two of us suspended in this charged moment. My heart raced, not just from the shock of his admission but also from the emotional whirlwind it stirred within me. I had always known Lucas as my steadfast friend, someone who was there for me through thick and thin, but this revelation transformed my perception of him, of us.

His words lingered between us, each syllable echoing louder in my mind than the last. Lucas's admission wasn't merely about his feelings; it was also a raw, unfiltered display of his inner turmoil. The way he spoke, with a mix of desperation and hope, revealed layers of emotion I hadn't fully appreciated before. It was as though a veil had been lifted, allowing me to see the depth of his affections and the extent of his inner conflict. His vulnerability was both compelling and disconcerting. I had always seen him as a pillar of strength, and now he stood before me, exposed and unguarded.

I tried to process his confession, but my thoughts were a chaotic jumble of confusion and self-reflection. How had I missed the signs of his feelings? Was I so absorbed in my own uncertainties that I failed to recognize the depth of Lucas's emotions? His declaration of jealousy, the pain he felt seeing me with Tyler—it all pointed to a side of him that I had never fully acknowledged. The realization that Lucas had been struggling with these feelings, that he had been trying to hide his hurt behind a mask of friendship, was deeply unsettling. It was both humbling and disorienting to understand how much my presence, my actions, had impacted him.

As I stood there, grappling with the weight of his confession, Tyler's advances seemed to fade into the background. The attention he had given me, once so flattering and distracting, now felt insignificant compared to the depth of what I was hearing from Lucas. The contrast between Tyler's overt and often intrusive attention and Lucas's quiet, heartfelt vulnerability could not have been starker. Tyler had been persistent, almost aggressive in his pursuit, but it was Lucas's sincere admission that made me confront the reality of my feelings and the choices I needed to make.

I looked into Lucas's eyes, searching for the right words to respond, to acknowledge his feelings without causing further pain. "Lucas, I..." My voice faltered as I struggled to articulate the storm of emotions inside me. I wanted to assure him, to explain that his feelings were not misplaced, but the complexity of my own emotions made it difficult to speak clearly. The boundaries between friendship and something more had blurred so significantly that I wasn't sure how to navigate them.

Lucas's face was a study in anxiety and hope. He watched me intently, waiting for a response, his usual confident demeanor replaced by a palpable uncertainty. It was clear that this moment was a crossroads, one that could change the trajectory of our relationship. The prospect of acknowledging a deeper connection with Lucas was both exhilarating and terrifying. The comfort of our established friendship was at stake, and I was acutely aware of the risks involved.

In the midst of my internal struggle, I could see how deeply Lucas cared for me. His confession wasn't just about expressing his feelings; it was also an act of vulnerability, a willingness to risk the stability of our friendship for the chance of something more. This act of bravery, of laying his heart on the line, forced me to confront my own feelings and the choices I had been avoiding. It was clear that the easy path was no longer an option. The dynamics between us had irrevocably changed, and I had to decide how to navigate this new terrain.

The rehearsal room, which had once been a space of creative collaboration and casual interactions, now felt charged with unspoken tension. The lines between our professional roles in the play and our personal feelings had become indistinct.

What had been a routine rehearsal was now a battleground of emotions, with Lucas's confession casting a long shadow over everything.

As I took a deep breath, I realized that I needed to be honest, not just with Lucas but with myself. I had to confront the feelings I had been reluctant to acknowledge, to reconcile the affection I had for him with the turmoil caused by Tyler's advances. My response needed to be sincere and reflective of the complexity of my emotions, acknowledging both the depth of Lucas's feelings and my own evolving sentiments.

The silence that followed Lucas's confession was filled with the weight of unspoken truths and unresolved emotions. I knew that whatever I said next would not only address Lucas's feelings but also set the course for our future interactions. The path forward was uncertain, but it was clear that the foundation of our friendship had shifted, making way for new possibilities and challenges.

the way he had pursued me, but it was Lucas's quiet confession that now held my attention with an unshakable grip. I could no longer ignore the implications of his words. Every interaction we had shared, every moment of camaraderie, was now tinted with a new understanding. It was as if a hidden layer of meaning had been unveiled, altering the context of our entire relationship.

Lucas's gaze remained locked on mine, his expression a mixture of hope and trepidation. The earnestness in his eyes was undeniable, and it struck me deeply. His vulnerability was raw, a stark contrast to his usual demeanor. I could see the weight of his emotions in the way he stood, the tight grip on his own hands, and the way he avoided looking away, as if fearing that any movement might shatter the fragile moment.

I found myself grappling with a surge of conflicting emotions. On one hand, I was overwhelmed by the depth of Lucas's feelings and the courage it took for him to lay his heart bare. On the other hand, I was acutely aware of the complexities of my own feelings and the position I was in. The pressure of the situation seemed to bear down on me, accentuating my internal conflict. I was not only dealing with my own emotions but also with the weight of Lucas's expectations and the consequences of my next actions.

The rehearsal hall around us had fallen into a muted silence, as if the entire space had absorbed the tension between us. The other students, who had been bustling with their own pre-performance preparations, were now distant observers, their movements almost imperceptible in the background. The only sounds were the faint hum of the heating system and the distant echoes of footsteps from the corridor. This silence, while initially comforting, soon felt stifling, amplifying my own internal struggle.

I wanted to respond to Lucas, to provide him with some sense of clarity or reassurance, but my mind was clouded by the complexity of the situation. The words I might have said were entangled with uncertainty. My own feelings for Lucas had been growing, but I had been hesitant to acknowledge them fully. The confusion brought on by Tyler's attention had further complicated my understanding of my emotions. Now, with Lucas's confession, the need to confront these feelings head-on was undeniable.

In this moment of introspection, I realized the importance of honesty, both with myself and with Lucas. To navigate this intricate emotional landscape, I needed to confront my own feelings openly. It was not fair to Lucas or to myself to remain ambiguous or indecisive. The clarity I sought required more than just acknowledging Lucas's feelings; it necessitated a thorough examination of my own heart and a courageous confrontation of what I truly desired.

As I finally found my voice, the words that emerged were carefully chosen, reflecting both my own feelings and the respect I had for Lucas's vulnerability. I spoke with a mix of sincerity and caution, attempting to balance my own uncertainty with the need to be honest. I expressed how much I valued our friendship and how deeply moved I was by his admission. I also conveyed that, while I was still uncertain about the full extent of my feelings, I appreciated his courage and needed time to understand where my own heart truly lay.

Lucas listened intently, his expression a mixture of hope and concern. He nodded, as if understanding the need for patience and self-reflection. His demeanor shifted slightly, from the intensity of his confession to a more contemplative, accepting stance. It was evident that he was prepared to give me the space I needed, even if it meant enduring further emotional turbulence.

The resolution of this emotional confrontation did not bring immediate clarity or resolution. Instead, it opened a new chapter in our relationship, one that required continued exploration and understanding. The process of untangling my feelings for Lucas, while simultaneously dealing with the lingering effects of Tyler's advances, would be neither straightforward nor simple. However, the authenticity and depth of Lucas's confession had set a new standard for honesty and emotional engagement.

In the aftermath of this moment, I was left with the task of navigating my emotions with a newfound sense of clarity. The dynamic between Lucas and me had irrevocably shifted, and I was now faced with the challenge of reconciling my own feelings with the expectations and realities of our evolving relationship. The journey ahead would be one of introspection and open communication, with the hope that, through this process, we could both find a path forward that honored our individual feelings and our shared history.

CHAPTER 38: IMPLEMENTING WEBSOCKET AUTHENTICATION

In the realm of modern web applications, WebSockets provide a powerful mechanism for enabling real-time, two-way communication between the client and server. However, the introduction of WebSockets into an application architecture also necessitates careful consideration of security practices, particularly in the area of authentication. Implementing effective WebSocket authentication ensures that only authorized users can access the real-time features of your application, thus maintaining the integrity and confidentiality of the communication.

To begin with, it is crucial to understand that WebSocket connections differ fundamentally from traditional HTTP requests. While HTTP requests are stateless and each request must be independently authenticated, WebSocket connections are persistent and stateful. Once established, a WebSocket connection remains open for the duration of the session, which introduces unique challenges and considerations for authentication. This requires a nuanced approach to securely manage user sessions and verify identities throughout the duration of the WebSocket communication.

When implementing WebSocket authentication, one of the primary strategies is to leverage token-based authentication. This approach typically involves the use of JSON Web Tokens (JWTs) or similar mechanisms. The authentication process generally begins with the client sending a WebSocket connection request to the server, which includes an authorization token in the request headers or as part of the WebSocket handshake. The server then verifies this token to ensure that the client is authenticated before establishing the WebSocket connection.

The first step in this process is to ensure that your application can handle authentication tokens within WebSocket requests. Many WebSocket libraries and frameworks do not directly support token validation out of the box, so you may need to implement custom logic to process and validate these tokens. For instance, if you are using a popular WebSocket library like `ws` for Node.js or `websockets` for Python, you would typically need to extend the library's functionality to include token validation. This can be done by intercepting the WebSocket handshake and extracting the token from the request headers or URL parameters.

Once the token is extracted, the server must validate it to authenticate the user. This validation process involves checking the token's signature and expiration date, as well as ensuring that it is associated with a valid user session. In a typical implementation, this validation process would involve parsing the token, verifying its cryptographic signature, and checking the user's credentials against a database or authentication service. If the token is valid, the server establishes the WebSocket connection; if not, the connection is rejected, and the client is typically notified of the authentication failure.

After a WebSocket connection is established, maintaining

secure sessions is another critical aspect of WebSocket authentication. Unlike HTTP requests, which are short-lived and stateless, WebSocket connections persist over time. This means that once authenticated, the connection remains open, and any additional security measures must be implemented to ensure ongoing session integrity. One approach to managing secure WebSocket sessions is to implement session refresh mechanisms. For instance, you might periodically refresh the authentication token to ensure that it remains valid for the duration of the session. This can involve sending a refresh request from the client to the server and issuing a new token if the current one is nearing expiration.

Additionally, it is important to consider how to handle cases where a user's authentication status changes during an active WebSocket session. For example, if a user logs out or their session is terminated for any reason, the WebSocket connection should be appropriately managed to reflect these changes. This might involve implementing mechanisms to detect and respond to session invalidation, such as terminating the WebSocket connection or notifying the client of the session's invalidation.

Furthermore, securing WebSocket communication also involves addressing other potential vulnerabilities, such as ensuring that the connection is encrypted using TLS (Transport Layer Security). Just as with traditional HTTP requests, WebSocket connections should be encrypted to protect against eavesdropping and man-in-the-middle attacks. This requires configuring your WebSocket server to support and enforce secure WebSocket connections (wss://) and ensuring that clients are also configured to connect using this secure protocol.

In summary, implementing WebSocket authentication involves several critical steps: verifying authentication tokens during the WebSocket handshake, managing secure sessions through token refresh mechanisms, handling changes in user authentication status, and ensuring that communication is encrypted. By carefully addressing these aspects, you can ensure that your WebSocket connections remain secure and that only authorized users are able to access the real-time features of your application.

In the process of validating tokens, the server needs to handle several key tasks to ensure robust security. First, the server should verify that the token has not been tampered with. This typically involves checking the token's signature using the appropriate cryptographic keys. For instance, if using JSON Web Tokens (JWT), the server will decode the token and verify its signature against a pre-defined secret key or public key, depending on whether it is signed with HMAC or RSA algorithms. This step ensures that the token has not been altered since it was issued.

Next, the server must check the token's expiration time to ensure it is still valid. Tokens often have a time-to-live (TTL) associated with them, and it is crucial to enforce this expiration to prevent unauthorized access. This involves comparing the current time against the token's issued time and expiration time, and rejecting the token if it has expired. Additionally, it is prudent to consider the possibility of token revocation. If a token needs to be invalidated before its natural expiration—such as when a user logs out or changes their password—the server should have mechanisms in place to handle such scenarios.

Another important aspect of token validation is ensuring that the token corresponds to a valid user session. After verifying the token's authenticity, the server should check that the user associated with the token is authorized to access the requested WebSocket endpoint. This step typically involves looking up the user's details in a database or session store to confirm that they are allowed to engage in the specific WebSocket interaction.

Once token validation is complete and the user is authenticated, the WebSocket connection can be established. At this point, the server should maintain the session's security throughout the WebSocket communication. This involves managing the session state, monitoring for any anomalies, and ensuring that the connection is consistently secure. Because WebSocket connections are long-lived, it is essential to continuously monitor and protect the session against potential threats, such as session hijacking or unauthorized access attempts.

In practice, implementing secure WebSocket authentication involves integrating these components into your WebSocket server. For example, in a Node.js environment using the `ws` library, you might extend the server setup to include a middleware function that intercepts WebSocket handshake requests. This middleware function would extract and validate the token before allowing the WebSocket connection to proceed. Similarly, in a Python environment with the `websockets` library, you might create a custom authentication decorator or middleware that performs these validation steps during the handshake phase.

Moreover, it is essential to handle errors gracefully during the authentication process. If token validation fails, the server should reject the WebSocket connection and provide a clear, informative error message to the client. This approach helps maintain a secure environment by ensuring that unauthorized attempts are properly handled and does not leave room for ambiguity or confusion.

Beyond the initial authentication, ongoing security measures are necessary to protect WebSocket connections. Implementing additional layers of security, such as encryption and regular security audits, helps safeguard the communication channel. For instance, using Transport Layer Security (TLS) for WebSocket connections (commonly referred to as WSS) ensures that data transmitted between the client and server is encrypted, mitigating the risk of interception or eavesdropping.

Additionally, it is important to remain vigilant against potential security vulnerabilities specific to WebSocket communication. This includes being aware of common attack vectors such as Cross-Site WebSocket Hijacking (CSWSH) and ensuring that your WebSocket implementation adheres to best practices for security. Regularly updating your dependencies and libraries, conducting security reviews, and keeping abreast of emerging threats are crucial practices for maintaining a secure WebSocket environment.

In summary, implementing authentication for WebSocket connections requires a comprehensive approach that includes token validation, session management, and ongoing security practices. By integrating these elements effectively, you can ensure that your WebSocket-enabled application remains secure and resilient against unauthorized access and potential threats. The process involves not only validating authentication tokens but also managing secure sessions and protecting the integrity of real-time communication throughout the WebSocket lifecycle.

In a Python environment, specifically when using libraries such as `websockets`, the approach to integrating authentication involves a similar set of principles. The `websockets` library does not provide direct support for token validation out of the box, so you would need to implement your own authentication logic. This usually begins by overriding or extending the WebSocket server's connection handler to perform token validation before allowing a connection to be established.

To do this, you would create a custom connection handler

function that processes incoming WebSocket requests. Within this function, you would extract the token from the request headers or query parameters. The next step involves validating this token similarly to how you would in a Node.js environment: by verifying its signature and checking its expiration time. Once the token is validated and the user's credentials are confirmed, you proceed to establish the WebSocket connection.

Managing secure sessions for WebSocket connections is critical for maintaining the integrity and security of real-time communication. After establishing the connection, the server must ensure that the session remains secure throughout its lifecycle. This involves several best practices. First, ensure that all WebSocket connections are encrypted using TLS (Transport Layer Security). This prevents eavesdropping and man-in-the-middle attacks by encrypting the data transmitted between the client and the server.

Additionally, implement proper session management on the server side. This includes tracking active sessions and ensuring that each WebSocket connection is associated with a valid and authenticated user. For long-lived sessions, such as those established by WebSockets, consider implementing periodic token refresh mechanisms. This approach helps in mitigating risks associated with token theft or session hijacking, as it reduces the window of opportunity for an attacker to exploit a compromised token.

Another crucial aspect of WebSocket authentication is handling disconnections and reconnections. WebSocket connections are inherently more volatile than HTTP connections due to their persistent nature and the potential for network interruptions. Thus, your application should be prepared to handle scenarios where a connection is lost and later re-established. This includes re-authenticating the user upon reconnection and ensuring that the session state is properly maintained or restored. Implementing mechanisms for detecting and managing session interruptions can help in providing a seamless user experience despite these challenges.

It is also important to implement comprehensive logging and monitoring for WebSocket connections. By keeping detailed logs of connection attempts, authentication processes, and session activities, you can identify and respond to security incidents more effectively. Monitoring tools can alert you to unusual patterns or potential security threats, allowing you to take timely actions to protect your application.

In summary, implementing WebSocket authentication requires a multi-faceted approach that addresses token validation, secure session management, and robust handling of real-time communication challenges. By ensuring that your WebSocket connections are properly authenticated and monitored, you can maintain a secure environment for your application and its users. Whether working with Node.js or Python, the principles remain consistent: validate tokens, secure sessions, and stay vigilant against potential security threats.

CHAPTER 39: SUPPORTING MULTIPLE DATA FORMATS

In modern software development, the ability of an API to handle multiple data formats is crucial for ensuring interoperability and flexibility. APIs are integral to enabling different systems and applications to communicate effectively. As a result, developers often encounter scenarios where they need to support various data formats for both request and response payloads. This chapter will explore how to manage different data formats, including JSON, XML, and custom data formats. We will delve into parsing and serialization techniques, and discuss strategies for maintaining compatibility across diverse data interchange formats.

Handling different data formats begins with understanding the primary formats used in web APIs. JSON (JavaScript Object Notation) and XML (Extensible Markup Language) are two of the most widely used formats for data interchange. JSON, known for its simplicity and readability, is favored for its ease of use in web applications. XML, on the other hand, offers a more structured approach with a strong schema definition, making it useful in contexts where data validation and hierarchical data representation are important.

To start, let's discuss JSON, a format that is both lightweight and easy to parse. JSON data is represented as a string that is organized into key-value pairs. For instance, a JSON object might look like this:

```json
{
 "name": "John Doe",
 "age": 30,
 "isStudent": false,
 "courses": ["Math", "Science", "History"]
}
```

In this example, the JSON object contains several key-value pairs: `"name"` maps to a string, `"age"` maps to a number, `"isStudent"` maps to a boolean, and `"courses"` maps to an array of strings. Parsing JSON involves converting this string into a data structure that can be manipulated programmatically. In many programming languages, this process is handled by built-in libraries. For instance, in JavaScript, `JSON.parse()` is used to convert a JSON string into a JavaScript object, while `JSON.stringify()` converts a JavaScript object back into a JSON string.

Serialization, the reverse process, involves converting a data structure or object into a JSON string. This is essential for transmitting data over the network or saving it to a file. To ensure compatibility and proper handling, it's crucial to validate JSON input and output. This can be achieved by using schema validation tools or libraries that check for the correctness of the JSON structure before processing.

XML is another prevalent format that offers a different set of features compared to JSON. XML provides a markup language with a rich set of features, including the ability to define custom tags and attributes, which can be beneficial for representing complex data structures. A typical XML document might look like this:

```xml
<person>
 <name>John Doe</name>
 <age>30</age>
 <isStudent>false</isStudent>
 <courses>
  <course>Math</course>
  <course>Science</course>
  <course>History</course>
 </courses>
</person>
```

In XML, data is organized into a hierarchy of elements and attributes, which allows for more detailed representation of relationships between different data components. Parsing XML involves converting this structured text into a format that can be programmatically accessed. Many languages provide libraries for XML parsing, such as `xml.etree.ElementTree` in Python or `DOMParser` in JavaScript. These libraries typically support DOM (Document Object Model) and SAX (Simple API for XML) parsing methods.

Serialization of XML data involves converting the data structure back into an XML string. Similar to JSON, it's important to ensure that the XML data adheres to the expected schema or structure. XML also supports schema validation through technologies like XML Schema Definition (XSD), which can be used to enforce rules and constraints on the XML data.

Beyond JSON and XML, custom data formats may also be required depending on the specific needs of an API. Custom formats can be designed to optimize performance, accommodate unique data structures, or integrate with legacy systems. For instance, an API might use a custom binary format for efficient data transmission or a specialized format for integrating with a proprietary system.

Handling custom data formats involves defining a clear specification for the format and implementing parsing and serialization logic according to this specification. It is crucial to document the format thoroughly and provide robust error handling to deal with any inconsistencies or unexpected data. This might involve creating custom parsers and serializers that adhere to the defined format and ensuring that the data can be accurately interpreted by both the API and its clients.

In summary, supporting multiple data formats in an API requires a comprehensive understanding of how to parse and serialize different formats, including JSON, XML, and custom data formats. Ensuring compatibility involves validating data structures, using appropriate libraries and tools, and adhering to specified schemas or formats. By effectively managing these aspects, developers can create APIs that are flexible, reliable, and capable of integrating with a wide range of systems and applications.

To ensure compatibility and proper handling, it's crucial to validate JSON input and output. This can be achieved through schema validation or by using libraries designed to enforce structural constraints on the data. For instance, in JavaScript, libraries such as Joi or AJV provide functionality to define and validate schemas, ensuring that incoming data adheres to expected formats and constraints.

While JSON is prevalent, XML remains a significant format, especially in legacy systems and enterprise environments. XML offers extensive capabilities for describing complex data structures with nested elements and attributes. Its verbose nature and the need for strict syntax adherence can make it less intuitive compared to JSON. Nonetheless, XML's strengths lie in its ability to represent hierarchical data and its support for namespaces, which are beneficial in scenarios involving multiple data schemas.

An example of XML data might look like this:

```xml
<person>
 <name>John Doe</name>
 <age>30</age>
 <isStudent>false</isStudent>
 <courses>
  <course>Math</course>
  <course>Science</course>
  <course>History</course>
 </courses>
</person>
```

In this XML example, data is organized into elements nested within other elements, providing a clear hierarchical structure. Parsing XML requires an understanding of the Document Object Model (DOM) or streaming parsing approaches, such as SAX (Simple API for XML). Many programming languages provide built-in libraries or APIs for XML parsing. For example, in Python, the `xml.etree.ElementTree` module allows for easy parsing and manipulation of XML data.

Serialization in XML involves converting data structures into XML format for transmission or storage. This process is more complex than JSON serialization due to XML's richer set of features, including attributes and mixed content. Properly handling XML serialization requires attention to detail to ensure that all relevant data is accurately represented, and that the XML is well-formed and valid according to any associated schemas or DTDs (Document Type Definitions).

Custom data formats may also be required in specific scenarios where standard formats like JSON or XML do not meet all requirements. Custom formats can be designed to optimize performance or to handle unique data structures that are not easily represented by traditional formats. When working with custom formats, it is essential to define a clear specification and ensure that both serialization and deserialization processes are well-documented and robust.

Custom formats might involve defining bespoke data structures or encoding schemes. For instance, a custom binary format might be used to efficiently transmit large amounts of data, where a compact binary representation is preferred over textual formats. In this case, serialization would involve converting data into a binary format that can be written to a file or sent over a network, while deserialization would involve reading the binary data and reconstructing it into a usable format.

When developing APIs that support multiple data formats, it is important to implement robust error handling and validation mechanisms. This includes not only checking for syntactical correctness but also ensuring that the data adheres to any semantic rules or business logic. For example, when accepting JSON input, an API should verify that required fields are present and that the data types match expectations. Similarly, for XML, it should ensure that the data adheres to any schema definitions and that required elements are correctly populated.

Versioning is another critical aspect when supporting multiple data formats. As APIs evolve, changes in data formats might be necessary. Implementing versioning strategies allows for backward compatibility and smooth transitions. This can involve using versioned endpoints or incorporating version information into the request headers or payloads.

Additionally, documentation plays a key role in managing

APIs that support various data formats. Comprehensive documentation should include detailed descriptions of the supported formats, example requests and responses, and information on how to handle errors or invalid data. Clear documentation helps developers understand how to interact with the API effectively and reduces the likelihood of integration issues.

Testing is equally important when dealing with multiple data formats. Automated tests should cover different scenarios and edge cases for each supported format. This ensures that the API behaves correctly and consistently regardless of the format used. Testing should also include validation of error handling, performance considerations, and the compatibility of different formats with existing systems.

In summary, supporting multiple data formats involves a thorough understanding of different data interchange standards, such as JSON and XML, as well as the ability to handle custom formats. Effective parsing and serialization, along with robust validation and error handling, are crucial to ensuring that APIs can manage diverse data formats seamlessly. By incorporating versioning strategies, comprehensive documentation, and rigorous testing, developers can create APIs that are flexible, reliable, and capable of meeting the needs of various systems and applications.

When designing an API to handle multiple data formats, careful consideration must be given to how data is parsed, serialized, and validated. The goal is to ensure that the API can seamlessly handle requests and responses in different formats while maintaining consistency and correctness. This involves implementing robust mechanisms for parsing incoming data, serializing responses, and ensuring compatibility across formats.

Custom data formats, although less common than JSON

and XML, can be highly beneficial in certain contexts. They offer the advantage of tailoring data representation to the specific needs of an application or system. However, working with custom formats requires a thorough understanding of both the data structure and the encoding/decoding processes. Developing a custom format involves defining a specification that clearly outlines how data should be formatted, parsed, and serialized. This specification must be rigorously documented to ensure that all parties involved in using the API can accurately interpret and manipulate the data.

To illustrate the process of handling custom data formats, consider a scenario where a custom binary format is used for efficient data transfer. Binary formats can be compact and fast to parse, but they are less human-readable than text-based formats like JSON or XML. Implementing support for a custom binary format involves creating a custom parser that can interpret the binary data and convert it into a usable data structure. Similarly, a custom serializer must be implemented to convert data structures into the binary format.

Parsing custom formats requires an understanding of the specific encoding rules and data structures defined in the format's specification. For example, if the custom format uses fixed-length fields or specific delimiters, the parser must be designed to recognize and handle these elements correctly. Serialization, on the other hand, involves converting data structures into the custom format, which often requires encoding data according to the defined rules and handling various edge cases.

In addition to parsing and serialization, validating data is a critical aspect of supporting multiple formats. Data validation ensures that incoming requests adhere to the expected format and constraints, reducing the risk of errors and inconsistencies. For JSON and XML, schema validation can be employed to enforce data structure and type constraints.

For custom formats, validation may involve custom logic to check the correctness of the data according to the format's specification.

When developing APIs, it is also essential to consider how to handle errors and edge cases that may arise when dealing with various data formats. Error handling should be implemented to provide meaningful feedback to clients when they submit data in an unsupported or incorrect format. This includes returning appropriate HTTP status codes and error messages that clearly indicate the nature of the problem.

In practice, APIs often need to provide support for negotiating the data format between the client and server. This negotiation process is typically managed through HTTP headers, such as `Accept` and `Content-Type`. The `Accept` header in the client's request specifies the desired data format for the response, while the `Content-Type` header indicates the format of the data being sent to the server. By examining these headers, the server can determine how to process the request and what format to use for the response.

Furthermore, versioning can be a valuable strategy when dealing with multiple data formats. By versioning the API, developers can introduce new formats or changes to existing formats without disrupting existing clients. Each version of the API can support different data formats, allowing clients to choose the version that best meets their needs.

Testing is another crucial aspect of ensuring that an API correctly handles multiple data formats. Comprehensive testing should include scenarios involving all supported formats, as well as edge cases and error conditions. Automated tests can help verify that the API behaves as expected and handles various data formats correctly. These tests should cover parsing, serialization, validation, and error handling to ensure that the API remains robust and reliable.

In conclusion, supporting multiple data formats in an API involves implementing robust parsing and serialization mechanisms, ensuring compatibility across formats, and validating data to maintain consistency and correctness. By understanding the requirements and intricacies of different data formats, including JSON, XML, and custom formats, developers can create APIs that are flexible, efficient, and capable of handling a wide range of data interchange scenarios. This approach not only enhances the interoperability of the API but also ensures that it meets the diverse needs of its clients.

CHAPTER 40: CUSTOMIZING API DOCUMENTATION

FastAPI provides robust automatic documentation generation through its integration with OpenAPI and Swagger UI, but there are instances when customization of this documentation becomes necessary to better align with specific project requirements or improve user experience. Customizing API documentation can involve several aspects, including adding custom metadata, modifying the user interface, and enhancing the overall user experience for API consumers. This chapter will delve into these elements, providing a comprehensive guide on how to effectively customize API documentation in FastAPI.

To start, adding custom metadata to the API documentation can significantly enhance its clarity and usefulness. Metadata includes additional information about the API, such as descriptions, terms of service, contact information, and license details. FastAPI allows for the inclusion of this metadata through the `openapi_tags` parameter and the `description`, `terms_of_service`, `contact`, and `license` attributes within the `FastAPI` class.

For example, you can include a general description and contact information directly in your FastAPI app initialization as follows:

```python
from fastapi import FastAPI

app FastAPI(
  title"My API",
   description"This API allows you to interact with the service in various ways.",
  version"1.0.0",
  terms_of_service"https://example.com/terms/",
  contact{
    "name": "API Support",
    "url": "https://example.com/support",
    "email": "support@example.com",
  },
  license_info{
    "name": "MIT License",
    "url": "https://opensource.org/licenses/MIT",
  },
)
```

In this setup, `title`, `description`, and `version` offer fundamental information about the API. The `terms_of_service`, `contact`, and `license_info` fields provide additional context and support information, which can be particularly useful for users navigating the documentation. This approach not only makes the documentation more informative but also helps in establishing trust and transparency with API consumers.

Customizing the user interface (UI) of the API documentation can further enhance the user experience. FastAPI uses Swagger UI by default, which offers a user-friendly, interactive interface for exploring the API. However, you might want to customize this UI to better fit your branding or to streamline the documentation's appearance. Customizing Swagger UI involves modifying its underlying configuration, which can be achieved by creating custom HTML templates or by using external CSS and JavaScript files.

To implement UI customizations, you can start by creating a new `swagger_ui.html` file with your desired HTML and styling. This file should include any custom CSS or JavaScript required to modify the appearance and behavior of the Swagger UI. You can then configure FastAPI to use this custom template by specifying the path to your file when initializing the `FastAPI` app:

```python
from fastapi import FastAPI

app FastAPI(
  docs_url"/custom-docs",  Custom path for Swagger UI
  redoc_urlNone,  Disable ReDoc if not needed
)
```

You would place the custom `swagger_ui.html` file in the appropriate directory, typically in the `static` folder of your FastAPI application. This approach allows you to have full control over the Swagger UI's look and feel, ensuring that it aligns with your application's branding and design guidelines.

Enhancing the user experience for API consumers involves more than just visual customizations. It requires ensuring that the documentation is comprehensive, intuitive, and easy to navigate. One way to achieve this is by adding detailed descriptions and examples for each endpoint. FastAPI allows you to include detailed descriptions and examples directly in your endpoint definitions. This can be done using the `description` and `response_model` parameters within your route decorators.

For instance:

```python
from fastapi import FastAPI, HTTPException
from pydantic import BaseModel

app FastAPI()

class Item(BaseModel):
  name: str
  description: str  None

@app.post("/items/", response_modelItem)
async def create_item(item: Item):
  """
  Create a new item.

    - name: Name of the item.
  - description: Optional description of the item.
  """
  return item
```

In this example, the `create_item` function is documented with an in-line description explaining the purpose of the endpoint and the data it expects. This detailed documentation helps API consumers understand how to use the endpoint effectively, providing clarity on what each field represents and what kind of data is required.

In addition to these methods, incorporating interactive elements like code samples or live request/response examples can further enhance the user experience. This could involve using tools such as Swagger UI's built-in functionality to run example requests directly from the documentation or including interactive playgrounds where users can test API calls.

By carefully customizing metadata, UI, and documentation content, you can ensure that your API documentation is not only informative but also user-friendly and aligned with your application's goals. This approach not only improves the overall usability of the API but also helps in establishing a positive experience for API consumers, ultimately contributing to the success and adoption of the API.

Customizing the user interface of the API documentation in FastAPI is an important step in tailoring the documentation experience to better meet the needs of users. FastAPI leverages Swagger UI by default for interactive API documentation, but there are occasions when modifying or extending this UI can provide a more tailored experience. Customization can include altering the appearance, layout, and behavior of the documentation interface to align with specific design requirements or organizational branding.

One of the primary ways to customize Swagger UI in FastAPI is by injecting custom JavaScript and CSS. This approach allows for modifications such as changing the color scheme, adjusting layout components, or adding custom functionality. To achieve this, you can utilize FastAPI's `swagger_ui_parameters` and `swagger_ui_oauth2_redirect_url` parameters to configure Swagger UI settings.

For instance, if you need to include custom CSS or JavaScript, you can provide the URL of these resources using the `swagger_ui_parameters` parameter. This parameter accepts a dictionary where you can specify the URL to your custom styles and scripts. Here’s an example of how to include custom CSS and JavaScript:

```python
from fastapi import FastAPI

app FastAPI(
  swagger_ui_parameters{
    "customCssUrl": "https://example.com/custom.css",
```

```
    "customJsUrl": "https://example.com/custom.js",
  }
)
```

In this configuration, `customCssUrl` points to a URL where your custom CSS file is hosted, and `customJsUrl` points to a URL for your custom JavaScript file. This allows you to inject styles and scripts that modify the appearance and behavior of Swagger UI according to your specific needs.

Beyond basic visual customizations, you might also want to adjust the functionality or features provided by the documentation interface. For example, integrating OAuth2 authorization into Swagger UI can be done by setting the `swagger_ui_oauth2_redirect_url` parameter. This URL directs Swagger UI to handle OAuth2 authentication flows, which can be crucial for APIs requiring secure access.

Another aspect of customization involves adding custom documentation sections or information. FastAPI provides mechanisms for including detailed descriptions, examples, and interactive elements directly in the documentation. You can use the `description` parameter of the `FastAPI` class to provide a detailed explanation of the API, its features, and usage guidelines. Furthermore, you can enhance specific endpoints with additional descriptions and examples using FastAPI's path operation decorators.

For example, to add a detailed description and example to a specific endpoint, you can use the `description` and `examples` parameters of the path operation decorators like `@app.get`:

```python
from fastapi import FastAPI

app FastAPI()
```

```
@app.get("/items/{item_id}",
        description"Retrieve an item by its ID. Provides detailed information about the item.",
     responses{
        200: {
           "description": "Successful response",
           "content": {
              "application/json": {
                 "example": {
                    "item_id": 1,
                    "name": "Sample Item",
                    "description": "This is a detailed description of the sample item.",
                    "price": 100.0
                 }
              }
           }
        }
     })
async def get_item(item_id: int):
        return {"item_id": item_id, "name": "Sample Item", "description": "Detailed description", "price": 100.0}
```

In this example, the `description` parameter provides an overview of what the endpoint does, while the `responses` dictionary includes an example response payload. This enhances the documentation by offering users a clear understanding of what to expect from the API response.

Furthermore, customizing documentation involves ensuring that the user experience is intuitive and accessible. This can be achieved by organizing the documentation effectively, providing clear and concise descriptions, and including examples and usage scenarios. Proper organization can involve grouping related endpoints into logical sections, using tags to categorize operations, and providing search functionality to help users quickly find relevant information.

To optimize the documentation experience, it is also beneficial to test the documentation interface from the perspective of different user roles, such as developers, testers, or end-users. Gathering feedback from these users can provide valuable insights into how the documentation can be further improved or refined.

In summary, customizing API documentation in FastAPI involves a multifaceted approach that includes adding custom metadata, modifying the Swagger UI, and enhancing the user experience. By leveraging FastAPI's configuration options and path operation decorators, you can tailor the documentation to better meet the needs of users, improve accessibility, and ensure that the API is both well-documented and user-friendly.

To further enhance API documentation beyond UI and metadata customizations, consider the addition of interactive features and detailed examples. FastAPI provides facilities to enrich the documentation with more extensive examples and interactive capabilities, making it easier for users to understand and interact with the API.

One effective way to improve documentation is by including detailed request and response examples for each endpoint. This can be done using FastAPI's built-in support for example data in the endpoint definitions. The `response_model` and `responses` parameters of the route decorators enable you to define response models and examples. Providing examples helps users understand the expected input and output formats, which can significantly enhance the usability of the API.

For instance, if you have an endpoint that returns user information, you can define a detailed response example like this:

```python
from fastapi import FastAPI
from pydantic import BaseModel
from typing import List

app FastAPI()

class User(BaseModel):
  id: int
  name: str
  email: str

@app.get("/users/{user_id}", response_modelUser,
response_description"The user details", responses{
  200: {
    "description": "Successful response",
    "content": {
      "application/json": {
        "example": {
          "id": 1,
          "name": "John Doe",
          "email": "john.doe@example.com"
        }
      }
    }
  }
})
async def get_user(user_id: int):
    return {"id": user_id, "name": "John Doe", "email":
"john.doe@example.com"}
```

In this example, the `responses` parameter includes a JSON example that demonstrates what a successful response would look like. This example is presented directly in the documentation, allowing users to see concrete examples of the data format.

Another important aspect of customizing API documentation is managing and documenting request parameters and query options. Providing clear descriptions and examples for request parameters can help users construct valid requests. FastAPI's path, query, and body parameters can be documented with detailed descriptions and examples, which improves the overall clarity of the API.

For example, you might include descriptions for query parameters as follows:

```python
from fastapi import FastAPI, Query
from typing import Optional

app FastAPI()

@app.get("/items/")
async def read_items(skip: int  Query(0, description"Number of items to skip"), limit: int  Query(10, description"Maximum number of items to return")):
  return {"skip": skip, "limit": limit}
```

Here, the `Query` function is used to specify default values and descriptions for query parameters, which are reflected in the generated documentation. This approach ensures that users understand the purpose and constraints of each parameter, reducing ambiguity.

Furthermore, implementing versioning and deprecation notices in the API documentation can also be beneficial. As APIs evolve, it's important to communicate changes and maintain backward compatibility. FastAPI allows you to add version information and deprecation warnings through the documentation metadata and endpoint descriptions. This helps users understand which versions of the API are supported and when certain features might be phased out.

To include versioning information, you can use the `title` and `description` parameters of the `FastAPI` class to indicate the version of the API:

```python
app FastAPI(
  title"My API v2",
   description"This is version 2 of My API. Please refer to the documentation for details on new features and changes.",
  version"2.0.0"
)
```

For endpoints that are deprecated, you can include notes in the endpoint descriptions and use response descriptions to inform users of the deprecation status:

```python
@app.get("/old-endpoint", deprecatedTrue)
async def old_endpoint():
   return {"message": "This endpoint is deprecated and will be removed in future versions."}
```

In this case, the `deprecated` parameter is used to indicate that the endpoint is no longer recommended for use, and additional information about its deprecation is provided in the endpoint's response description.

Customizing API documentation in FastAPI offers numerous possibilities for improving the clarity, functionality, and user experience of your API. By incorporating custom metadata, modifying the UI, adding detailed examples, managing request parameters, and implementing versioning and deprecation notices, you can create a comprehensive and user-friendly documentation experience. These enhancements not only make your API more accessible but also help in fostering better communication and understanding between API developers and users.

CHAPTER 41: BUILDING REUSABLE COMPONENTS AND LIBRARIES

Creating reusable components and libraries is a fundamental practice in software development that enhances efficiency and maintainability. In the context of FastAPI, this involves designing components that can be shared across multiple projects, reducing redundancy, and promoting consistency. This chapter will delve into best practices for building reusable FastAPI components, focusing on middleware, dependency injections, and utility functions.

To begin with, middleware is a powerful feature in FastAPI that allows you to execute code before and after the request and response cycle. Middleware can be used for a variety of purposes, such as logging, authentication, or modifying requests and responses. Creating reusable middleware involves defining classes or functions that encapsulate specific functionalities and then integrating them into multiple FastAPI applications.

Consider an example of a middleware component for logging request details. This middleware might be implemented as follows:

```python
from starlette.middleware.base import BaseHTTPMiddleware
from starlette.requests import Request
from starlette.responses import Response
import logging

class LoggingMiddleware(BaseHTTPMiddleware):
  async def dispatch(self, request: Request, call_next):
    logger logging.getLogger("my_logger")
    logger.info(f"Request: {request.method} {request.url}")
    response await call_next(request)
    logger.info(f"Response status: {response.status_code}")
    return response
```

In this example, `LoggingMiddleware` logs the HTTP method and URL of incoming requests as well as the status code of outgoing responses. By encapsulating this functionality within a class, it becomes reusable across different FastAPI applications by simply adding it to the middleware stack of each application.

Moving on to dependency injections, FastAPI provides a flexible system for managing dependencies that can be reused across various endpoints and applications. Dependencies are functions or classes that are injected into route handlers, providing common functionality such as database connections, authentication, or configuration settings. Creating reusable dependencies involves defining these components as standalone functions or classes and then injecting them into multiple endpoints.

For instance, consider a dependency for database access:

```python
from typing import Generator
from sqlalchemy.orm import Session
```

```
from myapp.database import SessionLocal

def get_db() -> Generator[Session, None, None]:
    db SessionLocal()
    try:
        yield db
    finally:
        db.close()
```

In this example, `get_db` is a generator function that provides a database session to route handlers. It ensures that each request gets a fresh session and that the session is properly closed after use. This dependency can be injected into any route handler requiring database access:

```python
from fastapi import Depends, FastAPI
from sqlalchemy.orm import Session

app FastAPI()

@app.get("/items/")
def read_items(db: Session Depends(get_db)):
    return {"items": db.query(Item).all()}
```

This approach allows for a clean separation of concerns and promotes code reuse across different endpoints and projects.

Utility functions are another critical aspect of building reusable components. These are functions that encapsulate common logic or operations that are not specific to a single endpoint but are used across multiple parts of the application. Utility functions can include operations such as data validation, formatting, or transformation. By placing these functions in a separate module or library, they can be easily imported and used across different parts of the application.

For example, a utility function for validating email addresses might look like this:

```python
import re
from typing import Optional

def is_valid_email(email: str) -> bool:
    pattern r"^[a-zA-Z0-9._%+-]+@[a-zA-Z0-9.-]+\.[a-zA-Z]{2,}$"
    return re.match(pattern, email) is not None
```

This function checks if a given email address matches a standard pattern. It can be imported and used in various endpoints or services that require email validation.

When building reusable components and libraries, it is important to follow best practices for structuring and organizing your code. Components should be modular, with a clear separation of responsibilities. Documentation is also crucial, as it helps other developers understand how to use and integrate the components into their projects. Providing clear docstrings, usage examples, and API references will improve the usability and maintainability of your reusable components.

Furthermore, versioning and testing are essential practices when developing reusable libraries. Versioning helps track changes and manage compatibility between different versions of the library. Testing ensures that the components work correctly and continue to function as expected as the codebase evolves. By incorporating unit tests and integration tests, you can validate the functionality of your reusable components and ensure their reliability.

In conclusion, building reusable components and libraries in FastAPI involves creating modular middleware, managing dependencies, and developing utility functions. By following best practices for modular design, documentation, versioning, and testing, you can develop a library of components that enhances efficiency, consistency, and maintainability across multiple projects.

Continuing from our discussion on middleware and dependency injections, it is crucial to consider utility functions as another cornerstone of building reusable components in FastAPI. Utility functions are those that provide common functionalities or perform repetitive tasks that can be used across different parts of your application or even across different projects. These functions can simplify your codebase, reduce duplication, and promote a modular architecture.

Utility functions can encompass a wide range of tasks, from data validation and transformation to logging and error handling. For example, suppose you frequently need to validate email addresses throughout your application. Instead of repeating the validation logic, you can create a reusable utility function:

```python
import re
from typing import Optional

def validate_email(email: str) -> Optional[str]:
  """Validate email address format."""
  email_regex r'^[\w\.-]+@[\w\.-]+\.\w+$'
  if re.match(email_regex, email):
    return None
  return "Invalid email format"
```

In this example, the `validate_email` function uses a regular expression to check the validity of an email address. By encapsulating this logic within a utility function, you ensure that the validation is consistent and easily maintainable. This function can be imported and used wherever email validation is required in your FastAPI project.

Building a library of reusable components involves more than just creating individual pieces; it requires organizing them effectively. Consider structuring your components into a well-defined module or package. For instance, you might create a `utils` package containing various utility functions, a `middleware` package for middleware components, and a `dependencies` package for dependency injections. This modular approach helps in managing the codebase and ensures that each component can be easily located and maintained.

Here is how you might organize a project with reusable components:

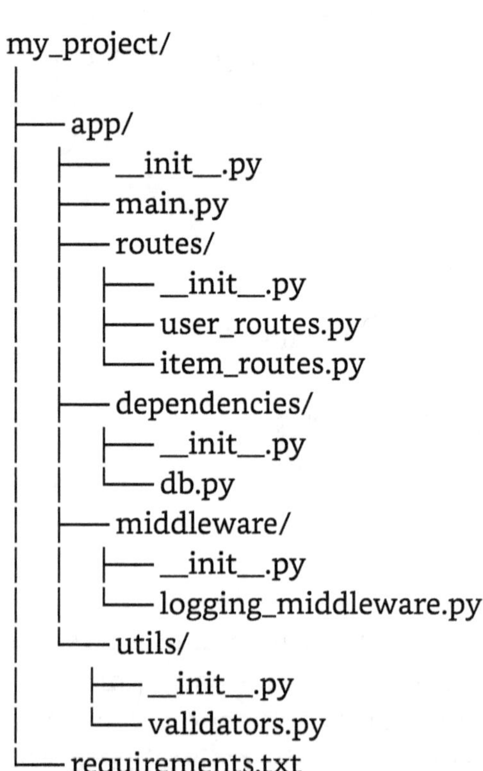

```
my_project/
│
├── app/
│   ├── __init__.py
│   ├── main.py
│   ├── routes/
│   │   ├── __init__.py
│   │   ├── user_routes.py
│   │   └── item_routes.py
│   ├── dependencies/
│   │   ├── __init__.py
│   │   └── db.py
│   ├── middleware/
│   │   ├── __init__.py
│   │   └── logging_middleware.py
│   └── utils/
│       ├── __init__.py
│       └── validators.py
└── requirements.txt
```

```

In this directory structure, `user_routes.py` and `item_routes.py` would contain route definitions, `db.py` would include reusable database-related dependencies, `logging_middleware.py` would define the logging middleware, and `validators.py` would house utility functions for validation tasks.

Another key practice in building reusable components is ensuring that they are well-documented. Proper documentation enhances the usability and maintainability of your components, allowing other developers to understand how to use them effectively. Documenting each component should include a clear description of its purpose, usage examples, and any parameters or return values it handles. This can be achieved through docstrings in Python, which can be rendered into documentation formats using tools such as Sphinx or MkDocs.

For example, adding a docstring to the `validate_email` function might look like this:

```python
def validate_email(email: str) -> Optional[str]:
  """
  Validate the format of an email address.

    Args:
     email (str): The email address to validate.

    Returns:
     Optional[str]: Returns None if the email format is valid,
     otherwise returns an error message.
  """
  email_regex r'^[\w\.-]+@[\w\.-]+\.\w+$'
  if re.match(email_regex, email):
    return None
```
```

```
    return "Invalid email format"
```

By documenting the function in this manner, you provide clear guidance on its usage and expected behavior, which is invaluable for both current and future developers working with the code.

In summary, creating reusable components in FastAPI involves designing middleware, dependencies, and utility functions that can be shared across projects. Proper organization of these components into a modular structure, along with thorough documentation, ensures that they are maintainable, understandable, and easily integrable into different applications. Through these practices, you can significantly enhance development efficiency, reduce code duplication, and promote consistency across projects.

When developing a library of reusable components for FastAPI, attention to documentation and testing is paramount. Proper documentation ensures that your components are understandable and easy to use, while comprehensive testing guarantees that they function correctly across different scenarios. Both aspects are essential for maintaining the reliability and usability of your reusable components and libraries.

Documentation should provide clear and concise information on how to use each component, including setup instructions, usage examples, and explanations of parameters and return values. For instance, if you have created a middleware component, the documentation should include details on what the middleware does, how to configure it, and examples of how it can be used within a FastAPI application. Here's an example of how documentation might look for a middleware component:

```markdown
```

LoggingMiddleware

`LoggingMiddleware` is a middleware component that logs incoming requests and outgoing responses.

Setup

To use `LoggingMiddleware` in your FastAPI application, you need to add it to the middleware stack:

```python
from fastapi import FastAPI
from my_project.middleware.logging import LoggingMiddleware

app FastAPI()
app.add_middleware(LoggingMiddleware)
```

Configuration

`LoggingMiddleware` does not require additional configuration. It automatically logs request and response details.

Example

When a request is made to your API, `LoggingMiddleware` will log the following:

- HTTP method and URL of the request
- Response status code

` ` `

This level of detail helps users understand the purpose and usage of the middleware, making it easier for them to integrate it into their projects.

Testing is equally crucial to ensure that your components behave as expected under various conditions. Comprehensive tests should cover different use cases, edge cases, and potential failure scenarios. FastAPI, combined with testing frameworks such as Pytest, provides a robust environment for testing API components.

For example, if you are testing a utility function like `validate_email`, you should write tests that cover valid email formats, invalid formats, and edge cases. Here's how you might write tests for the `validate_email` function:

```python
import pytest
from my_project.utils.email_validator import validate_email

def test_valid_email():
  assert validate_email("test@example.com") is None

def test_invalid_email():
  assert validate_email("invalid-email") "Invalid email format"

def test_edge_case_email():
  assert validate_email("user@domain") "Invalid email format"
```

These tests ensure that the `validate_email` function correctly identifies valid and invalid email formats. Running these tests regularly as part of your development process helps catch any issues early and ensures the reliability of your utility functions.

In addition to documenting and testing individual components, consider creating a comprehensive overview of your reusable library. This overview should describe the purpose of the library, the components it includes, and how to integrate and use them. A well-structured README file or equivalent documentation can serve as a central resource for users of the library, providing a quick reference for setting up and using the components.

To further enhance the usability of your library, consider implementing version control and maintaining a changelog. Version control allows you to track changes to your library over time, while a changelog provides a record of updates, bug fixes, and new features. This practice helps users understand the evolution of the library and manage upgrades in their projects.

In summary, building reusable components and libraries in FastAPI involves creating middleware, dependencies, and utility functions that are modular, well-documented, and thoroughly tested. By focusing on clear documentation and rigorous testing, you ensure that your components are reliable and easy to integrate into various projects. This approach not only improves development efficiency but also promotes best practices in software design and maintenance.

CHAPTER 42: IMPLEMENTING RATE LIMITING AND THROTTLING

Rate limiting and throttling are critical strategies in API management that help control the load on your API and protect it from abuse or overuse. By implementing these strategies, you can ensure that your API remains responsive and available even under high traffic conditions. This discussion will cover the principles of rate limiting and throttling, and provide a detailed guide on how to implement these strategies in FastAPI. We will explore various methods of setting limits based on criteria such as IP addresses, user accounts, or other relevant factors.

Rate limiting involves setting a maximum number of requests that a client can make to your API within a specified time frame. This is typically done to prevent abuse and ensure fair usage among all clients. Throttling, on the other hand, refers to the process of controlling the rate of requests that can be processed by the server, often to maintain performance and prevent overloading.

In FastAPI, implementing rate limiting and throttling requires the use of middleware or third-party libraries that manage request quotas and track usage patterns. One common approach is to use a rate limiting library like `slowapi`, which provides an easy way to apply rate limits using various criteria.

To get started, you first need to install the `slowapi` library, which integrates seamlessly with FastAPI:

```bash
pip install slowapi
```

Once installed, you can configure and use `slowapi` to implement rate limiting in your FastAPI application. Here's an example of how to set up rate limiting using `slowapi`:

```python
from fastapi import FastAPI, Request
from slowapi import Limiter
from slowapi.util import get_remote_address

app FastAPI()
limiter Limiter(key_funcget_remote_address)

@app.get("/items/")
@limiter.limit("5/minute")
async def read_items(request: Request):
  return {"message": "This endpoint is rate limited to 5 requests per minute per IP address."}
```

In this example, the `@limiter.limit("5/minute")` decorator applies a rate limit of 5 requests per minute per IP address to the `/items/` endpoint. The `get_remote_address` function extracts the client's IP address, which is used to enforce the rate limit. The `slowapi` library handles the logic of tracking requests and applying limits, making it easy to implement rate limiting with minimal configuration.

Beyond IP-based rate limiting, you might want to implement more complex strategies based on user accounts or other criteria. For example, you could use authentication tokens to track and limit requests on a per-user basis. To achieve this, you would need to modify the `key_func` used by the rate limiter to extract user-specific information from the request.

Here's an example of how to apply rate limits based on user authentication tokens:

```python
from fastapi import FastAPI, Request, Depends
from fastapi.security import OAuth2PasswordBearer
from slowapi import Limiter
from slowapi.util import get_remote_address

app FastAPI()
oauth2_scheme OAuth2PasswordBearer(tokenUrl"token")
limiter Limiter(key_funclambda request: get_user_from_token(request))

def get_user_from_token(request: Request):
  token request.headers.get("Authorization")
   Assume a function to decode token and retrieve user ID
  user_id decode_token_and_get_user_id(token)
  return user_id

@app.get("/user-data/")
@limiter.limit("10/minute")
async def read_user_data(request: Request, token: str Depends(oauth2_scheme)):
    return {"message": "This endpoint is rate limited to 10 requests per minute per user."}
```

In this setup, the `get_user_from_token` function extracts the user ID from the authentication token and is used as the key for rate limiting. This approach ensures that rate limits are applied on a per-user basis, rather than per IP address.

It is also essential to handle cases where users exceed the rate limits. Typically, the response should indicate that the rate limit has been exceeded, providing information about when the user can make their next request. This is usually done by returning a 429 Too Many Requests status code along with a relevant message.

Implementing rate limiting and throttling is not only about setting limits but also about ensuring that your API provides a good user experience even when limits are enforced. Providing informative error messages and allowing users to understand their usage patterns can help mitigate frustration and improve the overall interaction with your API.

In summary, effective implementation of rate limiting and throttling in FastAPI involves using appropriate libraries and configuring them based on your specific needs. By setting limits based on IP addresses, user accounts, or other criteria, and handling rate limit breaches gracefully, you can protect your API from abuse, manage traffic loads, and ensure a reliable and fair service for all users.

In order to effectively manage and safeguard your API from potential misuse, implementing rate limiting and throttling is crucial. These mechanisms help regulate the number of requests a user or system can make in a given period, ensuring that your API remains responsive and available for all users. FastAPI provides a flexible framework for integrating these controls, allowing you to set limits based on various criteria such as IP addresses, user accounts, or other identifiers.

To begin with, understanding the basic concepts of rate limiting and throttling is essential. Rate limiting refers to the practice of setting a maximum number of requests that a user or system can make to an API within a specified timeframe. This prevents any single user from overwhelming the server with excessive requests. Throttling, on the other hand, involves controlling the rate at which requests are processed. It can be used to delay the processing of requests that exceed certain thresholds, thereby managing the load on your API.

In FastAPI, rate limiting can be implemented using several approaches. One common method is to use middleware that intercepts incoming requests and enforces rate limits based on configurable parameters. Middleware in FastAPI allows you to execute code before and after the request processing, making it an ideal place to implement rate limiting logic.

To illustrate, let's consider how to set up a simple rate limiter using FastAPI and the `slowapi` library, which provides built-in support for rate limiting. First, you need to install `slowapi`:

```bash
pip install slowapi
```

Once installed, you can integrate `slowapi` into your FastAPI application. Start by importing the necessary components and initializing the rate limiter:

```python
from fastapi import FastAPI, Request
from slowapi import Limiter
from slowapi.util import get_remote_address

app FastAPI()
limiter Limiter(key_funcget_remote_address)
```

In this example, `get_remote_address` is a function provided by `slowapi` that extracts the IP address of the incoming request. The `Limiter` object is initialized with this function to ensure that rate limits are enforced based on the client's IP address.

Next, apply the rate limiter to your routes. You can use the `@limiter.limit` decorator to specify the rate limits for individual endpoints. For instance:

```python
from slowapi.errors import RateLimitExceeded

@app.get("/items/")
@limiter.limit("5/minute")
async def read_items(request: Request):
    return {"message": "This is a rate-limited endpoint"}
```

In this example, the `read_items` endpoint is restricted to a maximum of 5 requests per minute per IP address. If a client exceeds this limit, `slowapi` will automatically handle the rate limit exception, returning a `429 Too Many Requests` response.

For more granular control, you might want to set different rate limits for different users or based on other criteria. This can be achieved by customizing the `key_func` parameter in the `Limiter` initialization. For instance, if you want to apply rate limits based on user accounts rather than IP addresses, you would need to modify the `key_func` to extract and use user-specific identifiers.

Consider the following example where we assume users are authenticated and their IDs are available in the request. The `key_func` function could be modified as follows:

```python
def get_user_id(request: Request):
        Assume user ID is stored in the request state after
authentication
    return request.state.user_id
```

Then, initialize the `Limiter` with this function:

```python
```

limiter Limiter(key_funcget_user_id)
```

Now, the rate limits will be applied based on user IDs, allowing for more customized control of API usage.

In addition to rate limiting, throttling can be implemented to further manage request processing. While rate limiting restricts the number of requests, throttling can control how quickly requests are handled after a certain threshold is reached. This can be particularly useful to prevent abuse and ensure fair resource allocation.

Implementing throttling typically involves introducing delays or queuing mechanisms. FastAPI does not provide built-in throttling capabilities, but you can achieve this through custom middleware or by using additional libraries. One approach is to use a token bucket algorithm or a leaky bucket algorithm to manage request rates and introduce delays when thresholds are exceeded.

For example, you might create a middleware component that checks the rate of incoming requests and introduces a delay if the rate exceeds certain limits. Here's a simplified example of how you might implement such a middleware:

```python
from starlette.middleware.base import BaseHTTPMiddleware
import time

class ThrottleMiddleware(BaseHTTPMiddleware):
  def __init__(self, app, max_requests: int, per_seconds: int):
    super().__init__(app)
    self.max_requests max_requests
    self.per_seconds per_seconds
    self.timestamps {}

   async def dispatch(self, request: Request, call_next):
    client_ip get_remote_address(request)
```
```

```
    current_time  time.time()
    if client_ip not in self.timestamps:
      self.timestamps[client_ip] []
                              self.timestamps[client_ip]        [t    for
t  in  self.timestamps[client_ip]  if  t  >  current_time  -
self.per_seconds]
    if len(self.timestamps[client_ip]) > self.max_requests:
              time_to_wait  self.per_seconds - (current_time -
self.timestamps[client_ip][0])
      if time_to_wait > 0:
        time.sleep(time_to_wait)
    self.timestamps[client_ip].append(time.time())
    response  await call_next(request)
    return response
```

In this middleware, requests from the same IP address are tracked, and delays are introduced if the number of requests exceeds the allowed limit within a specified period. This approach provides a basic form of throttling, but more advanced solutions may be required for complex use cases.

In summary, implementing rate limiting and throttling in FastAPI involves integrating middleware and libraries to enforce and manage request rates. By setting appropriate limits and handling exceptions or delays, you can protect your API from abuse and ensure a fair and reliable service for all users.

When implementing rate limiting and throttling, it is crucial to consider not only the basic configurations but also the nuances of how they interact with your API's overall performance and user experience. While the previous discussion covered the integration of rate limiting using the `slowapi` library, this segment will delve deeper into more advanced techniques and configurations, including how to handle different types of rate limiting, custom strategies, and how to ensure that throttling does not negatively impact the usability of your API.

After configuring basic rate limiting, the next step is to handle error responses effectively. When a user exceeds the allowed request limits, it is essential to provide meaningful feedback. Typically, a `429 Too Many Requests` status code is used to indicate that the rate limit has been exceeded. You can customize the error message to include details such as the remaining time before the user can make new requests. Here's an example of how you might handle this:

```python
from slowapi.errors import RateLimitExceeded
from fastapi.responses import JSONResponse

@app.exception_handler(RateLimitExceeded)
async def rate_limit_error_handler(request: Request, exc: RateLimitExceeded):
  return JSONResponse(
    status_code429,
    content{
      "message": "Rate limit exceeded. Please try again later.",
      "retry_after": exc.retry_after,
    },
  )
```

This custom error handler will ensure that users receive a clear and actionable message when they hit the rate limit, improving their experience and understanding of the limitation.

In addition to IP-based rate limiting, you might need to implement rate limits based on user accounts or other criteria, such as API keys or user roles. FastAPI does not provide built-in support for user-based rate limiting out of the box, but you can extend the `slowapi` library's functionality to achieve this. For example, you could create a custom key function that generates rate limit keys based on user identifiers instead of IP addresses.

Consider the following example, where we use a custom key function to apply rate limits based on a user ID retrieved from a request header:

```python
def get_user_key(request: Request) -> str:
  user_id request.headers.get("X-User-ID")
  return user_id if user_id else get_remote_address(request)

user_limiter Limiter(key_funcget_user_key)

@app.get("/user-data")
@user_limiter.limit("5/minute")
async def get_user_data(request: Request):
  return {"data": "This is user-specific data"}
```

In this example, the rate limit is applied based on the `X-User-ID` header. If the header is not present, the limiter defaults to using the IP address. This approach allows for more granular control over rate limits, accommodating different types of users or scenarios.

Another important consideration is how to handle rate limits across distributed systems or microservices. In a distributed environment, rate limiting needs to be consistent across all instances of your service. One approach is to use a shared store such as Redis to maintain and check rate limit counters. Redis is well-suited for this purpose due to its fast in-memory data structure and support for atomic operations.

To integrate Redis with FastAPI for rate limiting, you can use the `redis-py` library along with `slowapi`. First, install the required packages:

```bash
pip install redis slowapi
```

Next, configure Redis and modify the rate limiter setup to use Redis as the backend for storing rate limit counters:

```python
import redis
from slowapi import Limiter
from slowapi.util import get_remote_address

redis_client redis.StrictRedis(host'localhost', port6379, db0)
limiter Limiter(key_funcget_remote_address, storageredis_client)
```

This configuration will ensure that rate limit data is stored and accessed from Redis, allowing for consistent rate limiting across multiple instances of your service.

Beyond rate limiting, throttling can also be implemented to manage request processing rates. Throttling involves delaying the processing of requests when the system is under high load. This can be achieved by introducing a delay in request handling or by queuing requests. FastAPI does not have built-in support for throttling, but you can implement a throttling mechanism by combining middleware with asynchronous tasks.

For example, you can create a middleware that introduces a delay for requests when certain conditions are met:

```python
from fastapi.middleware.base import BaseHTTPMiddleware
import asyncio

class ThrottleMiddleware(BaseHTTPMiddleware):
  async def dispatch(self, request, call_next):
```

```
 Simulate throttling by introducing a delay
 await asyncio.sleep(1) Delay of 1 second
 response await call_next(request)
 return response

app.add_middleware(ThrottleMiddleware)
```

This middleware introduces a delay of 1 second for each request. You can adjust the delay or implement more sophisticated throttling logic based on your needs.

In conclusion, implementing rate limiting and throttling in FastAPI requires careful consideration of your API's requirements and user needs. By using middleware, libraries like `slowapi`, and external storage solutions like Redis, you can create a robust system that manages request rates effectively while maintaining a positive user experience. It's important to tailor your rate limiting and throttling strategies to fit the specific context and usage patterns of your API, ensuring both performance and security are optimized.

CHAPTER 43: HANDLING API DEPRECATION AND SUNSET

In the lifecycle of an API, deprecation and eventual sunset of older versions are inevitable as improvements and changes are made. Managing these transitions effectively is crucial to maintaining a positive experience for your users and ensuring a smooth migration process. This section will explore comprehensive strategies for handling API deprecation, including clear communication with users, providing structured migration paths, and gracefully sunsetting outdated API versions while striving to maintain backward compatibility where feasible.

The first step in managing API deprecation is to establish a clear and consistent communication strategy. Users need to be informed well in advance about the impending deprecation of API versions to allow them ample time to adapt. This communication should be multi-faceted, leveraging various channels to ensure the message reaches all affected users. It is advisable to use direct notifications via email or dashboard alerts for registered users, complemented by public announcements on your API documentation site and developer forums.

When announcing deprecation, it is essential to provide detailed information regarding the reasons for deprecation, the timeline, and the steps users need to take. A typical deprecation announcement should include a deprecation date, a final date after which the API will be sunsetted, and a description of what changes or new versions are available. For example:

"Version 1.0 of the API will be deprecated as of March 1, 2025. We recommend transitioning to Version 2.0, which includes enhanced features and improved performance. Please review the migration guide available at [link] to understand the changes and update your applications accordingly."

Providing a migration path is a critical component of the deprecation process. A migration path should outline the steps necessary for users to move from the deprecated version to the new one. This guide should cover the following aspects: differences between the old and new versions, changes in endpoints, updates required in request and response formats, and any new authentication or authorization methods. It should also include sample code snippets and troubleshooting tips to assist users in making the transition smoothly.

To facilitate the migration process, it is helpful to provide version-specific documentation and tools. For instance, you might offer a version comparison tool that highlights differences between the deprecated and new versions. Additionally, providing a sandbox environment where users can test their applications against the new API version before making the full switch can be extremely beneficial.

Graceful sunset of older API versions involves ensuring that even after deprecation, the API continues to function correctly for existing users while encouraging migration to newer versions. During this phase, it is essential to maintain backward compatibility to a reasonable extent. This means that while you may introduce new features and improvements in the latest version, the older versions should continue to operate as expected until the official sunset date.

To manage backward compatibility effectively, you can implement versioning strategies within your API. One common approach is to use URL versioning, where the version number is included as part of the API endpoint URL (e.g., `/api/v1/resource`). This method allows you to maintain multiple versions of the API concurrently, making it easier for users to transition at their own pace. Another approach is header-based versioning, where the version information is included in the request headers (e.g., `Accept-Version: 1.0`). This method can help keep URLs cleaner and avoid clutter but requires users to be aware of and configure headers correctly.

As the sunset date approaches, it is important to monitor usage of the deprecated API versions closely. This monitoring can help identify which users are still relying on the old versions and may require additional support during the migration process. Tools for API analytics and logging can provide insights into usage patterns and help prioritize support efforts.

Finally, after the sunset date, it is crucial to ensure that the deprecated API versions are fully removed from service. This removal should be handled in a manner that minimizes disruption. Typically, this involves disabling the endpoints and providing users with a final notification that the version has been retired. It is also helpful to archive documentation and migration guides for historical reference, in case users need to revisit the transition process.

By implementing these strategies for handling API deprecation and sunset, you can facilitate a smoother transition for your users, reduce the risk of disruptions, and ensure that your API continues to evolve in a manner that supports both innovation and user satisfaction.

To ensure a smooth transition during the deprecation and sunset process, maintaining backward compatibility is essential, especially when you are dealing with a large user base that may not be able to migrate immediately. While it is often impossible to keep support for every deprecated feature indefinitely, a thoughtful approach can minimize disruptions and maintain user trust.

One effective strategy is to introduce a deprecation warning mechanism in the API itself. When a user accesses deprecated endpoints or uses features slated for removal, the API should return a warning message indicating that the feature is outdated and provide guidance on the recommended alternatives. This proactive approach informs users of the upcoming changes in real-time, giving them immediate feedback and prompting them to take action. The response could include a `Deprecation-Notice` header or an explicit warning message in the response body. For example:

```json
{
 "warning": "This endpoint is deprecated and will be removed in Version 3.0. Please use the new endpoint at /v2/new-endpoint.",
 "details": {
  "migration_guide": "http://example.com/migration-guide"
 }
}
```

By embedding these warnings directly into the API responses, you ensure that users are constantly reminded of the need to update their integration without relying solely on external communications.

In addition to warnings, you should also provide a grace

period during which both the old and new versions of the API are available simultaneously. This overlap allows users to transition at their own pace without experiencing service interruptions. During this grace period, it is important to monitor usage patterns and gather feedback to address any issues users might encounter while migrating.

Graceful sunset procedures involve not only providing advance notice but also implementing a structured plan for removing deprecated features. This plan should outline key milestones, such as the end of the grace period, the final removal date, and any necessary post-sunset support. It is beneficial to continue offering limited support for deprecated features after their removal date, allowing users who may have missed the transition to seek assistance and resolve any migration issues.

Support during and after the sunset period can take various forms. For instance, providing an extended support window for critical users who are unable to transition immediately can be valuable. This support might include additional troubleshooting assistance, temporary workarounds, or custom migration support to address specific needs. Clear documentation of these support options, along with an accessible support team, ensures that users are not left stranded after the deprecation of features.

Another critical aspect of handling deprecation and sunset is managing the versioning of your API effectively. Clearly delineating different versions and maintaining separate documentation for each helps users understand which features are available in which version. It is essential to establish a robust versioning scheme that accommodates future changes and provides clear guidance on which versions are actively supported, deprecated, or sunsetted.

Implementing API versioning involves deciding on a

versioning strategy that best fits your API's needs. Common strategies include path versioning, where the version number is included in the URL path (e.g., `/api/v1/resource`), and header versioning, where the version is specified in the HTTP headers. Each approach has its benefits and trade-offs. Path versioning is straightforward and easily understood by users, while header versioning can help keep URLs clean and can be useful when version changes are frequent or minor.

Finally, continuous monitoring and feedback collection play a crucial role in managing the deprecation and sunset process. By actively soliciting user feedback and analyzing API usage data, you can identify potential issues early and address them promptly. Regularly reviewing the deprecation and sunset process and making adjustments based on user experiences ensures that the transition remains as smooth as possible and that any unforeseen challenges are promptly addressed.

In summary, handling API deprecation and sunset requires a combination of clear communication, structured migration paths, backward compatibility, and ongoing support. By implementing deprecation warnings, providing a grace period, maintaining separate versioning, and offering continued support, you can manage the transition process effectively and minimize disruptions for your users. Through these strategies, you can ensure that the evolution of your API is both user-friendly and efficient, maintaining the integrity of your service while accommodating the needs of your user base.

When it comes to the actual removal of deprecated API versions, a thoughtful approach is essential to avoid disrupting services and ensure that users are adequately prepared. The transition should be executed in stages, with a final deprecation deadline that is communicated clearly and frequently.

A critical aspect of this transition involves the maintenance of documentation. As you prepare to sunset older versions, it is crucial to keep the documentation for deprecated APIs accessible for a period of time. This ensures that users who are in the process of migrating or who have not yet completed the transition can still reference the necessary information. Documentation should clearly state that the version is deprecated and provide pointers to the updated API versions. This archival of documentation, while ensuring that the deprecated version is marked as outdated, should still be readily available to users.

Another important consideration is managing the deprecation of features within an API version. In many cases, it's not the entire version that needs to be deprecated but specific features or endpoints. For these scenarios, an effective strategy is to deprecate features gradually. Inform users about the deprecation of specific features with ample lead time and provide alternatives or replacements within the same API version if possible. When these features are eventually removed, ensure that users are notified and that any remaining support is handled smoothly.

When planning for the final shutdown of deprecated API versions, consider implementing a phased approach where you first disable the ability to create new instances or access new data through the deprecated endpoints. This phase allows users to complete their migration while still being able to interact with existing data. Subsequently, you can move to a phase where the deprecated endpoints are no longer available for any interaction, including reading data.

To further ease the transition, provide tools or scripts that assist users in migrating their data or configurations to the new API version. These tools can automate the conversion process, reducing the manual effort required by users and minimizing potential errors during migration. For example, a data migration script might help users convert old data formats into the new schema used by the updated API.

Throughout the deprecation and sunset process, maintaining open lines of communication with users is vital. Regular updates through various channels such as email newsletters, blog posts, and community forums can help keep users informed about the progress of the deprecation and any new developments. Additionally, consider establishing a dedicated support channel specifically for migration issues. This could be a dedicated support email, a community forum, or even live chat support during critical periods.

It is also beneficial to gather feedback from users who are going through the migration process. This feedback can provide valuable insights into any challenges or issues that users are facing and can inform further improvements to the migration process or documentation. Actively addressing these concerns and iterating on your approach based on user feedback can greatly enhance the effectiveness of your deprecation strategy.

Finally, after the sunset of an API version, it is crucial to perform a post-deprecation review. This review should assess the impact of the deprecation on users and evaluate the effectiveness of the migration support provided. Analyzing metrics such as user adoption of the new API version, any residual support requests related to the deprecated version, and overall user satisfaction can provide insights into how well the deprecation was managed and where improvements might be needed for future deprecations.

By employing a comprehensive and well-structured approach to handling API deprecation and sunset, you ensure a smooth transition for your users while maintaining the integrity and usability of your API. Clear communication, structured migration paths, and robust support mechanisms are key components in facilitating this process and minimizing any potential disruptions. As the landscape of your API evolves, these practices will not only help manage deprecations effectively but also foster trust and satisfaction among your user base.

CHAPTER 44: EXPLORING FUTURE TRENDS AND INNOVATIONS

As the landscape of API development evolves, keeping abreast of future trends and innovations is essential for maintaining relevance and leveraging new opportunities. This final exploration delves into the emerging technologies, evolving best practices, and potential advancements within the FastAPI ecosystem. Understanding these elements will not only help in adapting to future changes but also in continuously refining and improving API strategies.

One prominent trend in API development is the increasing emphasis on machine learning and artificial intelligence (AI). As these technologies advance, APIs are becoming integral in enabling machine learning models and AI-driven services. FastAPI, with its support for asynchronous programming and high performance, is well-positioned to take advantage of this trend. Future innovations may include more seamless integration with machine learning frameworks and libraries, allowing for more efficient deployment of AI models through APIs. For instance, APIs could directly interface with TensorFlow or PyTorch models, providing real-time inference capabilities.

Another significant trend is the rise of serverless architectures. Serverless computing abstracts away infrastructure management, allowing developers to focus solely on writing code. This model can be particularly advantageous for APIs, offering scalability and cost-efficiency. FastAPI's compatibility with asynchronous programming complements serverless environments by handling concurrent requests efficiently. Future advancements may include better integration with serverless platforms such as AWS Lambda or Google Cloud Functions, enabling developers to deploy FastAPI applications in a serverless manner with minimal configuration.

GraphQL is also gaining traction as an alternative to traditional REST APIs. Unlike REST, which uses fixed endpoints, GraphQL allows clients to request exactly the data they need, reducing the amount of data transferred and improving performance. FastAPI has been evolving to support GraphQL alongside its RESTful capabilities, and future developments may further enhance this support. This includes improving tools for schema generation, query optimization, and integration with GraphQL libraries. For developers working with FastAPI, adopting GraphQL can provide more flexibility and efficiency in data fetching.

API security remains a critical concern, and advancements in security practices are continually emerging. As threats become more sophisticated, APIs need to adopt advanced security measures. This includes enhanced authentication mechanisms, such as OAuth 2.1 and improved encryption standards. FastAPI's support for OAuth 2.0 and other authentication protocols is likely to evolve to incorporate these new standards, ensuring that APIs remain secure against emerging threats. Future trends may also see the adoption of AI-driven security solutions that can detect and mitigate vulnerabilities in real-time.

Additionally, the concept of API versioning is evolving. Traditional versioning approaches, such as including version numbers in URLs, are being supplemented with more dynamic methods. For example, versioning through headers or query parameters is gaining popularity. FastAPI's flexibility allows developers to experiment with these newer methods while maintaining backward compatibility. Future innovations might include more sophisticated tools for managing API versions, making it easier to handle deprecations and transitions seamlessly.

As the API ecosystem grows, interoperability between different APIs and systems is becoming increasingly important. This involves creating standards and protocols that enable APIs from different sources to work together seamlessly. FastAPI's adherence to open standards like OpenAPI facilitates this interoperability. Future developments may focus on enhancing support for emerging standards and protocols, enabling more seamless integrations and interactions between disparate systems.

The evolution of best practices in API development is also a crucial consideration. As the field matures, new best practices are emerging for designing, implementing, and maintaining APIs. This includes practices related to API documentation, testing, and performance optimization. FastAPI's emphasis on automatic documentation generation and testing tools aligns well with these evolving best practices. Staying current with these practices will be essential for maintaining high-quality APIs and ensuring they meet user expectations.

To stay current with new developments and continuously improve API strategies, developers should engage with the FastAPI community and broader API development communities. Participating in forums, attending conferences, and following industry publications can provide valuable insights into emerging trends and best practices. Additionally, actively contributing to open-source projects and collaborating with other developers can help in staying at the forefront of innovation.

In summary, the future of API development is shaped by advancements in machine learning, serverless computing, GraphQL, security practices, and interoperability. FastAPI is well-positioned to adapt to these trends, with ongoing improvements and innovations expected to enhance its capabilities. By staying informed about emerging technologies and best practices, developers can ensure that their APIs remain relevant, efficient, and effective in an ever-evolving landscape.

As we delve deeper into the future of API development, another significant trend to consider is the growing importance of API management and orchestration tools. These tools help organizations manage their APIs more effectively by providing features such as monitoring, analytics, security, and governance. They also facilitate the orchestration of complex API interactions, which is increasingly relevant as APIs become integral to multi-service architectures.

In this evolving landscape, FastAPI's integration with API management platforms will likely become more robust. For instance, tools like Apigee, AWS API Gateway, and Kong provide capabilities for traffic management, authentication, and rate limiting. Future advancements in these tools may include enhanced support for FastAPI's asynchronous features, allowing for better performance monitoring and more granular control over API traffic. These integrations will enable developers to leverage advanced analytics and monitoring capabilities directly within their FastAPI applications, providing insights into usage patterns and potential bottlenecks.

Another trend that is reshaping the API development landscape is the increasing adoption of API-first design principles. This approach emphasizes designing APIs before developing the underlying implementation, which promotes better planning, documentation, and consistency. Tools and practices associated with API-first design, such as OpenAPI specifications, are becoming standard in modern API development. FastAPI inherently supports OpenAPI, which provides a foundation for designing and documenting APIs in a structured manner. Future developments may further enhance FastAPI's capabilities in this area, potentially incorporating advanced features for validating and testing APIs based on OpenAPI definitions.

In parallel, the emphasis on developer experience (DX) is becoming more pronounced. Ensuring that APIs are easy to use, well-documented, and developer-friendly can significantly impact adoption and satisfaction. Future innovations may focus on improving the tooling and frameworks around FastAPI to enhance the developer experience. This could include better integration with development environments, enhanced code generation tools, and more intuitive debugging and testing capabilities. By focusing on DX, FastAPI can continue to attract and retain developers who value efficiency and ease of use in their API development workflows.

The integration of APIs with emerging technologies such as the Internet of Things (IoT) and edge computing also represents a key area of growth. As IoT devices proliferate, APIs will play a crucial role in managing and interacting with these devices. Similarly, edge computing, which involves processing data closer to the source rather than in a centralized cloud environment, requires APIs that can handle distributed data and computational tasks. FastAPI's support for high-performance and asynchronous operations positions it well to handle these scenarios. Future advancements may include optimized libraries and frameworks that facilitate seamless interaction between FastAPI applications and IoT or edge devices, enabling real-time data processing and interaction.

Another evolving area is the adoption of low-code and no-code platforms, which aim to simplify the development process by allowing users to build applications with minimal coding. These platforms often integrate with APIs to provide functionality without requiring deep technical knowledge from users. For FastAPI developers, staying abreast of how these platforms interact with APIs can provide opportunities to offer more accessible solutions or integrations. This may involve developing user-friendly interfaces or tools that enable non-technical users to interact with FastAPI-based applications more easily.

As API ecosystems continue to expand, the concept of API composability is gaining traction. Composable APIs allow different services or APIs to be combined in a modular fashion, enabling more flexible and scalable application architectures. FastAPI's modular design supports this trend by allowing developers to build and integrate various components efficiently. Future innovations may include enhanced support for creating and managing composable API services, which could further streamline the development and integration processes.

Finally, staying current with new developments in API strategies and technologies requires ongoing learning and adaptation. Following industry trends, participating in developer communities, and engaging with FastAPI's evolving ecosystem are essential practices for continuous improvement. Regularly reviewing updates to FastAPI and related technologies, attending conferences, and contributing to open-source projects can help developers remain at the forefront of API innovation. By embracing these practices, you can ensure that your API strategies are aligned with the latest advancements and continue to deliver value in an ever-changing technological landscape.

As we look further into the future of API development, the role of APIs in supporting decentralized technologies, such as blockchain and distributed ledgers, is becoming increasingly prominent. These technologies, known for their robustness and transparency, are finding applications in areas like finance, supply chain management, and digital identity. APIs will be essential for interacting with blockchain networks and distributed ledger systems, providing access to functionalities such as transaction processing, smart contract execution, and ledger queries.

In the context of FastAPI, adapting to these technologies could involve integrating with blockchain protocols and decentralized networks. For instance, FastAPI could provide built-in support for common blockchain operations or include libraries that facilitate interactions with blockchain networks. This would enable developers to build applications that leverage the benefits of blockchain technology, such as enhanced security and transparency, directly through FastAPI interfaces. Future developments might see FastAPI evolving to offer more streamlined methods for interacting with these decentralized systems, perhaps through dedicated libraries or plugins.

Another evolving area is the concept of API composability, which focuses on the creation of modular APIs that can be combined and reconfigured to build complex functionalities. This approach aligns well with microservices architecture, where APIs serve as the building blocks for larger systems. By emphasizing composability, FastAPI could enable developers to design APIs that are more flexible and easier to integrate with other services. Innovations in this space may include better support for defining and managing modular API components, tools for composing and orchestrating APIs, and improved mechanisms for handling dependencies between different API modules.

The continued growth of data privacy regulations, such as the General Data Protection Regulation (GDPR) and the California Consumer Privacy Act (CCPA), underscores the importance of incorporating privacy and compliance features into API development. Future trends may include more advanced mechanisms for managing user consent, data anonymization, and secure data handling within APIs. FastAPI could benefit from enhancements that facilitate compliance with these regulations, such as built-in support for privacy controls and tools for auditing and reporting data access.

Additionally, the rise of API ecosystems and marketplaces represents a shift towards more collaborative and open API development environments. These ecosystems allow developers to publish, discover, and integrate APIs more easily, fostering innovation and reducing duplication of effort. FastAPI could play a role in this ecosystem by providing tools for creating, documenting, and managing APIs in a way that aligns with marketplace standards. Future advancements might involve features that support API publishing and integration within these marketplaces, as well as improved discoverability and interaction with other APIs in the ecosystem.

To stay current with these developments and continuously improve your API strategies, it is crucial to adopt a proactive approach to learning and adaptation. Engaging with industry trends, participating in relevant communities, and experimenting with new technologies will help you stay ahead of the curve. Regularly reviewing and updating your API practices to incorporate emerging best practices and tools is also essential. By remaining agile and informed, you can ensure that your APIs not only meet current demands but also anticipate and adapt to future challenges and opportunities.

In conclusion, the future of API development is shaped by a range of dynamic trends and innovations. Embracing advancements in machine learning, serverless architectures, GraphQL, security practices, and decentralized technologies will be key to leveraging new opportunities and addressing emerging challenges. FastAPI, with its flexibility and performance, is well-positioned to adapt to these changes, and staying informed and agile will enable you to continue refining and improving your API strategies effectively.

www.ingramcontent.com/pod-product-compliance
Lightning Source LLC
LaVergne TN
LVHW051349050326
832903LV00030B/2902